THE NEW VOICE

THE NEW VOICE

Religion, Literature, Hermeneutics

Amos N. Wilder

Including
The First Paul Tillich Commemorative Lectures, 1968

Herder and Herder

1969
HERDER AND HERDER
232 Madison Avenue, New York 10016

Library of Congress Catalog Card Number: 76–87775
© 1969 by Herder and Herder, Inc.
Manufactured in the United States

Contents

To
The Society for the Arts, Religion and Contemporary Culture
and its Founder and First Director
Marvin P. Halverson
1913–1967

THE NEW VOICE

Preface

The present volume represents a large amplification of the material and themes presented as the first Paul Tillich Commemoration Lectures under the title, "Modern Reality and the Renewal of the Word." I am grateful to the sponsoring bodies and the publisher for this opportunity to expand the presentation.

The lectures in question, which constitute Part II of the book, were delivered at New Harmony, Indiana, in May 1968. New Harmony is the site not only of Tillich's burial but also of the restoration of the buildings and other survivals of the older community foundations of the Rappites ("Harmonists") of 1814–24 and of Robert Owen, 1824 following, crowned today by the Roofless Church designed by Philip Johnson and the sculpture of Jacques Lipchitz. This cultural restoration carried out by the Robert Lee Blaffer Trust of Houston, Texas and New Harmony, and by other initiatives, has been recognized by the State of Indiana, and the town was designated as a National Landmark by the Secretary of the Interior in 1965.

The lectureship was sponsored by the Society for the Arts, Religion and Contemporary Culture whose office is in New York City. This society which honors Tillich as one of its founders

11

designated the lecturer and defined the purpose of the lectures: "to encourage others to further the work of Paul Tillich, who made great strides in uniting theological thought with the arts, sciences and psychiatry." The lectures were funded by the Blaffer Trust, and a company of artists, scholars and theologians was invited from all parts of the country. Besides the lectures the program included a panel discussion, worship in the Roofless Church, a concert by the Collegium Musicum of Indiana University, and a presentation of the Japanese Tea Ceremony.

I wish therefore to express my appreciation to the Society and to the Blaffer Trust for the opportunity to share my thought in such exceptionally favoring circumstances. The presence of my former friend and colleague, Paul Tillich, was constantly felt, particularly because of the attendance at the events of Mrs. Tillich. The cultural and spiritual concerns of the Trust were represented in the person of Jane Blaffer Owen, whose kindnesses Mrs. Wilder and I had known when teaching at Rice University in 1963, and by whose hospitality we were guests in the "Poets' House" during the meeting. The Society was represented by its Executive Secretary, Finley Eversole, and many Board members and Fellows, including Dr. Rollo May, who presided over the sessions and served as a link between the Trust and the Society.

For permission to republish here material of my own I am indebted to the following: to the editor of *Soundings,* New Haven, Connecticut, for the use of my article, "The Uses of a Theological Criticism," published in that quarterly, vol. LII, no. 1 (Spring 1969), included here with slight revisions in the introductory chapter; to the Society for the Arts, Religion and Contemporary Culture for the use of my paper, "Myth and Dream in Christian Scripture," one in a series of lectures shortly to be published by Dutton & Co. for the Society, edited by Joseph Campbell. I have used this paper with revision in Chapter IV; to the editor of the *Harvard Theological Review* for the use of my Ingersoll Lecture on the Immortality of Man entitled "Mortality and Contemporary Literature" (copyright 1965 by the President and Fellows of Harvard College), published in that journal, vol. 58, no. 1 (January 1965), here used with slight revisions in Chapter VIII; to the editor of the *Union Seminary Quarterly Review* for the use of my article, "Art and Theological Meaning," published in that quarterly, vol. XIII, no. 1 (November 1962), and included here in Chapter IX; and to the editor of *The New Republic* for several pages from my article, "The Anterooms of Faith," in vol. 141, no. 11, issue 2339 (September 14, 1959).

Part II of the book represents an extensive recasting and supplementation of lectures given at Yale University in 1956 under the auspices of the William Lyon Phelps Lectureship, and I take this occasion to acknowledge my appreciation again of that appointment. I also wish to thank Irene Walsh of the Harvard Divinity School staff for her assistance in preparing the typescript for the lectures and for the present book, and Jane Kingman and Dorothy Doty for their help in the office of the Society in connection with the Tillich Lectureship.

In including the name of Marvin Halverson in the dedication I wish to join my homage to that of many who remember his genius for bringing together the image-makers of the future from many isolated guilds and disciplines, beginning with the years when he was the Executive Director of the Department of Worship and the Arts of the National Council of Churches, 1952–1962 and later as Director of the Society.

These chapters explore the language crisis of our time. Tillich, speaking of the need of "a semantic clearing-up of the concepts" in use in our period, stated that "we are living in Babylon after the tower has been cast down and after the languages of men have been disturbed and dispersed all over the world." This suggests both the incoherence of our culture and the hiatus between past and present.

Though I deal mainly with the literary arts, I understand

13

language here in the widest sense of all the vehicles of meaning and communication. The fateful role of language and the modes of language for our grasp of reality has become especially clear to those of us who have been involved in the recent developments of biblical hermeneutics.

Anyone dealing with modern letters in such a general context as I do here places himself in an impossible situation, so illimitable are the relevant texts in all genres and schools. One can only hope by his own selection to identify illuminating features and issues.

Apart from changes in idiom and style the most stubborn problem in our material for any student of culture has to do with the vicissitudes of our inherited symbol. We observe in many quarters today, both in the arts and in religion, an understandable impulse to look within or forward and not back. A primary concern is that of liberation. At the most the imaginative motifs and vehicles of the past are available as elements of an eclectic spirituality in the sense of the creative act. In the baffling complexities of our modern reality the demand, therefore, is for some new dimension of experience rather than for the reordering of experience in its totality. This means a relativization of the cultural images and world images of the past.

But here again I would quote Tillich against any too free-floating a view of the imagination. In his last lecture at Chicago on the study of the religions of the world he said: "Religious symbols are not stones falling from heaven. They have their roots in the totality of human experience including . . . the political and the economic." It would follow that the nature of man is illuminated by such symbols from all faiths and cultures, but the illumination requires recognition of their rootedness, and each past must be accorded its own concrete and idiosyncratic rights. Creativity should not slight the past just as transcendence should not scorn the diurnal (the political and the economic). The archetypes are not only within us but also on the tablets and scrolls of man's immemorial pilgrimage.

14

In this book I have defended the engagement of the modern artist with the nihilist experience of our era. Yet it is to be recognized that many features of the current drama, novel, cinema, and so forth, are chiefly important for the light which they throw upon the immediate crisis.

The reader will note that I have placed a positive sign over against that whole western exploration and continuing revolution which has led to our present disarray and anomie. Like David Jones I continue to believe that this exploration will come through (though "it's a nice thing / as near a thing as ever you saw"). Like Frost I consent that we should continue to "trespass and encroach" on the unknown or the forbidden "without self-reproach." Like Perse I can believe that "the great age at length opens to us . . . as we are caught up in a prodigious blast and tide of things to come." But lest this be construed as an unconscionable blinking at evil I would like to safeguard myself.

I acknowledge that I must for my part appeal over and beyond the long view of the humanist to the mystery of the "remnant." This view sees with Hölderlin (as will appear in what follows) the immitigable limits of Promethean striving, limits accepted without cynicism or a "separate peace." It sees with Robert Penn Warren the "turpitude of time" and creation "gone astray," yet also that it is always the destroyer "who has most need of love" and "therefore destroys," and that the beginning of innocence for all us is "the recognition of complicity." The remnant located in incognito in all levels of society is free from the avidities and emulations which infect all groups, and its members are therefore all the more enduring in their witness to justice and freedom. This view can in consequence absorb the tragic disorders and costs of the period without nihilism. The violent and the rapacious ravage themselves and each other and the meek shall inherit the earth. Much of our literature carries out a surgical dissection of the processes by which the illusions of power are eroded, dissection especially of the private violences that are inseparable from the public. These arenas of aggression and phantasy of course always involve multitudes of the innocent or less responsible in their costs.

But this view also finds a cable or life-line of survival and promise running through the years, identified not so much with the dreams of men which are so likely to turn sanguinary, but with some aboriginal increment of health from the beginning, some prior fiat of life itself. In man's conscious history it can be recognized as an archetypal covenant, not only between man and man but between man and the stones of the field—as in Job—and between man and the stars: that is, a covenant between man and the powers. Earthly hopes as well as spiritual are sustained by this diffused and anonymous remnant which not only suffers with the miscarriages of time but is served by them. The best of our literature evokes this core of history all the more genuinely if the dramas of the psyche are not dealt with in isolation from such creaturely realities as tool-making and husbandry and from that whole rich gamut of the generic human passions and traits as is exhibited for example in Cervantes and in ancient epic, not forgetting the biblical narratives.

Andover Hall
Cambridge, Massachusetts

INTRODUCTION

I. Theological Criticism and Rhetorical Criteria

Since I write as a theologian by training and by profession (in two senses) my literary assessment in these studies will properly enough be assigned to that ambiguous category, "theological criticism." This category suggests that the critic in question not only is versed in religious learning but approaches literary works with certain Christian presuppositions. It may also suggest that as first of all a theologian he is a layman in the disciplines of literary criticism. This is not true of all those engaged in this interdisciplinary pursuit, but the suspicion holds until evidence is produced to the contrary. On this point, however, there should be some mitigation of the handicap if as in my own case the writer is a biblical theologian, specialized, that is, in the biblical literature. Sacred letters no doubt are not humane letters in the usual sense, but there is much overlapping in tools, methods and discriminations. One can cite notable instances of the carry-over not only of philological but of specifically literary methods from their use on modern texts to the clarification of the Scriptures. But the morphology and language features of the latter have called forth their own special range of observation. It would be highly desirable if these could be incorporated into our disciplines in ways more contemporary than those that interested Matthew Arnold.

In any case at the beginning of these inquiries I would like to define my own understanding of theological criticism as one that seeks constantly to keep in mind the basic considerations of language and rhetoric. This does not mean that matters of ideology, world-view, ethics are necessarily excluded. Form and content are inseparable. Styles are revealing of more than style. Genres and the transformation of genres answer to prior cultural factors and attitudes. Just as the basic syntax of a language and the prominence of certain parts of speech reflect a particular version of world-understanding, so these traits in a modern writer betray a particular stance. Basic life options often unconscious lie behind the media employed in the arts. The use of a particular rhyme scheme or nostalgic cadence in a poem is just as revealing of the author's values as any assertion more on the surface of the work. Particular ways of dealing with the time-dimension in a novel, or even the particular use of such details as the adjective, capitalization, the full stop or the exclamation point, all such are just as significant as any more overt ideological element. One major aspect of rhetoric, moreover, is that of its symbolics, and these are a touchstone again as to the presuppositions conscious or unconscious of a writer. All in all basic apperceptions of an artist and his age transpire in all such features of style and medium. The critic should remain attentive to all such properly literary and language criteria. If in what follows, however, I sometimes appear to be interpreting or assessing at a non-literary or even theological level, I trust that it will be evident that the connection with rhetorical considerations is not far to seek.

I.

This introductory chapter, then, seeks in this and other respects to clarify further that special approach to literary assessment often designated as a "theological criticism" or even a "Christian criticism." Though there is properly only one kind of criticism, only one cumulative discipline of criticism, yet contributions to it can be and have been made from various perspectives. It is to be recognized from the start that dogmatic shortcuts are impermissible, but this veto should apply to any and all imperialistic strategies from any quarter. Any serious artistic assessment, whether that of an individual or of a particular school of criticism, has its acknowledged or latent presuppositions, and all such can further the common task.

Discriminations in the arts, oriented to the Christian tradition, may indeed involve a clash of criteria and judgments as in all vigorous wrestling with our humanistic legacies or with contemporary works. But such discriminations need not be dogmatic in any sense other than those arising from other long-espoused and passionately maintained traditions in culture which appeal to their own various archetypes and classics and summarizing formulas.

In what follows, therefore, it should be understood that I reject the idea of a specifically Christian criticism whether in terms of the experience of the believer or of theological categories. The analogy of a Marxist criticism may be useful. This can only mean the contribution that a Marxist can bring to the common undertaking. So it is with what for shorthand purposes can be spoken of as a "Christian" criticism. When I use the expression it is to be understood in this sense.

Some preliminary considerations can be offered in favor or in explanation of that rather extensive activity referred to as theological criticism which has developed in England and America now for several decades. There surely can be no objection to the concern in some theological faculties since the thirties to alert the churches to the significance of modern letters. Nor can objection be made to the efforts of the theologian-critic to repossess his religious tradition and to renew its language

21

through an engagement with the contemporary arts and sensibility. Nothing but good, moreover, could come from his critique of the blighting effects of the inherited patterns of asceticism in certain religious traditions, nor from his critique of the bad taste associated with a more recent religious aestheticism. In all such areas qualified churchmen have sought first of all to carry over into the consciousness of the religious institutions and into the religious arts the standards of excellence and of artistic integrity defined by the most perceptive critical circles of the time.

More debatable has been the increasingly sophisticated participation of the theologian in the forums of general criticism. Since such activity has at first been associated with theological faculties and with commissions, lectureships and conferences under religious auspices, and its publication with religious journals and the religious departments of the various presses, it could be construed as mainly apologetic and partisan, even when participated in by leading secular critics. In England F. R. Leavis voiced a vigorous indictment of the phenomenon known as "Christian discrimination" identified with the title of a book by the Anglican critic, Brother George Every. It would be interesting to analyze the totally different context of these issues in France where theological polemic has had so prominent a place in general criticism. In the United States in any case we have not had to reckon with a self-proclaimed Catholic or confessional group of writers and critics of the order of Mauriac, Bernanos and Claudel. Eliot's literary criticism largely transcended any such dogmatic partisanship, and W. H. Auden has gone out of his way in his critical writings to set a Kierkegaardian gulf between all aesthetic activity and the existential dimension of faith.

But the situation is changing today and the role of the theologian in criticism appears in a new light. We see an increasing number of religious scholars who are also trained in literary studies. Their base of operations is often now in the college and the university rather than in the seminary, and in departments in the humanities rather than of those in religion. Meanwhile teachers in departments of language and literature, especially in dealing with our modern classics, often find themselves involved in issues which even under strictly literary assessment require religious and theological expertise and empathy.

Still more fundamentally we observe that the very conditions of contemporary culture tend to relativize critical orthodoxies, to require inter-disciplinary resources, and to open the interpretation of the arts of language to a total anthropological and linguistic approach. Literary criticism has had to take account of new explorations of the whole phenomenon of language, not only in the global sense of comparative literature and the history of genres, and not only in the social-psychological dimension of the study of myth and symbol, but more fundamentally in all that has to do with the correlation of language and reality. Western humanism and its canons are compromised by a new experience and our critical repertoire must be widened. But this richer and more baffling context of the arts at many points involves the category of religion, so inseparably linked with those older vicissitudes of language and consciousness which have now again in strange ways become contemporary for us.

The epochal character of the cultural transformation now in process has brought with it a crisis in language and in the arts, reflected in the revolution and dissolution of literary forms, in a combination of both iconoclastic impulse and ontological power, and even in the surfacing of archaic structures and motifs. The interrelation of the disorders in society and the arts places the critic in a difficult position. It is not easy to safeguard the proper autonomy of his discipline when his literary texts are so closely related to the anomie of the age. This embarrassment has led recently to even shrill forms of moralistic revulsion against current critical schools and to diatribes against the Academy generally. One may sympathize at many points with

23

any such exposure of the complicity of the artist or critic today with contemporary nihilism, but any critique of criticism at this fateful level requires grounded humanistic sanctions. At this point the relevance of the religious sources of culture cannot well be denied.

II.

Modern letters and the modern arts as a whole testify to the changing experience of mankind, at least in the West. A concern with this change is one legitimate approach to literature since language and reality are so closely related. The vicissitudes of the word open up to us today as in all periods basic issues with respect to past and present, tradition and revolt, meaning and vitality. What we are going through can be seen as a crucible of language, a crucible of images, a testing and transformation of signs and symbols, a revolution of sensibility. This situation is one which engages all our disciplines, all our traditions, all our vocations in mutual illumination.

The modern reality here testified is a new thing, but it is related to the realities of the past. It is in process and it has many facets. It is transient and relative, and only one window on any true or final reality. Therefore while the first task is that of knowing it and examining its witnesses, we cannot stop with that. We must assess it, defend it, criticize it and seek as participants to shape it. So far as such discrimination relates to the arts, especially the arts of language, this means an aesthetic criticism, but a criticism that finally rejoins all the fateful issues of language and is therefore more than aesthetic, is total. Here, however open our hospitality may be to all the voices and all the inspirations and all the traditions, we finally judge as we see things. We bring the contribution of our own perspective into the arena, into the weighing of choices, into the war of myths if such it be. So we instruct each other, challenge each other, crystallize new fronts, find unexpected allies.

In this engagement with our modern reality and its literary registers I find myself willy-nilly determined by ultimate Christian presuppositions. But this calls for clarification. Whether such presuppositions are genuinely Christian is always a prior question which should trouble the theologian-critic. Even at this basic level he should be open to instruction not only by other theologians but by his whole continuing life-experience, precisely in our modern context. For even presuppositions, not to mention doctrines, must be repossessed in every new situation.

The theologian-critic has been found especially vulnerable at two points. On one side he has often made the mistake also found in other critics of violating proper method by a prior dogmatic. Even in the domains of politics or morality it is only by a highly simplistic procedure that the Christian can pretend to assert norms directly from his doctrines or confessions. In questions of jurisprudence it is recognized that decisions and interpretations can properly be reached only by laboring with the precedents in all their complexity. The judge may not leap directly from Magna Charta or the Bill of Rights to the matter in hand. The moral theologian should not leap directly from the Sermon on the Mount to the present ethical decision. So also in the field of letters there is no shortcut for the believer.

But the theologian-critic has also been vulnerable on the other side. If his orientation has a contribution to make to the total undertaking he should be as clear and candid as possible about his ultimate criteria and maintain their cutting edge. Too often he has been uncertain about his base of operations. He has leaned over backwards to show his breadth and tolerance. This kind of protective coloring can relate to the regnant mood and horizon of current writing. Or it can relate to critical fashion. But by such acquiescence any profitable dialogue is frustrated. The modern situation with its special art forms, from the greatest to the least, from the modern classics to the popular floods in the mass-media, surely present us with competing options and these demand discrimination at every level.

When all is said and done, one cannot finally separate life-attitudes from aesthetic judgments. Behind every poem, novel or play there is a man. Behind every critical assessment of whatever school or method there is a man. Behind the artistic production of a decade or a period there is the fathomless reality of mankind. Admitted that every art has its own refined disciplines, whose independence is to be jealously guarded; admitted that literary criticism has its own sophisticated and scrupulous procedures; yet all such rightful autonomy can only be penultimate. Art and letters are too important not to be referred back finally to what is at stake in the human story. Inevitably, therefore, fundamental perspectives will and do affect particular judgments even of detail, and all such prior visions have their rightful place in court.

III.

Even when some such plausible case can be made for the uses of a theological criticism, the real crux remains. How does such a critic move properly and convincingly from his faith to his literary judgments? I do not, indeed, accept that view which insists upon the total incommensurability of divine and human things. But I agree that the theologian-critic should explain how he can pass in a persuasive way from those assurances of revelation and their corollaries which are indisputable to him to their particular application in the free market of literary discussion. It is not enough to have a stance or a perspective or some claimed world-epiphany or baptism. The *homo religiosus* cannot enter into the forum of life-decisions arbitrarily. Even the prophet and the martyr engage with the language of their contemporaries.

The difficulties if not the scandal of such a participation should be frankly recognized. After all the Christian view of the world carries with it axioms and assumptions which are widely held to be incredible today. Nor can such matters be excluded as extra-aesthetic unless we wish to dehumanize the arts and assign them that kind of immaculate autonomy which, experience has shown, only ends in their being credited with a religious or sacred character, whether hermetic or vatic. Life and language at whatever level cannot finally evade or deny the dimension of the sacred, and it therefore here again becomes a question of appropriate criteria. Aesthetic criticism cannot stop short of a total criticism and such ultimate sanctions should be as explicit as possible.

To suggest some of the disparities between the basis of a Christian criticism and the reality-view underlying much contemporary evaluation one could in rough fashion marshal a few models or pointers, distinguishing between several levels of language.

In ordinary language, then, the Christian believes that "no sparrow falls to the ground without your Father's will," and that "even the hairs of your head are numbered"; in dogmatic language, in personal providence; in mythological language, that "in everything God works for good with those who love him, who are called according to his purpose."

In ordinary language, the Christian believes that history has meaning and that the meek shall inherit the earth; in dogmatic language that God has disclosed himself and his purpose in the historical process; and mythologically, that God has elected Israel for the blessing of the Gentiles and has chosen the "community" as the means by which a disordered creation shall be reconstituted in unity.

In ordinary language the Christian believes that the health

and fulfillment of human society are linked with some aboriginal pattern of atonement at the heart of things; in dogmatic terms, that the world is redeemed by the death of Christ; and in mythological terms, that on the cross Christ overcame the principalities and powers of evil.

In ordinary language the Christian believes that in life or death we are the Lord's; in dogmatic terms, in the resurrection of the body; and in mythological terms, that He that raised Jesus from among the dead will also raise us.

One could add other axioms, especially such as seem to have a special timeliness: a Christian believes in the kind of love of God that is compatible with inexorable judgment, for example on every idle word. Like the Buddha he believes that "the liar digs up his own root" (for "liar" here read the purveyor of toxic or self-flattering images, of fraudulent rhetorics). He believes in non-violence psychological as well as overt, but he also believes that inherent civil authority and its sanctions of force are ordained by God. He believes in the essential innocence and goodness of created things, and therefore of the sensuous and sexual and economic orders, as well as of the rational faculties. But he warns against daemonic crafts and towers of Babel, looks on acquisitiveness as idolatry and equates the lustful eye with adultery. He draws a sharp line down through all agitations for freedom and all claims on property, distinguishing between covenant-rights and brotherly bonds on the one hand and secular emancipationism or emulation, avidity and invidiousness on the other.

Thus the theological critic should not compromise or disguise his disagreement with the widespread scepticism and nihilism and intoxication of our time, nor with widely regnant ideologies, programs and attitudes with their aesthetic presuppositions, all of which find expression in contemporary literature. But as in the social-ethical domain so in the field of letters, such a critic must identify himself with the givens of the occasion. That particular and austere criterion that is his can only validate itself meaningfully, even for himself, in the process, and not in some hortatory or moralistic intervention. A Christian presence in literary or artistic discussion surely involves no other law than that of the embodied Word as exemplified in both aspects of his Scripture.

I would like to explore what such a proper procedure would be by selecting the first of the Christian convictions listed, that having to do with personal providence. In dealing with writings in which exposure of the self to sheer fortuity and meaningless- ness is central a theological criticism will certainly not first of all indict the negative portrayal as such. It will indeed commend as truer to reality a work which recognizes disguised operations of grace in the enigmas of personal tragedy. But before all else it will ask whether the experience in question, however am- biguous, is adequately rendered. As Beckett admonishes in *All That Fall:* "Tell all! Tell all!" Does the author present the protagonist, the action, the impasse with some dense sense of all the contexts, complexities, imponderables that envelop all hu- man situations? In artistic terms does he have at his command the palette for this kind of exhaustive faithfulness? Does he em- ploy a full complement of the registers and manuals for a nuanced portrayal of the inwardness and ramifications of the matter?

In the case of the Book of Job—which imposes itself in this connection—meaningfulness here emerges not first of all out of the eventual intervention of God but out of the dialogue and the full gamut of affective-imaginative apperceptions evoked in it. The divine vindication that follows is to be seen as rhetorical stratagem enforcing the postulate of faith which speaks through the expostulation and tone of the hero. The prosodic as well as the religious matrix of Job's accents are to be traced to such older texts as Dt. 32:10,

> He found [Jacob] in a desert land,
>   and in the howling waste of the wilderness;

29

> he encircled him, he cared for him,
> he kept him as the apple of his eye.

The genre of the work, moreover, with its antecedents in the ancient world, governs the import of the dialogue.

But I would like to apply these considerations to two recent writings. Peter De Vries' novel, *The Blood of the Lamb*,[1] deals with the problem of meaninglessness in perhaps its most acute form, the suffering of a child. The Christian reader will sympathize with the assault on the stultifying dogma, "it is God's will," pilloried in the book. He will also respect the bereaved father's alternative: an agnostic celebration of the ephemeral beauty and delight of human intimacy in all its precariousness. He will, however, find the problem handled in a truncated way: the full octaves of imaginative and affective context and the prior ambivalences of our total human situation are missing. In literary terms these lacks can be related to the genre employed, that of the novel *á thèse*. Indeed, any satisfactory dealing with this subject-matter for our contemporary sensibility would rule out the conventional novelistic form here adopted, a form which belongs to "last year's language." Related to this incongruity is the occasional resort to the melodramatic as well as the tone and tenor which fail to move beyond the plangent to the deep diapason familiar to us in works that could be cited.

A better test case is afforded by Beckett's *All That Fall.*[2] This radio play is all the more to the purpose since its title cites the 143rd Psalm, "The Lord upholdeth all that fall." I cannot agree with the view that the "wild laughter" of Dan and Maddy Rooney on recalling this text represents nothing but derision of it on the part of the author, granted that life is, indeed, lived "under the wheels." The work is greater than any such part. The incandescence of the detail, the humanity of the characteri-

1. New York, 1961.
2. London, 1957.

30

zation, the irony and desperation suggested through the colloquial and the grotesque, the abysses of silence behind the words and gestures; all these suggest what we find even more movingly in the wonderful companion-piece, *Embers,* that motif of famishment and prayer, that Breugelesque *de profundis,* which keeps open the incursions of grace. A Christian criticism of the work will know how to recognize in the rhetoric what faith itself knows in extra-aesthetic wrestling with the enigmas of personal providence. If it be objected that any sound criticism can make such comments as I have made upon such writings I would reply that this illustrates the fact that a "Christian" criticism rightly carried out will coincide at many points with any grounded humanistic criticism, but, secondly, that it can also alert such criticism to the resonances of a profounder anthropology.

IV.

There is one point at which the Christian or any profoundly religious perspective can introduce an important element into the assessment of the modern arts. It is not predisposed to exaggerate the importance of the contemporary, even granted the stature of the works in question. This can become a matter of far-reaching consequence in a time like ours. The critic with this perspective will certainly not take lightly the signs of the times, the creativity of the moment. It is the peculiar genius of biblical religion to assign fatefulness to every present and to attribute significance to the present act or neglect whether of life or of the imagination. But such a critic will read all the witnesses and symptoms of this "now" in a wider context.

What makes him keep his distance, despite his admiration for contemporary voices, indeed his deep involvement in their explorations, is an old wisdom that has repeatedly justified itself

31

in riding out the gyrations of strange times, a wisdom which refers back to what Walt Whitman, no doubt in a different context, called the kelson of creation. These insights mean more than that a long history is recalled to relativize the present. They mean that the most intimate texture of contemporary work becomes subject to subtle apperceptions otherwise absent.

We find an analogy to this theme in remarks of Proust's alter ego in the closing section of the great novel. Marcel here is defending his at that time unappreciated art and questioning the reigning authorities and reputations. He suggests that the anonymous multitudes of mankind have a truer flair for what is important in literature than the current parties and schools "whose logomachy is renewed every ten years," the kaleidoscope being composed not only of the successive "modern groups," but of the social, political and religious ideas which successively take on a momentary amplitude and prestige.

There is a greater analogy between the instinctive life of the wider public and the talent of the great writer . . . than in the superficial verbiage and the changing criteria of the official judges.[3]

Proust's pursuit of a deeper sensibility and portrayal of society than that of Anatole France and other contemporaries suggests the detachment of a Christian discernment for which something of Vanity Fair is found in all cultures and something of the Cities of the Plain. In this view the fashions of criticism are part of the carnival and many of the critics represent the town criers of this or that Babylon. At short range they may have immense subtlety in dealing with the works symptomatic of the crisis and this is a valuable service. But in a wider frame of reference though they may see the writing on the wall at the feast of Belshazzar they are not able to decipher it.

3. *À la recherche du temps perdu,* vol. III (Pléiade ed.), Paris, 1954, pp. 893–894.

In any period or decade the observer of current letters inevitably has his attention called to highly publicized schools, personalities and movements which may, indeed, have undeniable significance and which rightfully demand not only his attention but often also his defense. Such movements characteristically iconoclastic and controversial, and the works that represent them, dominate the scene and focus the attention of sophisticated circles. They are important because they touch the nerve of the modern consciousness and reflect the changing sensibility of the period. There are, however, many considerations which argue for reserve on the part of the critic and point to the complexity of his task.

For one thing, without denying the fateful importance of the more searching and talented avant-garde voices of the time, we cannot but remember the cultural pluralism of our society. The modern world is made up of many communities and traditions and what speaks for one does not speak for another. The arts that crystallize the ethos of one group may not answer for another. Nor is it only a question of lag or ripeness, as though the culture moved as a whole towards only one kind of experience and sensibility. Our world with its many strata and legacies solves its inherited problems in various ways and is creative in various ways. In retrospect the more visible trends in art, and even those most rightfully authoritative for the historical moment, must take their place in a wider context. There are more permanent aspects of man than are evoked in our modern classics or evoked in other ways. The critic should be alert to this pluralism of the situation.

V.

It is a special feature of our time that the shaping of critical opinion tends to fall disproportionately into the hands of the most deracinated intellectuals of our society and their forums and media of publication. We can understand such deracination and recognize that it makes possible a disabused assessment of art and life that brings its own illumination. Perhaps it is always true that in any age the most sensitive groups are likely to be disaffected with prevailing patterns and attentive to those who are in revolt. But in our present disorder this phenomenon is maximized. For in our situation a wide public even of the discerning is so unsettled as to be open to the most radically oriented of those who shape our images and our opinions. In a time of disarray the most iconoclastic voices have the most appeal. In one aspect Proust, again, accounts for this prestige of a criticism over-impressed by contemporary fashion. "It consecrates as a prophet a writer who brings no new substance just because of his peremptory tone and the scorn he affects for the school that has preceded him."[4]

One sees susceptibility to extreme opinion today especially among students. Often our faculties in the humanities lend themselves to such unbalance. Thus it has been remarked that "too many brilliant students come out knowing Kafka but not Plato, Sartre but not Shakespeare, Black Power but not the French Revolution . . . and believing that American history began with John F. Kennedy."

There is still another consideration which weighs with the "Christian" critic who would keep some detachment from the sway of the contemporary. This has to do with certain extreme manifestations. When the revolt against tradition takes the form of blasphemy, pornography, gleeful or vindictive profanation, however justified such extremes may well appear in view of the aesthetic or moral insipidity of what is attacked, here a grounded even if sympathetic criticism will detect the symptoms of phantasy and guilt which accompany extreme deracination. The common charge that such features in the arts

4. *Ibid.,* p. 893.

are motivated by a desire for attention, and thus by shock-tactics and exhibitionism, is hardly relevant to the more serious artists. Among these moreover wide latitude must be allowed where the engagement with such ambiguous areas is responsibly conducted. But the resort to nihilism and outrage often represents a covert displacement of self-destruction in the author and in his society. This is related to an impulse to profane our human bonds especially with the fathers. Relevant here is the commandment to honor father and mother.

Deeply embedded in the work of Proust is the tortured theme of *les mères profanées.* As we shall see in Chapter III, following the lead of Harry Levin, it was this author's eventual remorse for the unfeeling cruelty of his earlier relationships especially to his mother which added a final clairvoyance and magnanimity to his great work. "The years of desecration had to be atoned for by a long and testing consecration."[5] But there are many writers of talent today, talent which for the moment disorients both criticism and self-criticism, whose garish impulse and whose fascination with the destructive element has never thus been chastened. One crucial test of the artist even when dealing with the worst tyrannies of our situation is an ultimate deportment of holy fear or *pietas* before the final mysteries. Or, as Charles Péguy observed in his *Saints Innocents,* "All life comes from tenderness."[6] It is not only the Christian in criticism who insists on the ultimate sanctities of life. And it is not only as a moralist that he does so.

A great many modern artists and critics speak for special new strata, new kinds of men, produced by the conditions of our society: the disordered family, neighborhood, livelihood. If there is an ecological crisis which calls our attention to the balance of

5. *The Gates of Horn,* New York, 1963, p. 439; see below, pp. 95–96.
6. *Cahiers de la Quinzaine,* XIII, 12 (1912); *God Speaks* (translation by Julian Green), New York, 1945, p. 66.

nature, we may say that there is a human ecological disturbance which has already for some time been determining a new kind of human breed within the wider culture. These groups have little or no memory—and what they have highly distorted—of that older world and its continuities which are still so real for many of us. But this means that they are not capable of relating old and new or of making just comparisons. We have every right therefore to assign their witness only limited authority. Yet the forces which have shaped these more deracinated groups have of course also played upon society as a whole in our time. The dilemmas so occasioned are indivisible and the responses to them in any quarter must be taken account of.

VI.

There is, finally, one major consideration bearing on the role of the Christian in criticism today or at any time. His perspective is one that assigns purpose and meaning to the human story and is confident that grace operates in the most baffling labyrinths of the life of the individual or of societies. It is here, indeed, that the charge of dogmatism seems most clearly justified, but the believer can blunt the charge by moving the discussion to the literary level and by invoking the evidence precisely of the supreme literature and literary forms provided by the charters of his faith. The Christian reads human experience and judges the monuments of time in terms of the biblical epic and its vision of providential strategies.

It is to be granted that the special nurture of the theological critic has been in only one of the main religio-cultural traditions of mankind. Yet it is one whose literary classics are interwoven with a rich variety of other religious patterns and their rhetorics. Indeed one may say that his engagement with contemporary culture has a background of three thousand years of encounter and discrimination, receptivity and rejection, vis-à-vis the cultures of the past. But it is precisely as a man of letters that the instructed Christian, initiated into the paideia and language repertory of the Hebrew and Christian charters, may offer some credentials as an interpreter of any literature.

It is not merely a question of widening the field of comparative literature and calling attention to genres and styles often neglected. One important range of observations has indeed been opened up by Erich Auerbach in his demonstrations of the influence of the Scriptures upon the history of realism and the western understanding of reality itself. More significant is the fact that this religious tradition has from the tenth century B.C. been peculiarly identified with the word and with the arts of the word. Through successive epochs it has been associated with profound revolutions of language and with new modes of oral and written communication, whether the schooling of the laity (from the first emergence of the synagogue in the period of the Exile), or refined disciplines of commentary, or extensive translation, or the exploiting of new arts of diffusion and publication such as codex, illustration and printing. Thus even granted his particular commitment the theologian like the Jewish intellectual (if he cherishes his tradition) has special habituations for opening up dimensions of reality associated with the language arts.

But more important than these considerations in qualifying the "Christian" critic is the concretely human character of his faith and its rhetorics. In the act of criticism it is language that we are concerned with. But from beginning to end the language of Scripture is wedded to all the dynamics of human experience, to the many-layered reality of man's life whether private or social, whether historical or cosmic. Immersion in this linguistic world provides an indispensable resource for the assessment of the rhetorics of any culture or period. Quite apart from any formal theological or moral dimensions of these classics the

37

Christian brings with him to his reading apperceptions and literary expectations which are a unique equipment for any kind of humanistic discrimination.

In the final analysis those of us who have been identified with the theological criticism would like to see all such activity merged with the one common pursuit. What properly literary illumination it may contribute should become part of the resources of any critic. At least the task of wrestling with any such perceptions falls on any interpreter of whatever confession or no confession. The case is like that of sociological criticism. There was a period in which the sociological approach to letters, indeed to all the humanities including history, was so valuable a corrective that it was proper to speak of the sociological critic or the sociological historian. When the insights in question had been, as it were, digested in the discipline as a whole there was no longer need to distinguish that particular approach.

Yet however instructive such an analogy may be, the case is not the same. The Christian approach to all cultural creativity and fabulation will no doubt continue to have its own critical perspective. The humanism associated with the Jewish and Christian vision of the world will continue to remain in productive tension if not in contradiction with all other humanisms and anthropologies, even when in a "post-Christian" epoch all such traditions will have been radically restructured.

PART ONE

Biblical Genres and Archetypes

... modern man lives with an increasing burden of subjectivity,
at the expense of his sense of the reality of the world.

Susan Sontag, *Against Interpretation*

Unique and individual perceptions require to be "grounded," in
both the ontological and electrical senses of the metaphor
"ground." . . . If there is anything to the master Christian
images, it is a carnal and dusty bond we have with historical
universality; as it is in flesh of our flesh and bone of our bone
that God has put in potency before us what it is to be before
him as his man.

Ray L. Hart, *Unfinished Man and the Imagination*

II. Biblical Epos and Modern Narrative

> . . . si l'un de nous avait eu la tête épique!
> Proust, *Du côté de chez Swann*

> Tell all! Tell all!
> Beckett, *All That Fall*

Our introductory chapter has urged that a proper theological assessment of literature should direct itself first of all to matters of language and rhetoric. But we have also seen that the theological critic could well take account of the literary heritage of his faith and its special modes of language. If one considers the momentous influence of the Hebraic and early Christian writings upon western culture we cannot but be struck by the anomaly that in general literary criticism such small attention has been paid relatively to these antecedents at this level. The fact that these classics have been assigned to the category of sacred texts has meant that their specifically linguistic and rhetorical features have not received the kind of attention in the study of letters and of comparative literature that have been given, for example, to the Greek classics.

We propose, therefore, in Part One of this book to deal with aspects of the Scripture in this perspective, keeping in mind their bearing on contemporary literature and its forms. The present chapter will be devoted to the Old Testament in respect to its narrative. The succeeding chapter will pursue this matter further by examining a major modern novelist in the light of the findings, and in such a way as to illuminate the cultural factors which condition the scope of modern narrative. In Chapter IV we shall turn to the symbolic imagination especially of the New Testament.

Our purpose, then, in the present chapter is to observe certain features of Hebrew narrative and use these as tests or queries directed to contemporary narrative or fiction. It is to be granted that the writings in question are separated by millenniums in point of time and by other radical disparities. But if we approach the task as a scrutiny of language, disregarding formal dogmatic considerations, my proposal may have some justification in the modern interest in the study of genres, in comparative rhetorics, and in the ultimate shaping of our language and apperceptions by the biblical texts.

I shall be concerned with style and rhetorical modes, and with the kinds of realism or particular reality-sense associated with them. But my project also offers an opportunity to reflect upon the dilemma of the epic form in our period, or at least on such features of epic as may have an after-life in our changed world. This topic is one that well highlights the special character if not the limitations of modern narrative, and may well therefore be briefly considered at the beginning of the discussion.

The larger cycles of the Old Testament histories represent a kind of epic as we shall see in what follows, and Milton for one could base his Puritan-humanist epics upon the biblical story-telling. It is generally recognized that the conditions of our own period are not propitious for any such larger plotting of experience. Yet the modern writer is attracted to the older epics, as he

42

is to Greek tragedy or to archaic mythical patterns, and we can detect a deep impulse even in the midst of our age of incoherence to achieve some universal pattern of fabulation by direct or indirect appeal to the structures of Homer or Dante or the Bible.

There is something poignant about the struggle to relate our modern anomie to these older stories of man, for our climate is surely uncongenial to such confident world-recital as those of the *Odyssey* or the *Divine Comedy.* We have here on one scale— in the work of Joyce or Pound or Proust—examples of that wrestling for meaning which in the less ambitious scope of most novels seeks through a close recital of experience and events to throw light on the enigmas of some more particular life-drama.

When we think of the major epics of the past we recognize a large-scale kind of recital in which the particular self-understanding of a society or an epoch is evoked, and one which gives order to its experience of time in particular. All such narrative-chartings of experience presuppose a confident and naïve sense of communal and world reality. But it is just here that our modern fictions have a different if not more limited scope.

We may illustrate by the case of Gertrude Stein who was all her life interested in the problem of narrative in our age, especially in America. She called her *Making of Americans* an "epic" and related it to Joyce's *Ulysses* and to the work of Proust. What makes this case specially appropriate here is that she also cited the Old Testament, praising it as an analogy of her idea of contemporary narrative, as against the kinds of narrative that have obtained in the past.[1]

1. *Narrative: Four Lectures,* Chicago, 1935, p. 19. Note the remarks of Carl Van Vechten in a letter to her about *The Making of Americans:* "To me, now, it is a little like the Book of Genesis. There is something Biblical about you, Gertrude. Certainly there is something Biblical about you." Cited by Elizabeth Sprigge, *Gertrude Stein: Her Life and Work,* New York, 1957, p. 135.

What Stein meant by "epic" and how it suits or departs from the classic understanding appear in the character of this work and in her general reflections on narrative.

The *Making of Americans* began as a thinly disguised history of three generations of Gertrude Stein's own family of Jewish immigrant stock, grew to include the histories of everybody the family knew, and ended up as an attempt to encompass the history of "all who ever were or are or could be living," described according to "personality traits." For the author, the "bottom nature" of human beings, the reflexes of the complete characters of individuals, were reflected not in their words and thoughts, but in the movement of words and thoughts, "endlessly the same and endlessly different." Yet she also emphasized that there is a hero in the work and a hero who dies.[2]

In her lectures entitled *Narrative,* Stein clarifies her intention as a way of writing which deals with reality as "immediately existing" and as immediately "known" in the recital rather than told at a remove. The excitement lies in the lived apprehension of the actuality of things and events. While there is sequence in any narrative it is not the important thing; and she especially decries the banality of the pattern of beginning, middle and ending. What is specially surprising here is her view that

in a kind of way what has made the Old Testament such permanently good reading is that really in a way in the Old Testament writing there really was not any such thing there was not really any succession of anything and really in the Old Testament there is no sentence existing and no paragraphing, think about this thing; . . .[3]

In the Old Testament, she writes:

2. "Announcement of *The Making of Americans: The Complete Version,*" New York, 1966. Cf. T. N. Wilder, Introduction to her *Four Americans,* New Haven, 1947.
3. *Narrative,* p. 19.

they told what they were and they felt what they saw and they knew
how they knew and everything they had to say came as it had to
come to do what it had to do.[4]

Evidently, Gertrude Stein's view here appears to fly in the
face of the usual view, and one which we shall stress later, that
the narrative of the Bible takes time and its events seriously and
above all provides a world-plot with a beginning, middle and
end. But her emphasis on reality in "existing" and on language
as event in the now has its parallels even in theology today.
We have here in any case a good specimen of the direction in
which the man and artist of our time, conditioned by modern
subjectivity, seek a different kind of structure for epic or for any
major narrative work than has been true in the past. Moreover
we recognize in Stein's way of putting it the modern revulsion,
so clearly stated and practiced by D. H. Lawrence, against the
staleness of the usual plot of good and bad fortune, and the
determination to go deeper into psychological or moral constants.

These observations on the fate of the epic mode in our day
lead me to a theme that is basic to my further discussion. For
better or worse the problems set for men in the West have long
focussed about what we speak of as his subjectivity, and this has
been increasingly true with the passage of time. This category
has many facets and its sense varies in different contexts. In the
present connection we have been led to it by the contrast between
a public arena of significant action in time and a more inward
one. This is related to loss of authority of older social and
cosmic assumptions and their structures with the result that
meaning must locate itself in the dramas of the psyche. In our
fifth chapter below we shall examine the vicissitudes of our
western sensibility especially as it bears on the resulting dilemma
of language. From the negative point of view emphasis can be
placed on the accompanying loss of the sense of the reality of

4. *Ibid.,* p. 27.

the world and the alienation of our *unbehauste Mensch.* From the positive point of view the emphasis may fall on the liberated powers of the self. The consequences for literature and its genres have been correspondingly diverse. Not only is the individual artist conditioned by his own particular form and degree of exposure to the cultural shift but various aesthetic and philo-sophical versions of the situation have their influence: surrealism, apocalypticism, psychologism, existentialism. The main point to bear in mind, however, is that all such psychodrama and cre-ativity seek contact with the real. The order of art itself pre-supposes a wider order. And any such rediscovered ceremony and orientation must have their profound correspondences with those of the past. In this sense the words of Herman Melville may guide the promptings of the modern artist:

> Not innovating wilfulness,
> But reverence for the Archetype.[5]

In this connection we shall give attention at a later point to one recent poetic narrative of epic scope which takes public history and its successions seriously and links the import of private experience with a world-plot, and that is *The Anathémata* of David Jones[6] which is at once a cult-epic and a celebration of *homo faber.* Here the achievement is all the more remarkable because this rehearsal of man's ceremonies and technics is the work of one thoroughly initiated into the modern sensibility. One evidence of this is the specific acknowledgement he makes to Eliot and Joyce in his preface. The work may be taken as one clue to the various solutions sought today both in art and in life in the attempt not to transcend psychologism and sub-jectivity but to exploit what we may learn from them for the sake of more adequate structures.

5. *The Works of Herman Melville,* vol. XVI, *Poems,* London, 1924, p. 287.
6. New York, n.d. (English edition, 1952). See Chapter VII, sec-tion III, below, for a more detailed discussion.

Although I intend to deal with the biblical material in this chapter in a non-dogmatic way I nevertheless invite the reader once again to look upon the undertaking as an exploration in theological criticism. In focussing upon the language I am not conscious of surrendering my confessional premises. I am going behind doctrine and confession to their matrix in the life-process and its recitals, to the biblical humanism which nourished the faith.

Theology, in any case, often neglects this sub-soil of the tradition, and in two senses. Its changing formulations may proceed without constant reimmersion in the elemental experience of man precisely as here narrated and fabled. What Christianity is taken to be in various periods forfeits its continuity with the fateful early vicissitudes of the people of God at the quasi-secular level, especially as evoked in the older annals. More specifically, biblical theology operates selectively in its appeal to Scripture. What is taken as normative for faith, and therewith for liturgy and ethics, tends to abstract from the wholeness of the canon. Thus the substance of Christianity is spiritualized, not only by a focus on the New Testament at the expense of the Old, but in the Old Testament itself by a neglect of those generically human strata represented by the narrative as well as the wisdom deposits.

Thus theology tends to shortcut the concrete human givens that are basic to doctrine, especially as they are manifest in the Old Testament story-telling. But such obscuring of the "human nature" in the Bible immediately frustrates any proper grasp of the relation of theology to culture, and particularly of theology to the arts. The plain reader of the Bible, nourished on the stories of the Pentateuch and the books of Samuel and the episodes in the Gospels and the Book of Acts, is already initiated into an implicit theology all the more negotiable in his own setting for being a matter of vivid story and poetry rather than of abstractions.

It is in the biblical epos, especially in the older records, that

47

we find ourselves face to face with man as the arts also reveal him, man the creature, man the maker, symbol-maker and fabulist, and man the political animal. The arts also are directly concerned with natural man and his endowments and dynamics. No theology will be adequate that obscures these. It is true that Hebrew man is distinctive. There are many differing humanisms, and we have here one remarkable instance. The unique narratives and epics of different peoples and ages expose all such differences in a most revealing way. This is clear in the case of the biblical epos, and the differences can serve as an appropriate basis for theological criticism of narrative literature generally.

To anticipate by one example. Let us suppose that one thing we look for in an account of some course of human events, fictional or not, is completeness[7]—not necessarily quantitative, but the full dimension of the event, with some suggestion of its deeper and wider context, and of those significant intangibles so easily overlooked. We cry out to the reporter: "But that's not the whole story! Tell the whole story!" As Mr. Rooney charges his wife in Beckett's *All That Fall,* "Tell all! Tell all!" May it not be that biblical story-telling will provide a test here?[8]

7. Gertrude Stein, again, witnesses to one version of this, for it is in connection with her method in writing *The Making of Americans* and her attempt to get at the "bottom nature" of men and women that she explained, "When I was working with William James, I completely learned one thing, that science is continuously busy with the complete description of something, with ultimately the complete description of anything with ultimately the complete description of everything." Cited by Elizabeth Sprigge, *Gertrude Stein,* p. 73.

8. In the case of Mr. Rooney (as we have noted above, pp. 30–31), to "tell all" is not to omit that the baby in question fell under the wheels of the train. Beckett wants among other things to rebuke dishonest sentimentalism and pietism, as suggested by the ironic use in his title of the words of the Psalm, "The Lord upholdeth all that fall" (Ps. 154:14). When the Christian asks that the whole story be told —"Tell all!"—he also insists with Beckett that all such fatalities be told without blinking them. But in the demand, "Tell all!" he expects a great deal more. In fact he may precisely ask the narrator to do

In a first section (I) we shall introduce the claim that the Hebrew epos as compelling language and world-story, in its combination of realism and holism, has served countless generations as a "house of being" or cable of order and survival across the centuries. And we shall confront it with the understandably restricted scope of contemporary rhetorics. In following sections, after noting the prominence of the narrative mode in Israel's Scriptures and its relation to this people's self-understanding, we shall consider more in detail (II) the world-plot character of the narrative cycles or movement from first to last things, (III) the richly concrete historical realism of the narratives, and (IV) matters of style corresponding to these features. We shall be led to observe that the ultimate motivation of the biblical recitals and the urgency of the fabulation are associated with defense of the human order against chaos. It is this also which drives the narrators to some kind of total history both in scope and in empiricism. So we are led to ask (V) what relevant queries can be brought from this kind of story-telling to contemporary fiction. In particular we shall observe that there is a striking analogy between the biblical rhetoric and that dimension of personal reality (intentionality, dialogical movement, cf. dialectical or epic theatre) which emerges as so telling a feature in much recent work.

I. BIBLICAL HUMANISM AND MODERN SUBJECTIVITY

A theologian reflecting on the modern novel may well find himself driven back to a review of the whole phenomenon of story-telling and recital as one of the primordial modes of language. The prominence and character of this vein of rhetoric in a given

---

justice to the insight that "the Lord upholdeth all that fall." As a matter of fact Beckett himself does not shut this door finally and is by no means the voice of despair and derision that many critics suppose.

society is a significant index of the culture. Those concerned with theology and literature will ask themselves especially about narrative genres in various religious contexts. The biblical theologian will naturally be led to scrutinize the special role of narrative in Scripture beginning with its dominant place in the literature of Israel.

Since we put modern fiction under the microscope and bring to bear upon it so many diverse interests, it is surely not far-fetched to invoke the biblical narrative as a foil and see what observations may be forthcoming. Indeed, we may here find ourselves on the track of a theological criticism more appropriate than some others. In assessing any particular literary form certainly one appropriate test should be that of any corresponding Christian or biblical genre. It is to this end that we make a first appeal not to dogmatic tests but to the Hebrew recitals, their styles and rhetorics. Here we can operate at a literary level rather than a theological, or, better, we can operate theologically at a literary level. Rather than test the modern novel by biblical truth, let us test it by biblical story-telling.

We have in view here first of all the narrative of the Old Testament beginning with the Pentateuch. Again one will ask: if we leave out theology and confine ourselves to this narrative as a literary genre, how can we profitably compare it with the modern novel after almost three millenniums? Yet let us remember that even in the smaller units of story-telling there are significant differences, morphologically, in the stories of different cultures. And we can look farther. When Auerbach compares biblical and classical narrative units he includes more than style in the narrow sense. Without going into theology he identifies in the rhetoric itself different types of realism, perspective, sensibility—all reflecting different cultural and anthropological presuppositions inseparable from style.[9] But if this holds for

9. *Mimesis,* Princeton, N.J., 1953, Chapters I and II. For example: "But even the human beings in the Biblical stories have greater depths

the unit story it holds also for a succession or cycle of such stories. With this kind of development recital evokes more and more clearly a particular version of world-awareness. When one enters into the epics of Homer or India it is not only the inventory of daily life and not only the repertoire of psychological responses that differ but basic apperception. This has to do with such fundamental matters as time, orientation, causation and reality-sense generally.

But these considerations also answer the objection that it is not meaningful thus to confront modern *fiction* with biblical *history*. I could argue that fiction and history always encroach on each other and in any case have a common root in what prompts to recital. But it is enough to urge that the two kinds of rehearsal can be compared—as could two kinds of history or two kinds of fiction—at the level of their respective realism, perspective, sensibility, apperception, and so forth, all having their bearing upon style and rhetoric. Auerbach's basic comparisons are between the *Odyssey* and Genesis on the one hand, and Petronius and the Gospel of Mark on the other. The fact that the pagan texts are fictional (epic and romance respectively) while the biblical texts are quasi-historical is of no significance for his study of realism.

In this context, then, we may anticipate and state our thesis. Since we are now concerned first of all with the arts of narration we push our search for criteria back behind the New Testament narrative to the Old, and make our appeal to the Hebrew anthropology, the biblical humanism, and venture our assessment from that basis. In Israel an earthy kind of realism came to birth such that its recitals encompass and interweave the whole story of heaven and earth and of man in unique fashion. If we speak of "epiphany" today in connection with those revela-

---

of time, fate and consciousness than do the human beings in Homer . . . their thoughts and feelings have more layers, are more entangled." P. 12.

tions that lie at the origin of religion or, technically, as a feature of modern fiction and lyric, Israel's "epiphany" was of such a kind that it had to be historized. Man was seen as a responsible actor in a world-story. Man's multi-dimensional nature is in view and a real world-theatre, and all in an ultimate context. This world-apperception, moreover, carries with it a dramatic element: the order in question is always threatened by anarchy, as the reality established is threatened by fantasy and false images or vain imaginations. Man is secured against these by fidelity to the revealed pattern or covenant which encompasses not only his "spiritual" faculties but also his social and somatic existence.

The biblical narrative perpetuates this epiphany and its vicissitudes and communicates its import. Indeed, the biblical epos remains as a kind of cable or life-line across the abysses of time and cultures, because man is here sustained over against anarchy, non-being and nescience. In this sense language is, indeed, a "house of being."

Other great cultural epiphanies or faiths have created their own ordering structures and rhetorics, testifying in various ways to particular endowments of our common human nature. But they differ in this matter of holism, in the realism and scope of their fabulation. In Israel we are confronted with a veritable mutation, to use a secular equivalent for "election." It is not surprising that its story of man engages his social sense and channels the vitalities of his biological inheritance towards personal fulfillment and viable community.[10] Is it not the con-

10. This is not the occasion to deal with the demurrer which would acquiesce in the fateful legacy of the biblical understanding of man but would also assign it responsibility, especially at a psychological level, for various disorders associated with it (and in contrast with other faiths, particularly of the East) such as moralism, diabolism, holy war mentality, etc. The point to make here is that the annals and ethic of any faith which truly relates itself to the dynamics of human nature and its irrational elements are bound to reflect the dramas of life against death, both private and public. It is, however, true that the

tinued story of Israel whether in the synagogue or the church
which until recently, in any case, has given history its substance,
though of course this historical fabric of reality has both its
visible and latent continuities.

To put it in another way, we can say that the ancient patterns
of rehearsal in the Bible—these genealogies of heaven and earth,
these paradigms of the human family, these vicissitudes of a
pilgrim people through ancient economies, these records of
conscience in the making, these annals of man's generic passions,
his wrestlings with the angel, the pride and miscarriage of his
his works and many inventions—we can say that these ancient
rehearsals may be recognized in some sort as the archetypal
molds of our own histories and fabulations. In these tracks our
own courses are run. Here we of the West find the world-old
syndrome that coerces us from the cradle to the grave. When
we come into the world in whatever century since, we find ourselves in a mystery that has been mapped, even if we disbelieve
it, and even if the ancient chart has all but faded away.[11] Never-

---

language and symbolics of the tradition have often been infected and
deformed in the course of its accepted engagements with the kingdoms
of misrule. I have discussed the perversion of Christian imagery of
sacrifice and atonement by alien motifs of masochism-sadism in "The
Cross: Social Trauma or Redemption," in my book, *Theology and
Modern Literature,* Cambridge, 1967, pp. 93–110.

11. Here we may cite one recent testimony, by the playwright Eugene Ionesco, all the more significant that it is not a Jew who is
writing: "I therefore believe that without the Jews, the world would
be harsh and sad. What keeps us alive? The hope that some day or
other, everyone will change, and everything will change and be good
and beautiful. Without the Jews, we should not have this belief: we
should not hope in the coming or the return of a Messiah, the saviour.
We still hope, knowing that the Messiah is behind the door: we hope
that he will open it one day and that the world will be flooded with
joy and light. We all hope in the ideal City, that is to say we all hope
that a new Jerusalem will rise up from the deserts and from death.
We hope for the transfiguration of the world, and we shall hope for
this as long as there are Jews. Without them, madness of crime;

theless, our inmost being, our genes, carry this imprint, suggested by such formulas as "lost and found," "from slave to royalty" and by such models as those of "pilgrim," "servant," "saint." If the biblical experience precisely as narrative carries this kind of meaning and this kind of holism, it is not far-fetched to take it as a basis of Christian discrimination over against other forms of story.

Yet we face here one consideration which may seem to block this kind of assessment today. Not only is our contemporary fiction removed by millenniums from the biblical recitals in question, but by comparison it deals with a very foreshortened reality, with one in which the self is alienated from a wider context, deals largely, in fact, with subjectivity.[12] Contemporary man and his accounts of himself forfeit the total perspectives of the biblical epic. We can understand this in the light of our western fate. But this radical disparity does not invalidate our procedure. No doubt the biblical holism judges our attenuated field of concern and challenges the restriction of so much of our fiction to the dramas of the self. Yet even within these limitations of the contemporary novelist, distinctions can be made. It is a question as to whether within them he nevertheless wrestles with the limits imposed, whether he seeks to move "beyond alienation," and to repossess in some new way the wider orientation.

Though the believer must regret the very special focus of the best contemporary fiction as compared with the perspectives of the biblical epic or the literature of other periods, one consideration should give him pause. He may himself be confident in his inherited affirmations of the total meaningfulness of the world,

---

without them darkness." "Journal," *Encounter* (London), vol. XXXI, no. 3 (September 1968), p. 14. The passage is dated in the year 1967.

12. Note the formulation of Susan Sontag: modern man's "increasing burden of subjectivity, at the expense of his sense of the reality of the world." *Against Interpretation*, New York, 1966, p. 134.

and in the bridges that he can build from his private experience
to the wider context of history and ultimate reality. But he
should ask himself whether this total grasp is actually earned
and operative. We know too well how a traditional Christian
idealism or pietism can affirm all this yet be quite blind to the
real givens and costs and corollaries of such a claim. The contemporary novelist at his best is wrestling with these givens and
impasses of our situation so as to make possible a genuine
repossession in new terms of the wider meaningfulness of the
world. Or, to say it in literary terms, he is seeking to tell the
whole story again in such a way that no stubborn elements need
be by-passed.

The difficulty of this today whether in life or in fiction
may be illustrated from Saul Bellow's *Augie March,* and I have
in view some remarks of Marcus Klein in his book, *After
Alienation.*[13] Augie is speaking of "the axial lines of life, with
respect to which you must be straight," and which are "Truth,
love, peace, bounty, usefulness, harmony!" which, he says, quiver
right through him when striving stops. And these, he observes,
are "not imaginary stuff . . . because I bring my whole life to
the test." Klein, citing this passage, goes on to remark, however,
that this is one of the moments when Augie's hopefulness becomes shrill. His whole life does not validate the perception. In
fact, "the novel is honest beyond Augie's knowing and it does
not permit him so easy an escape."[14] This instance illustrates
both the difficulty today of genuine as against cheap grace and
the integrity of the artist who in his own medium wrestles with
the problem of valid perspectives. What we look for in any
narrative, ancient or modern, is that kind of dense inner coherence which therefore moves towards whatever wider horizons
with convincing logic.

13. New York, 1965.
14. P. 53.

II. THE BIBLICAL EPOS
AS A "HOUSE OF BEING"

To clarify what is meant by the "holism" of the biblical epos we may begin by asking what might be called the prior question about narrative in general. What special aspect of our human reality discloses itself in the universal impulse to tell stories? We answer immediately: our sense of temporality and succession. An anecdote links a before and an after; a poem need not. But it goes deeper to say that a story posits a sense of orientation and coherence. The story, the fable, the myth assume a context, an order of some kind. They impose a graph upon chaos or nescience. They carve out a lighted space, a *zu-Hause,* in the darkness.

I am thinking of the primordial myth as the story that accompanied the mimetic ritual. The intense group experience of epiphany required meaningful extrapolation, explanation, in the narrative. One recalls Durkheim's description of the origin of the categories, the projection of particularized space and time, the process of world-making. To tell a story is to posit a meaningful order, however fragmentary, a degree of coherence. If the novel of today tends sometimes to refuse the story aspect, to transcribe chaotic impressions rather than woven sequence, to prefer epiphany over rehearsal, then we confront a significant symptom of our situation. The only redeeming feature of such a reversal would be that neglected ranges of experience were calling for recognition, thus for the moment disqualifying our inherited coherence patterns.

I am aware, of course, of the immense differences there can be in the kinds of coherence implicit in narration. The saga of different peoples differ radically in the kinds of reality they posit, the range or levels of human and cosmic relationship they incorporate, the dimensions of realism they represent.

In the Hebrew and Christian Scriptures the narrative mode has extraordinary importance, and not only quantitatively. If one looks at the classics and charters of other religions or religious philosophies the story aspect may be relatively marginal. Their sacred books often take the form rather of oracular aphorism or philosophical instruction or mystical treatise or didactic code. In the case of biblical man language moved towards recital, and all heaven and earth came into it. The community renewed its identity by its rehearsals, and by telling the world the way of the world as its members had heard it. The fact that narrative had such a constitutive part in Israel's faith points us back to a level of profound cultural apperception. But this bears also upon the kind of narrative. We speak of this as its holism. By this we mean the scope of awareness, the multidimensional reality and realism, the inclusion of private and public, of the inner life and the social-historical, of somatic and visionary, of ethical and metaphysical.

If we look now at the narrative-cycles of the Old Testament we find one or another kind of over-arching plot from beginnings to fulfillment, and, incorporated in it, a very dense portrayal of the human experience and existence in all its empirical reality. The oldest such cycle (taken up into the later Pentateuch) runs from the creation and the patriarchs through the Exodus from Egypt to the conquest of the Promised Land, all looking to the goal that the nations should be blessed through Israel's vocation. This graph of destiny is later enlarged so that its elements of myth and saga constitute the antecedents for the providential greatness of the reign of David. The *Aeneid* does something like this for the antecedents of imperial Rome, beginning at the fall of Troy. The two epics celebrate the divine predestination, discipline and blessing of their respective peoples, providing their different charts of time, thus enhancing the worth and pride of every member of the two commonwealths and lending meaning to their state rituals.

57

In the later Deuteronomic history, by means of the farewell discourses put in the mouth of Moses, the epic of the people is again rehearsed. Here the birth of the nation and its basic covenants are memorialized at a juncture between the great disasters to the northern and southern kingdoms. Only narrative, it seems, could serve the necessary self-understanding of Israel as the horizon opens beyond the recent apostasies and catastrophies to end with a call for the renewal of the covenant in a restored Jerusalem. The subsequent priestly narrative reshapes the total graph, now from creation to the post-exilic situation, though in a less realistic key. But the historian who combined and interwove these rehearsals into the form in which we have them in the Hebrew canon today gave to his people a total epos and a total orientation which was at the same time rooted in the richest kind of realistic humanism.

What I would like to emphasize here is that the employment of the narrative mode—a combination of myth, saga and history —provided not only orientation in the mysteries of time and existence, but therewith the structures of a human order against chaos, and of meaningfulness against unreason. The biblical epos secured life against death, being against non-being. In this sense again, language constituted a "house of being." Mythos and ethos were inseparable.

This crucial issue of human viability in the narrative appears also and especially in the bodies of law which are so deeply embedded in it. Just as the epic evokes the creation and the covenants of heaven and earth, that is, pledges of the stability of the cosmic order, over against the primeval chaos, so the laws set stern barriers and austere penalties against relapse into confusion. Characteristic for the laws is the sanction, "I am the Lord your God," in fuller form: "I am the Lord your God, who brought you forth from the land of Egypt to give you the land of Canaan, and to be your God" (Lev. 25:38). Thus the total narrative sanctions the commandments, evokes the self-understanding that bows to the obligation. We only recognize the full significance of this when we note that the demands so motivated reach to the fateful dividing line between creation and chaos, and between the human and the bestial. As the narrative represents the life-line of survival through flood and desert and foes natural and supernatural, so the mandates that appeal to it are directed against outrage, enormities and violations of nature. Both the narrative and the law reflect a dramatic sense of the jeopardies of the human community in existence, and this is evident in the attention given to incursions of the irrational, panics, abominations and hyperbolic penalties, bans and exterminations.[15] This defense of the human appears correspondingly in the law.

You shall not give any of your children to devote them by fire to Molock. . . . I am the Lord. (Lev. 18:21)

Everyone who curses his father or his mother shall be put to death. (20:9)

If your brother becomes poor, and cannot maintain himself with you, you shall maintain him . . . I am the Lord your God. (25:35, 38)

And so the prohibitions go on against removing landmarks,

15. Our modern outlook fails to see these elements of Scripture in context. Recently Robert Lowell in a lecture at the Harvard Divinity School dealing with the biblical literature registered his understandable revulsion at what he took to be the two most immoral books in the Bible, Joshua and the Apocalypse. He instanced the extermination of men, women and children in the former, and the blood up to the horses' bridles in the latter. But we should read ancient texts in terms of their rhetorical genres and cultural settings. Moreover, it is important to recognize the basic motive behind such hyperbolic dramatizations: all such sanguinary fictions whether in the form of history or prophetic anticipation reflect in the contemporary modes of the imagination men's acute sense of the struggle against the encroachments of the primeval chaos and for the viability of the human.

59

cutting down fruit trees, defrauding the laborer, giving a daughter in prostitution, falsifying weights and measures. All such orderings have their sanction in the narrative. They are more than morality. They are associated with the life-line of human order and sanity.[16] Thus the urgency and apodictic character of the laws match the powerful realism and dynamics of the total story.

We are noting the relation of narrative in Israel to other genres. How is it with the poem? The close of Moses' farewell discourses in Deuteronomy offers us an example. He concludes his rehearsal of God's ways with Israel by an injunction to treasure up "this book of the law" (that is, with its setting in the narrative) "that it may be there as a witness before you." It is to be rehearsed in the assemblies of the people "as long as you live in the land which you are going over the Jordan to possess" (Dt. 31:13). But then we read that in view of the anticipated breaking of the covenant God says to Moses:

Now therefore write this *song,* and teach it to the people of Israel; put it in their mouths, that this song may be a witness for me against the people of Israel. . . . for it will live unforgotten in the mouths of their descendents. (31:19, 21)

So we have the song of Moses in Deuteronomy 32. This is again a recital of God's favor to Israel and of her apostasy, followed by God's eventual vindication. But it is in the lyric and dramatic mode. Thus the self-understanding of Israel and the individual Israelite as brought home to them in the prose narrative is quickened to another degree of immediacy and responsibility by the visionary poetic vehicle. Is not this the role of the poetry in the Hebrew Scriptures as a whole, especially of the Psalter in relation to the total narrative ground plan?

16. Note Dt. 32:46–49. "Be careful to do all the words of this law. For it is no trifle for you, but it is your life."

60

Thus we have observed that the older Hebrew epos provided a total orientation and coherence. It was group-binding and time-binding. It offered a well-lighted place to the human being and the group against the incursions of the irrational in any theatre of experience. And we may add that it was this same map of existence which was taken over especially by the English and American Calvinists, and found later rehearsals in the work of Milton and Bunyan, and which has had its still later vicissitudes in American self-interpretation and literary fiction.

III. REALISM AND HOLISM

But we have in the story-telling of the Old Testament not only an over-arching world-plot but also a very rich dense portrayal of human experience. One way to identify the latter appears especially in the legends of Genesis. The fact that their origins can be assigned to archaic motifs associated with early epochs and transitions of society testifies to their realistic human substance. The usual typologies connect all such narrative lore with ancient culture-crises, tribal annals or ethnological and cultic history. In the stories as in the symbolic language a hermeneutic of symbol and myth brings to light very ancient strata of human conscience and consciousness reflecting the evolution of society and the self.[17]

But I would emphasize a more immediate kind of documentation of the human phenomenon in our narratives, one which also distinguishes the biblical recital from familiar kinds of fanciful or fabulous or gratuitous invention. Religion in the Old Testament roots in man's primordial drives and social bonds; it wrestles with the powerful, intractible but God-given raw materials of human nature. Why are the historical books so full of vivid and often shocking anecdotes about the elemental re-

17. Paul Ricoeur, *The Symbolism of Evil*, New York, 1967.

lationships, the a, b, c's of life as it were: sex, family, property, vendetta, heroism? To cite what I have written elsewhere:

It is not enough to say that here as in Homer we find a marvellous gamut of human nature portrayed. The point is rather this: the Bible recognizes that God finds his way to us, and we to Him, through the deep primordial cravings, hungers, loyalties, bonds, suggested by these relationships of parent and child, husband and wife, chieftain and follower.

These stories have to do with elemental relationships and natural yearnings like parental instinct, tribal and patriotic passion, hero worship and pride in skill or role, sentiments which involve our very entrails. They lay bare the roots of human vitality, the cables which carry the powerful voltage of human impluse and action, whether creative or destructive. The modern psychologist knows how important these ingredients in our make-up are. . . . The tree of Judaism has its roots in these kinds of human dynamics. The vitality and meaning of Messianic hopes and eschatological perspectives spring from these explosive forces in our nature.[18]

Now it is especially in the older stratum in the books of Samuel that this kind of holism can be seen. Here we follow the story of David's succession to Saul amid the strife of the tribes and war with the Philistines. We note the interweaving of Yahweh's over-ruling purpose with the raw material of human passions. Into the total web come not only dramas of intimate relationships but the play of historical determinations. The narrator is interested in the skills and occupations of men: the smith, the musician, the wise woman, the rancher; and in the traits of men: astuteness, magnanimity, melancholia, jealousy, emulation. We get the full gamut of social rank. We get prudential strategies and sagacity, but also resorts to divination and necromancy and mimetic exorcisms when normal controls

18. *Otherworldliness and the New Testament.* New York, 1954, pp. 32–36, abridged.

are swept away by incursions of the irrational or the horrors of
pestilence and famine.

There is one feature of this narrative which again seems to me
to be worth special consideration. The human actions recurrently
burst the wonted course of affairs and explode, as it were, into
the hyperbolic. They go over the limits of the human scale, in
heroism or immolation, in ecstasy or horror. We have a sense
of over-flowing human *virtu* or prodigality of creaturely vitality,
under brilliant realistic illumination, but it moves often into
the order of the arcane, disclosure of the prodigious. But even
such excursions beyond the normal are controlled in the
history. We have controlled frenzy, ritualized mania. The
irrational dimensions of life, above or below, are mastered but
their energies are acknowledged and channeled.

We have an example here in one theatre of what it is to tell
the whole story, such that private drama is only rightly grasped
in its public determination, and social rituals in their metaphysical relationship. Suggestive of this total vitality is the blessing of Joseph in Dt. 33:13;

> And of Joseph he said,
>   "Blessed by the Lord be his land,
>   with the choicest gifts of heaven above,
>   and of the deep that couches beneath."

What is the significance for our analysis of that great change
in the structure of the biblical epic that arose with Jewish
apocalyptic literature and that passed over into the New
Testament narrative? We can illustrate by the difference between
the Book of Ruth and the Book of Daniel. Ruth is by no means
only a pastoral idyll. With its exquisite old-Israelite realism it
is part of the total Hebrew epos, linking as it does the period of
the judges with ancestry of David. Kinship patterns and marriage, rural economy and judicial practice, private poignancy

and public, indeed international relationships, are all essential ingredients in a short story which has its place in that wider history that encompasses the whole course of the world. The Book of Ruth provides a signal example of how narrative provides orientation and coherence in the world, and how, for example, there is no truncation between the order of sexuality of the individual and a total context of meaning and value.

In the stories in the Book of Daniel: the lions' den, the fiery furnace, the feast of Belshazzar, but also in the mythological account of how one like a son of man succeeded to the world-rule of the beasts representing the empires of the East—in all these we again have a marriage of heaven and earth, of historical circumstance and a transcendental scheme. But we have entered here upon a kind of narrative reality and style that merge with those of the Book of Revelation and indeed with aspects of our Gospels.

Is there a loss of realism and holism when these eschatological and surreal features of language are introduced? But there is still a plot. Narrative is still the necessary medium to convey meaning and coherence. It is true that the goal of world-history is redefined. Alpha and Omega are reconceived. This calls for a revised version of the Hebrew world-story as a whole. Moreover, the story-teller and the hearers or readers now find themselves at the point of *dénouement,* in Act Five. But the New Testament is still basically narrative. Self-understanding and community-understanding are still mediated through recital. Even the poetry in the New Testament is often, again, confessional recital. And the law of the new movement in Israel is sanctioned by the recital.

Hans Käsemann in an often-quoted thesis has written that apocalyptic was the mother of theology—in the sense that the interim opened up by the portrayal of the end-time required new reflections on the meaning of the divine plan. This can be formulated in literary terms: the new vision of time and the world called forth new rhetorics.[19] But the Gospels show us that recital was still the inevitable medium; and that narrative, much of it of a very earthy kind like the parables of Jesus, was required to domesticate revelation in daily life. We see here the continuing Hebraic demand that epiphany be historized. In the Gospel narrative, the realism and the holism of Hebraic man is safeguarded and no truncation is allowed between the somatic and the spiritual, between the individual and the group, or between the historical and the transcendent. The narration makes men at home in the world, even when that world has entered upon its final transformation.

IV. STYLE AND THE RHETORICS OF THE HEART

A third aspect of the biblical narratives to be discussed is that of their styles. We have in mind the Old Testament material first of all. This evidences in many ways what we find in all ancient epic, the prior *oral* stage of recital, a feature which lends it an enlivening sense of actuality. With this goes the anonymity of the speaking voice of the writer, a feature again which lends prominence to the action itself as though events spoke for themselves, and one which conveys the community import of what is told. Much of it has, moreover, what is common to all cult-rehearsal as distinguished from universal story-telling, aspects of formality[20] which, at a second or third remove, reflect older cultic or ceremonial setting; in any case, features of sobriety and economy of language which are determined by the special sense of destiny associated with the tribes or the nation. No doubt one

19. See my *Language of the Gospel: Early Christian Rhetoric,* New York, 1964, especially Chapter IV, "The Story," 63–78.
20. "The prose is not the common colloquial language of everyday life, but is more artistic in its composition and has some sort of rhythmical construction." H. Gunkel, *The Legends of Genesis,* Chicago, 1901, p. 38.

can recognize elements in Genesis or the Book of Judges or II Samuel, and so on, which go back to a quasi-secular inspiration, but these have been subsequently metamorphosed by being taken up into the more fateful context of some larger cycle. An analogy is found in the way in which an archaic war-ballad and taunt-song has been transformed into what we now have in the Song of Deborah in Judges 5; a liturgical paean for use at one of the older Israelite sanctuaries as part of a cycle of *res gestae* or heroic rehearsals of the tribes.[21]

In recognizing the ways in which the styles of Hebrew narrative were variously colored by the cultic-factor or by the special apperceptions of Israel as a people with an historical calling I would not give the impression that we have to do with hieratic language, though the so-called priestly stratum has a special formality of this kind. We should not be misled by the way in which ideas of a sacred style have been falsely imposed on the Scriptures by later canonization and translation, and by special views of inspiration elaborated by synagogue and church. What distinguishes these histories from common story-telling and even from comparable culture-epic is finally the depth of motive that lies behind the utterance, the impulse behind the birth of language (behind what Ebeling and Fuchs call the *Sprach-Ereignis* or *Wort-Geschehen*), the urgency of the fabulation, all of which shape the narrative in the single episode and in the sequences.[22] I have spoken of this dynamic aspect of the narrative in another

21. J. Blenkinsopp, "Ballad Style and Psalm Style in the Song of Deborah," *Biblica* 42/1 (1961), pp. 61–76. Cited in my *Language of the Gospel*, p. 105. Another analogy is the way in which the old English ballads were transformed in the course of the Christianizing of the culture. Cf. M. Jarret-Kerr, *Studies in Literature and Belief*, London, n.d., Chapter II.

22. ". . . each successive member is linked to the preceding one . . . each preceding member appears as the natural cause or at least the antecedent of the succeeding one. . . . These narratives, then, are tense in their connection. The narrators do not like digressions, but press with all their energy toward the mark." Gunkel, *op. cit.*, p. 70.

way in saying that it was a special feature of Israel's epiphanies that they required historization.

But there are more specific features of style that can be identified. With respect to the Hebrew language itself the prominence of the verb commands first attention, as well as the plastic and sensuous character of the vocabulary. In both respects abstraction is largely still beyond the horizon. Syntax is paratactic, and clause is added to clause with the simplest construction. This is what Gertrude Stein has in mind when she writes that "really in the Old Testament there is no sentence existing and no paragraphing."[23] Her point is that the real import of the telling goes beyond conventional interest in the one-dimensional succession of events.[24] Gunkel commenting on the paratactic features associates it with the tenseness "of the connection of the successive clauses, and attributes it to the undeviating energy of the narrator."[25]

Yet while in one dimension experience is ordered in teleological succession its reality is also evoked in another dimension which we may call the dialogical. Style in this respect is not a matter of Hebrew syntax so much as one of the special sensibility and psychology of this people. Israel construed its world very much in terms of relationships, encounter, address and response, the confrontation of wills. Events and episodes have their import in this domain, in the aspect of transaction. It is not surprising therefore that narrative style is short on description and foregoes detailed portrayal and unbroken sequence of events. Reality is not here but at the level of personal and community

23. *Narrative: Four Lectures*, p. 19.
24. With respect to the rarity of the period in Beckett's later fiction Hugh Kenner writes: "No sequence of sentences can approximate the ultimate statement The Unnamable yearns to make, since every sentence must begin somewhere and end somewhere else (*abitus, transitus, aditus,* wrote Geulincx) and no choice of a beginning or an ending can fail to exclude a thousand others." *Samuel Beckett,* p. 188.
25. Cf. note 22 above.

response. With some over-simplification it has been claimed that Israel's genius is associated with the ear as that of other cultures and their epics is with the eye. In any case the "word" was evidently primary for the Hebrew religious experience, "word" not in the sense of language in general but in the sense of the word of address and of dialogue.

It follows that the subjectivity of the actors in the narratives is conveyed chiefly by their action, deportment and external indications, as well as by their speech.

The ancient story teller does not share the modern point of view that the most interesting and worthy theme for art is the soul-life of man; his childlike taste is fondest of the outward, objective facts. . . . He has an extraordinary capacity for selecting just the action which is most characteristic for the state of feeling of his hero. . . . Little as these primitive men could talk about their soul-life, we gain the impression that they are letting us look into the very hearts of their heroes.[26]

Gunkel is speaking here of the legends of Genesis, but the characterization applies more generally.

There is one other feature of the Hebrew language and syntax which is consonant with all that has been said, and this is the minor role of the adjective. But this is only one of the more striking indices of the absence in its narrative of elements familiar in other forms of saga and epic: circumstantial description, personal portraiture, detailed sensuous delineation. In these respects the Hebrew histories while they evoke an abundant and many-levelled humanity nevertheless focus on actions, relationships and their moral nexus. It follows, as Auerbach has shown, that the narrative styles lack the unbroken surface continuity and pictorial fullness of Homer. The continuity and the reality-sense lie deeper and are conveyed by a seemingly less developed gamut of language but by one well adapted to the dramatic

26. Gunkel, *op. cit.*, pp. 61–62.

transactions of the heart. We shall note at a later point certain analogies between this observation and some of the more recent explorations in modern fiction.

V. IMPLICATIONS FOR MODERN NARRATIVE

With these interrelated aspects of the biblical epos before us, world-plot, concreteness and style, we propose now to single out fundamental features of the biblical story-telling which might still fairly be used as tests of or as foil to modern narrative. After two millenniums and more we are not so foolish as to take it as a model in any narrow sense, least of all in its ideology. To make a relevant literary comparison we must go deeper.

One such challenge has to do with the motive for narration. This raises a question which is so elementary it is often not even thought of: why narrative at all! Why does narrative exist at all in the old Hebrew society and why in any case so much of it? Or, again, what prompts the modern fabulist? For what good reason are novels written in the first place? This is a good question because it points us back to what should be the profound life-relationship of this genre or mode of language. And it points us to the elemental compulsion which called forth precisely narration as a form of awareness among the early Hebrews, and determined the scope and realism of the recitals that followed. But this factor is connected with their survival power.

There is one basic test of all story-telling which again we are apt to forget, and that is that it should hold the auditor or reader. So the reader says, "I could not put it down," or, "I had to see how it came out." This feature of any extended narration points to something much deeper than contrivance. The act of telling must spring from a profound necessity. There must be an initial urgency, life-force, in the story-teller, an *Erzählerfreude*, that lends power like that of a spell to his fabulation, and enables him to order experience in persuasive designs. One of the most illuminating things ever said about a fabulist, and it was said about Ezra Pound, was that he provided humanity with incentives to *go on living.* I would put this beside that primordial secret of a narration which induces the reader to *go on reading.* This is not a truism. There are many stories which are not read or heard to the end. The world they create does not come into existence. It is not real enough. The biblical epos has continued to be read and the world it created has continued to be real for men of many kindreds and generations down to the present time. It has "held" the world in more senses than one. This first test, then, is a challenge to the ultimate springs of motivation of the novelist.

No doubt there is abundant justification for many of the less ambitious kinds of fiction which are written or told in all periods. But our concern here is with the ultimate criteria of the genre and therefore with its most important contemporary examples or directions. In the next chapter we shall turn to the example of Proust all the more because the question of motivation had a central importance for him and was determinative of his achievement as well as of his method and style.

A second test is that of what we have called holism. In the biblical narration no significant dimensions are scanted. The private and the public are interrelated, the psychological and the social, the empirical and the metaphysical. And there is a robust reality-sense, a power in being, and it is related to the fact that man in Scripture, precisely in his total perspectives, is still linked with the archaic hidden roots and fibres of his pre-historical and biological inheritance. This test is a challenge to any kind of truncation of man, whether naturalistic or spiritualizing or solipsist. It exposes particularly one dominant feature of modern letters, that which can be generally characterized as the "epiphany." For the epiphany moment in modern experience and the modern novel, which often has to carry the whole burden of

70

meaning, represents a highly fragmentary grasp of reality. The momentary vision in question may have a romanticist, an existentialist or a surrealist character, but in whatever form it evidences a forfeiture of relationships and so of holism. It testifies, indeed, to an impoverishment of vitality in the visionary rather than the contrary. For when epiphany is powerful it orders reality.

It is to be acknowledged that the imagination of our time meets all but insuperable obstacles in its tasks of ordering our confusions. In this dilemma it is more courageous for the artist to explore what authentic contacts with reality open up for him than to cling to structures and idioms that have lost their authority. Yet the impulse to "tell more" if not to "tell all" is ever present in modern letters, as indeed is testified by recurrent wrestlings with ancient epic including the Bible and by transformations of the novel-genre to bring it closer to the full range of experience new and old.

There is one further challenge presented by the biblical epos. It is difficult to state it without seeming to involve theology. We have already had it in view when discussing the "dialogical" dimension of that narrative. The question raised is that of doing justice to the full mystery of the self and its aliveness at the level of inter-personal encounter and mutuality. The unique humanism of the Old Testament would appear to rest upon some momentous cultural drama that moved the race along towards the personal.

Its narrative, therefore, evokes something more than the usual suspenseful turns of fortune of men and societies and something more than the joys and sorrows, hopes and disappointments of life. In such classic epic and fictions the deeper enigma of man is hardly touched. What is missing is some sense of that secret of his being where he is a mixture of freedom and helplessness, of loneliness and entanglement, and where all this carries with it a consciousness of responsibility, and where man is sensitive

71

not only to external approval or disapproval but to internal peace or shame. It is a question of the dramas of the heart, and of the share of men's willing and choosing in the fatefulness of the world.[27]

I can do no better to suggest this special awakening of the self than by noting how in the biblical episodes, in the Old Testament stories, God, as it were, looks man in the eye. This intense facet of awareness may be evoked for us if we remember occasions when our parents, desiring to track something down, bade us look them in the eye. "Eyeball to eyeball," we say. This kind of naked confrontation and searching of the human self can mean a calling to account. We think of Jesus looking at Peter after his denial. (Auerbach chooses this as an example of a new kind of realism in the ancient world; a banal police-court incident linked with world-significance.) Or we think of Nathan's words to David: "Thou art the man!" The kiss of Judas suggests this order of personal existence, or the handwriting on the wall in Daniel. But such moral reverberations of a positive character can also be evoked in the narrative: Joseph disclosing himself to his brothers, or the mutual magnanimity of David and the three mighty men who at the risk of their lives brought him water from the well which was by the gate of Bethlehem, to solace him at a moment of homesickness and dereliction. Quite apart from theology, all this represents a deeper kind of humanism, an existential kind of realism, such that the narrative pierces to the heart's core of the reader and binds us hand and foot. This test exposes a great deal of fiction,

27. I recur here to my discussion of the New Testament parable as narrative in *The Language of the Gospel*, p. 84. I note there also the observation of André Gide in *Les Faux-Monnayeurs:* "It seems to me that one kind of tragic dimension has for the most part been missing in literature up until now. The novel has concerned itself with the strokes of fate, with good and bad fortune, with social interchanges, with the conflict of passions, with characters, but not at all with the essence of the human being. To carry the drama over to the moral plan—this, however, was the task of Christianity." Paris, 1925, p. 160.

past and present, particularly today much that is inspired by a sub-personal aestheticism or an affective pathos whether athletic or sophisticated, or the novel of ideas, all of which by-pass this dimension. On the other hand, it is here that justice should be done to a Salinger who has the delicate registers to deal with the infinitely subtle and complex world of relationships at this level.

The dimension of involvement of which we have been speaking refers first of all to the characters in the given narrative. But the reader is also involved. We are reminded of Berthold Brecht therefore. For if it was his view that there must be a distance between the audience and the action it was to ensure that the spectator's responsibility was demanded. Transferred to the arts of narration this means that the hearer or reader should not be a victim of hypnotic compulsion or sorcery. Brecht spoke significantly therefore of a dialectical or epic theatre. The biblical epic has this character. It is not seductive, subjective, romantic. It does not work by a depersonalizing enchantment. When one finds sentiment in the Old Testament—as, for example, in the sacrifice of Isaac or the immolation of Jephthah's daughter—any evasion into common pathos is blocked by a high art of austerity, or any consent to disguised forms of masochism or sadism such as are invited in current novels and plays. The sufferer in such episodes is not a victim but an actor at a sacrifice.[28]

One could speak of this added dimension of narrative as that of intentionality. If a novelist is to "tell the whole story," it is not enough that we should have a richly circumstantialized account of all that happened, even if it include many levels of experience. Added to all such objectivities there should be the

28. Quoting Robert Frost, *A Masque of Reason*, New York, 1945, p. 12. God explains to Job why he had caused him to suffer:
> Society can never think things out:
> It has to see them acted out by actors,
> Devoted actors at a sacrifice.

baffling dimension of intentionality, ultimate freedom, personal reality in its movement. What is in view here is well suggested in remarks of Gertrude Stein:

Everybody's life is full of stories: your life is full of stories; my life is full of stories. They are very occupying, but they are not really interesting. What is interesting is the way everyone tells their stories; [and at the same time she was listening to the tellers' revelation of their "basic nature."] If you listen, really listen, you will hear people repeating themselves. You will hear their pleading nature or their attacking nature or their asserting nature.[29]

Miss Stein could speak of this as catching the "rhythm of personality." But if this dimension of personal reality is in the novel it will also involve the reader and his core of freedom.[30]

We find an echo of this dissatisfaction with mere stories today and a demand for that kind of personal dimension we have found in the biblical narrative in Samuel Beckett's play for radio, *Embers*.[31] Henry exclaims:

Stories, stories, years and years of stories, till the need came on me, for someone, to be with me, anyone, a stranger, to talk to, imagine he hears me, years of that, and then, now, for someone who . . .

29. As quoted in the introduction by Thornton Wilder to Gertrude Stein, *Four Americans,* New Haven, 1947, p. x.
30. "What Robbe-Grillet is after (and to a greater or lesser degree his colleagues in the form . . .) is not simply 'objectification of things,' but the forced inclusion of the reader in the process of inventing art, inventing stories, inventing experience. . . . It is a view that shows Robbe-Grillet, the chief propagandist of the nouveau roman, to be as stern a moralist as he is a rationalist . . . all of [his novels] do succeed in some degree in scattering one's preconceptions and thereby making one aware of the possibilities of a re-energized involvement on the reader's part in the invention of art and life." Eliot Fremont-Smith, reviewing *La maison de rendez-vous* in *The New York Times,* November 23, 1966.
31. *Krapp's Last Tape and Embers,* London, 1959.

74

knew me, in the old days, anyone, to be with me, imagine he hears me, what I am, now.[32]

What Henry craves is not "stories" but a voice. And here Henry and Beckett himself speak for an epoch, as Hugh Kenner suggests. For as to the "stories": "That is where the Newtonian universe belongs also: it was a story Europe told itself for many decades.[33] In *Embers* the character Bolton in a climax of tremendous poignancy pleads for "response, personal impingement as against mechanism," in asking mutely "for whatever cannot be specified, for whatever communion looks out of another's eyes."[34]

We have before us, then, these observations on the biblical epos and the literary tests it offers to modern narrative. We find the modern novel lacking in this kind of holism or total humanism. This is first of all a literary observation. We are not complaining that modern fiction does not present the biblical world-view or theology. We are saying that its humanism is partial or selective, narrowly focussed, for example, upon the dramas of the modern self. Or, if wider contexts are implicit, they are not integrally related, say the public world or the metaphysical. We know that there are good reasons for this. Nevertheless, a theological criticism must register this fact, and at a literary level. So Georg Lukacs can make an analogous literary criticism, though writing as a Marxist. Speaking of the dominance of *Angst* and alienation in modern fiction he says that the test is whether the writer's view is able to include—or, better, demands—a dynamic, complex analytical rendering of social relationships or whether it leads to loss of perspective and historicity."[35] A theological criticism can also make the same diagnosis and demand.

32. Pp. 24–25.
33. *Samuel Beckett,* New York, 1961, p. 184.
34. *Ibid.,* p. 186.
35. *Realism in Our Time,* New York, p. 82.

Even when a novelist seeks to incorporate metaphysical relationships into his work we can often observe that the procedure is not structurally persuasive. In one form it has the effect of an unconvincing *deus ex machina.* Thus in *The Counterfeiters* at the point of Bernard's deepest despair, André Gide introduces an angel of comfort to strengthen the youth in a vision. The passage is moving but has an aura of the romantic and the staged. Miracles in our time are difficult to bring off. In another form presentation of the metaphysical dimension is only effected at the expense of all others. In his *Reprieve* Sartre's hero, Mathieu, caught up in the mobilization on the eve of World War II, has an apocalyptic vision of the total devastation not only of Paris but of the world, an eschatological epiphany that confers on him an inhuman liberation of the self. This leap beyond all involvement of the person is determined by Sartre's view of freedom and is unpersuasive if we step outside the ideology which controls his fiction and drama.[36]

In all such cases the gulf between empirical and transcendental is not genuinely bridged. We have observed the same hiatus in the case of Augie March's "axial lines" in Bellow's novel. Our criticism will vary with particular novelists and works. For example, a case like that of James Baldwin's *Go Tell It on the Mountain* is particularly interesting because the metaphysical dimension is evoked in biblical categories. A powerful searchlight is beamed upon patterns of human relationship and transactions in the heart, viewed in their ultimate religious reference. In these dramas of soul-saving whose syndrome has been established by a long history of introvert piety in America, Baldwin's focus on subjectivity is dictated by his material. It

36. Proust offers a very much more persuasive parallel to Sartre. Marcel in Venice sees the whole city disintegrate before his eyes as an aspect of his moral anguish in allowing his mother to leave without him. Terrified by a sense of irrevocable solitude, all reality outside him becomes empty and devastated, and Venice is dissolved as his will is paralyzed. *Albertine disparue,* vol. II, Paris, 1925, pp. 147–8.

is to his credit that he attempts to relate this claustral dimension of religion to wider moral and social realities. Yet one remains dissatisfied with the novel because of recurrent features of haziness and conventionality in the characterizations and the language. What is missing becomes clearer if one recalls the way in which Faulkner handles analogous material in *The Sound and the Fury*. Another successful attempt to deal with Christian supernaturalism in terms of our modern sensibility is Frederick Buechner's novel, *The Final Beast*.[37]

All in all, it is to be recognized that the modern novelist has to work within the givens of his epoch. We cannot ask him to be a Cervantes or a Tolstoi. The engagement with subjectivity and alienation has fallen to him as by a kind of fate. This situation has perforce narrowed and reduced the field of observation, and has located the struggle for orientation and meaning in the self and its dramas, thereby for the time being placing in question all wider contexts and the more total perspectives of the past. Amid the relativities and disarray consequent on a long history of necessary emancipations he seeks the final ground of things. In literary terms this means that language must be kept close to all vicissitudes of his experience. Yet in the ultimate urgency of speech and of marrying the word to a changing reality the narrator may still find himself obscurely prompted by the profound categories and voices of the world-story of the Scriptures.

37. New York: Athenaeum, 1965. Cf. also Jerome Nilssen, *The Drowning and the Dancing*, Philadelphia, 1967.

III. From the Almanach de Gotha to the Old Testament: The Case of Marcel Proust

I have already had occasion to confront features of the biblical narrative with modern texts and to note both disparities as well as some surprising convergences. But to suggest how such a diagnostic might be carried out more fully it will be worth while to examine some major novelist of our century and we choose Marcel Proust. Though he is not a contemporary yet we would be obliged in any case to return to one of the modern classics to find a figure of sufficient stature to make our observations fully illuminating. Since Proust has such surprising gifts and scope and at the same time shares with contemporary novelists "our increasing burden of subjectivity at the expense of our sense of the reality of the world," he can serve as an instructive test.

We may recall at this point our admission at the outset that it may appear strange to set any modern work of fiction over against the biblical histories. Yet a preliminary justification for such a procedure can be found if the work in question proposes some kind of universality. In the case of Proust the anomaly of such a confrontation may seem at its greatest. Especially when we compare him with his predecessors, Balzac and Zola, we find here a characteristic modern version of psychologism, "the rediscovery of self through the modalities of art." More than that, the "universality" achieved in this work, as Harry Levin has pointed out, "is even more surprising because the premises are so idiosyncratic, so far-fetched and special."[1] Yet in the strange world of Proust we find ourselves on common ground with the biblical humanism so far as we receive an "enhanced awareness of the way things happen to happen, of how human beings respond or do not respond to one another,"[2] and of the deeper determinations of weal and woe.

I.

In *À la recherche du temps perdu* we find an incredibly nuanced fabric of life-stories, portraits, anecdotes, tableaux. The narrative is like an endless chain—though with aspects of the spiral or symphonic recurrence. The interior cinema carries us, as it were, through its own Thousand Islands. Involuntary memory is combined with voluntary, and both are counterpointed with reflection. The style and method allow for a revelation of the mind at different foci and levels of attention, or what William James called the "compounding of consciousness."[3] Our modern sophistications call forth their own styles seeking to do justice to a complex experience. As Proust remarks: "It is difficult when one is troubled by the ideas of Kant and the nostalgia of Baudelaire

1. *The Gates of Horn,* New York, 1963, p. 444.
2. *Ibid.*
3. Cf. Melvin Friedman, *Stream of Consciousness: A Study in Literary Method,* New Haven, 1955, p. 2. On Proust see especially pp. 92–98. As "stream of consciousness" Proust's style is identified with that type related to rational control called "internal analysis" rather than the bolder and more broken type identified as "sensory impression."

to write the exquisite French of Henry IV."[4] Yet already we may note that if this modern style carries us far from the tone of epic recital and its public theatre, yet what we have spoken of as the dialogical dimension in biblical narration has its analogies here.

In Proust we have an extraordinarily refined analysis of the heart, the passions and the mores. Moving behind older thresholds and reticences we enter into the underworld of society and the self. Yet the context in psychological and moral observation is not only that of the social tabus and their penalties but also that of deeply felt ethical sensitivities. With all this the corruption and suffering of the individual are to some degree woven into their social determinations. Proust's world includes aspects of the public history of his time, as is evident in the prominence of the Dreyfus case and World War I. Moreover, his interest in the salons of Paris is more than snobbism: he has here a laboratory for the dissection of the heart, and he can recall Saint-Simon's earlier scrutiny of *"le méchanique"* of the court of Versailles and its social-psychological obsessions.

Even the extensive attention given to Sodom and Gomorrha serves the passion for moral understanding. Here too the riddling maze of motivation in the life of society is surgically inspected with an infinite calculus. Behind the prodigious undertaking, indeed, is an insatiable quest for meaning and for the sources of plenitude.

If the more general formula of the entire work is the intolerable aridity of the soul ("la *sécheresse de l'âme"*) relieved by epiphany—human epiphanies, apparitions, recovered from the past by art and in terms of the "intermittences of the heart" —yet the basic problem of this modern self is vacuity, here

4. *À la recherche du temps perdu,* vol. II, p. 503. Our references hereafter will be to this edition, identified as "Pléiade" except where other editions are specifically identified.

studied especially in connection with the illusions of jealousy. Notably in *La Prisonnière* this excruciating passion is seen not only as a matter of possessiveness or wound to self-esteem, but one whose roots go down into ultimate existential insecurity and vertigo. The panic at betrayal feeds on avid calculation of appearances, real or imaginary, febrile probings in an unbounded space of ambiguities.

Jealousy writhes in a vacuum . . . We persist desperately in exploring the inconsistent debris of a dream, and meanwhile our life with our mistress goes on, a life oblivious of that whose importance for us we fail to recognize, attentive rather to that which perhaps has no importance, our life engrossed in a nightmare by beings who have no real relation to us, full of forgetfulness, lapses, vain anxieties, our life like that of a dream.[5]

Thus the author finds in the phenomenology of jealousy a paradigm of all human avidity and its illusions. His recurrent thesis that "suffering makes intelligent" lies behind his art, for it is only in the act of narrating that the maze can be threaded and the enigma exposed. We have here a classic example of the craving for understanding in the modern experience, as exemplified in fiction. All these explorations are determined by modern man's anxiety with the wearing thin of traditional codes, his disorientation between an old and a new ethos, and they are carried out with a whole lexicon of new bodies of knowledge. A revealing index of Proust's implacable urge towards explanation is found in a passage dealing with jealousy. Marcel reflects upon the impenetrable mass of false leads and ambiguities, the mixture of candor and mendacity, with which he is confronted in his attempt to get at the truth about Albertine. In the case of the Arabian Nights, he says, such a tissue of fictions charms us. But

5. *La Prisonnière,* vol. I, Paris, 1923, pp. 201–202; Pléiade, vol. III, p. 147.

in the case of a person that we love they make us suffer, and so
enable us to enter a little more deeply into the knowledge of human
nature instead of allowing us to play about upon the surface. The
hurt goes deep and in painful curiosity compels *us* to go deep.
Whence the truths that we feel that we have no right to conceal, to
the point that the dying atheist who has discoverd them—convinced
that only nothingness awaits him, and heedless of fame—nevertheless
spends his last hours trying to make them known.[6]

We have here a self-portrait of Proust himself in his last years
of hermetic and single-minded composition. Using the microscope of narration and the reagent of the imagination upon innumerable enigmatic life-histories of men and women and the
annals of his own heart he seeks to uncover the deeper patterns
of our nature. Nor should we underestimate the fatefulness of
the issues at stake for him. It is not as though he sought only
to redeem a landscape of vanity by the power of the imagination. What he met in the moral enigmas over which he pored
was in the last analysis the visage of death.

After the first irreparable quarrel with Albertine had taken
place and Marcel had the atrocious intimation that the breach
was definitive and that she was about to leave him, there is a
scene in which he steals into her room and sees her asleep. The
moment takes on surreal overtones; she lies in such a way as to
suggest that she was dead, with the bedclothes "rolled like a
winding-sheet about her body." And he confuses this vision with
that of his own death. "Thus I remained before the contorted
body, the allegorical figure of what? Of my death? Of my
love?"[7] Thus behind the figments and dramas of the passions
and behind the blindfolds of the social carnival Proust discovers
nothingness or the grimace of the death's head. But his task is
to disengage the mechanisms, and through art to rescue the

6. Pléiade, vol. III, p. 146.
7. *Ibid.*, p. 360.

ineluctable intimations of a deeper order, glimpsed especially in the intermittences of the heart and in the music of Vinteuil.

Thus Proust is faithful to the point of genius in seeking to tell the whole story as he sees it and can elicit it. Yet like other of our novelists he encounters the limits of our modern perspectives, especially those of our subjectivity. He hints at this when he observes that "events are vaster than the moments in which they occur and cannot be wholly contained within it."[8]

Again it is Proust who offers us a paradigm of the limitations of much modern narrative, and these go behind subjectivity to ultimate premises. In *La Fugitive* he is reflecting upon the factors which had led to his own misreading of reality, instanced here by his misreading of a fateful letter, actually his reading into it what was not there after mistaking its author. In such cases, he writes, given a reader who is preoccupied and already predisposed, and who

begins with the idea that the letter is from such and such a person—how many of the letters in a word does he actually read, how many of the words in a phrase? The fact is that in reading one divines, one creates; it all starts from an initial error; those that follow—and not only in the reading of letters and telegrams but in any kind of reading—are altogether natural, however extraordinary it may appear to one who does not start at the same point. A good part of what we believe—and so with the same combination of one-track thinking and good faith right down to the ultimate conclusion—arises out of an initial error in the premises.[9]

8. Pléiade, vol. III, p. 401. In the context in which the observation is made it refers to the fact that events cast their shadow before and after. The subsequent death of Albertine forced itself praeternaturally upon the consciousness of Marcel before the event even as it had an after-life in his later experience. But the ramifications of events have other dimensions than those of time, and their understanding and ordering, the grasp of their larger relationships whether by insight or in narrative require ever more total contexts.

9. *Ibid.*, p. 656.

In other connections Proust suggests what the mistake in the premises was. He had indeed sought in writing to go beyond the external notation of the Goncourts, however inimitable in richness, and beyond the aesthetic fiction of Bergotte, seen as a musical transcription of *"le vaine songe de la vie,"* and of *"l'inépuisable torrent de belles apparences."* But he was never able fully to extricate himself entirely from "that same idealist philosophy,"[10] which he had shared as a young man with the older author. That momentous later self-knowledge that came to him with a recognition of the sway of cruelty in himself and in others, a self-knowledge by which the masks of snobism and of *la vie mondaine* were removed, even this operated within the limits of a particular vision of the world. It was a vision defined by sentiment and idealism, carried over from the nineteenth century, and one which like all forms of romanticism, mysticism or psychologism, even when as here radically qualified, overlooks certain ranges of "how things happen to happen." We shall attempt to illustrate this in our third section below in comparing Proust's treatment of jealousy with that in Othello and that in the biblical account of King Saul. The limitation betrays itself in the affective categories in which Proust presents what were for him the ultimate data of truth. That dispassionate objectivity with which he scrutinizes experience falls short in important points. And though fiction of our own later decades sharply dissociates itself from the aesthetic lineage of Proust much of its harsher or more ironic realism still shares his limitations.

What the ultimate data of truth were for Proust is movingly noted when he discusses what music meant to Swann as capable of "changing the pattern of a man's existence" so that he is no longer "leaving out of account the ground of things,"[11] and is

10. *Du côté de chez Swann,* vol. I, Paris, 1911, 1939, p. 139; cf. *Le Temps retrouvé,* Pléiade, vol. III, p. 910.
11. *Ibid.,* p. 302.

like a convalescent "who begins to envisage the unexpected possibility of tardily beginning an entirely different life . . . and the impulse and almost the power to consecrate his life."[12] As we shall see in what follows, however, it was also through the resonances of the heart and the compunctions for violated human affections that Marcel was moved to a deeper grasp of reality than was afforded by art.

It is tempting to move out of its immediate context an expression of the author pointing towards a more holistic fiction than he ever was able to achieve. "*Si l'un de nous avait eu la tête épique,*"[13] he exclaims with a certain melancholy. We may extend its import to the modern novelist generally: "if only one of us had the epic gift!" The remark is made when the author is amusing himself with recollection of family rituals when he was a child in Combray. One such local, quasi-civic custom "could have been the already supplied germ of a legendary cycle." But this suggests a modern fiction escaping from the subjective or rather including it in epos that would bring all dimensions of life into mutually illuminating relation to one another as in the great epic of the past. If we press the passing remark of Proust in this way it is only to suggest the disquietude of the modern chronicler in his sense of alienation from the final ground of things and the conditions of an era which must postpone any such more total fabulation.

Such grasp on reality as we find in Proust has then the character of epiphany, though of a kind which transcends aestheticism. The novel records momentous apparitions of indisputable good. These are evoked in connection with the recovered memories of his mother, and in the emergence of "impressions which I discovered at distant intervals in my life as observation points, allurements to the construction of an authentic life,"[14] or the

12. P. 303.
13. Pp. 161–162.
14. Pléiade, vol. III, p. 261.

promise that came to him by way of music "that something else existed, realizable no doubt by art, than the nothingness that I found in all pleasures and in love itself."[15]

II.

To further our inquiry into the scope and limits of modern fiction and of Proust in particular we now venture to consider his work in the light of certain fundamental features we have identified in the biblical epos. We recognize that to use these ancient records as a reagent in this way can only be seen as exploratory. We shall also need to distinguish between what bears on Proust in particular rather than on other writers of our time.

We have urged that a prior question to raise with regard to any kind of story-telling whatever is that of the motive of the fabulation, the depth of the impulse to speech. This is more than a question of the talent of the narrator; it is one as to the power of the word in its time. The fact that the great masters of modern fiction have widely been recognized with all their limitations as purifiers of language, as secular prophets and as fashioners of order and conscience in our world testifies to the depth of their utterance. In the case of Proust we have noted the passage in which he speaks of the passion for understanding which animates the dying atheist so that he spends his last hours careless of fame in an effort to pass on his findings.

Yet Proust's identification with the full reality of his time and its travail has its very real limits, and the momentous summons to carry through his earlier project which came to him ten years before his death crystalized out of a somewhat partial if intense relation to the human drama. For one dimension of his age that could not find voice in him one would have to look elsewhere, for example to such a lesser artist as Charles Péguy.

15. *Ibid.*, p. 263.

Though Proust's world overlaps with that of politics and war, and though statesmen and soldiers and men and women of the common people are found in his dramatis personae, yet this social dimension of mankind is never part of the substance of his vision. His revelations were not of a kind, did not spring from a level, such as to involve or master these aspects of our relationships. Except for his attention to the Dreyfus case his dealings with political and economic realities are conventional if not naïve, and this lacuna inevitably limits the portrayal even of those circles and individuals he knows best.

In speaking of this lacuna we have already partly answered our second query, that as to the holism of Proust's narrative. But with respect to the full concrete density of human relationships we must also note another limitation. One aspect of his psychologism is that even the exhaustive dissection in depth of his own intimate circles makes of it a mirror of self-knowledge. The independent reality of his world thereby suffers in this respect also. Through his "psychology in time" he uncovers profound patterns of human life but in a restricted or penultimate way whose coordinates are set by his particular form of the modern sensibility. That further test of the biblical humanism, moreover, which links empirical and transcendental, earth and heaven, exposes a further limitation of scope. The dimension of the transmundane in Proust appears under the sign of the subjective and the aesthetic. What he speaks of as "the ultimate ground of life," of which he has indisputable disclosures, is not of a kind as to involve in a fateful nexus all the faculties of the self and all the orders and happenings of the wider world. At most these fully personal depths are only incompletely explored. Indicative is a kind of cecity with regard to the popular classes, portrayed (with rare exceptions as in the case of Françoise) in the key of the picturesque or the charming. More serious is the attitude to women. We have here the paradox that some women are the object of an incomparable analysis as well as homage

87

and gratitude, while on the other hand women in general and again those of the common people are the objects of a conventional disparagement as of the order of works of art if not playthings.[16]

This restriction of the total reality has its counterpart in the musical architecture of the entire work which follows the pattern ABA. The concluding third section thus rounds out the plot by a repossession or transfiguration of the first at a higher level. But this telos or homecoming of the last section represents the final vision and self-understanding of the artist rather than any movement or goal of the world-process. Meanwhile the style, characterized as that of a "waking dream" in its fluent, inexhaustible and poetic movement, and the complexity of its syntax, answers to the primary preoccupation with the history of the author's sensibility.

One becomes progressively awed by Proust's command over language. He appears to have an inexhaustible facility and compass of discourse, so as to be able to take up the given matter into words or contrariwise to superpose fittingly the reality of language upon a labyrinthine mystery of persons and events. All this seems to take place effortlessly, and we recognize in the author a large surplus of resources for the task in hand. The medium is narrative, and the "vocation" (as he calls it) is to understand through the telling: to present, survey, probe, analyze a world of sentiments, motives, avidities; to observe their compulsions, maladies, illusions, filiations; and to overcome their flux by distilling out their psychological laws. But the style called for, evidently, to match this maze of occasions and appearances must be at one level realistic, documentary, inquisitorial and abundant. Much of the work takes on the character of a clinical phenomenology—reminiscent of

16. A witticism like the following is not without its wider implications: "In the life of most women, everything, even the greatest sorrow, ends up in a matter of trying on a new dress." Pléiade, vol. II, p. 335.

investigators like Charcot, Bergson and Ribot—devoted to the scrutiny of memory, perception, sleep, dreams, the passions and the imagination. But what prompts him finally is not only such curiosities but a dedication to explore the eternal sources of plenitude and the extra-temporal "essence of things."[17] This justifies him, he insists, in turning from any social or political role of the writer to his private task as artist. But this inward quest for that which is extra-temporal qualifies the realism of the whole and widely determines its rhetoric. The deeper fatefulness of the personal life, in the sense of the historical reality of the human being, is not absent in Proust but its theatre is limited, and this is reflected in the style. In retrospect we can recognize how this level of existence demands different rhetorics in such writers as Joyce and Faulkner, including a less controlled form of "stream of consciousness." But Proust's fiction is only one form of much modern fabulation representing not public epic but the notation of the world through the mirrors of the self. As Roger Shattuck has observed, the work is to be placed as a chronicle of illusions and homecoming not with the epic or the historical memoir or historical novel, but with the "literary tradition of legends and folk tales we usually devour in childhood," and more particularly with the cycle of the *Arabian Nights*.[18]

The final area in which we presume to examine modern fiction in the light of the biblical epos is that which we have spoken of as the "dialogical" dimension, that level at which the full mystery of the person is disclosed and the relation of its choosing and willing to the fatefulness of the world. It will be recalled that we have cited the demand of Gertrude Stein and Beckett for something deeper than "stories," in the latter

17. ". . . *sollicité . . . de chercher la cause de cette felicité, du caractère de certitude avec lequel elle s'imposait*." Pléiade, vol. III, p. 871.

18. *Proust's Binoculars,* London, 1964, pp. 136–7.

case for genuine communion and a human voice. Here the theatre of what is real moves from the annals and intoxications of the soul to the transactions of our freedom and responsibility. In the case of Proust this latter dimension struggles for recognition through the prior limits of his sensibility. Marcel is almost neuresthenically impressionable to the whole order of sentiment in human relationships. This is one aspect of the sway over him of affectivity, evident in affection itself, friendship, tenderness, nostalgia, moods, as well as in the hyper-aestheticism of his responses to music, art, names, spectacle and the glamor of society. In this limited sense Proust's world is largely constituted of the resonances of the heart.

But a later and deeper ingredient entered into the vision, related as we shall see to a more austere epiphany than those associated with his "privileged moments." Or rather we can say that these finally mediate not only transcendence over time and death but also purification of the affections. In the outcome his portrayal of the high European bourgeoisie is a judgment and not only a dissection. In a particular case like that of Charlus, the poet of the social kaleidoscope, he can show not only the surpassing talent and virtuosity but also can trace the degeneration to the final obscenity.

III.

To push further this examination of Proust in the light of the biblical realism it will be profitable to select one area at the point of his strength, his treatment of jealousy. This is germane because the basic concern with illusion and reality in the entire work is closely linked up with Marcel's disclosure of the torments, irrationality and waste of this passion. Jealousy is connected as a form of suffering with intelligence, and therefore as mediating an understanding of man. Swann who observes that jealousy is the most atrocious of torments is also quoted as saying:

I, I have never been curious except when I have been in love and when I have been jealous. And as to what that has taught me![19]

But may we not say that in Proust jealousy is found throughout in the dimension of sensibility, under the bell-jar as it were of the affective life, so that certain wider ramifications of the passion are absent?

Here it would be suggestive to compare, granting all the differences, the portrayal of jealousy in other literary texts, such as *Othello*. Both in Shakespeare and Proust we find recognition of the irrationality of this passion, the gratuity of the phantasms that swarm in the imagination:

> They are not ever jealous for the cause,
> But jealous for they are jealous: 'tis a monster
> Begot upon itself, born on itself.
>
> (Act III, Scene iv)

> Trifles light as air
> Are to the jealous confirmations strong
> as proofs of holy writ.
>
> (Act III, Scene iii)

But in Othello jealousy appears to infect the full personal existence more radically and in ways not medicable by new distractions or the passage of time. We should of course keep in mind the different factors. Yet Marcel's malady, however profoundly it introduces him into psychological chaos and panic, does not reach the accents of Othello.

> But there, where I have garner'd up my heart,
> Where either I must live or bear no life,

19. *Sodome et Gomorrhe II,* vol. I, Paris 1922, p. 103.

The fountain from the which my current runs,
Or else dries up; to be discarded thence!
                              (Act IV, Scene ii)

Most significant of all for the assumptions of Shakespeare about human interrelatedness is the passage in which Othello even when his suspicions are only first aroused, exclaims,

              O, now for ever
Farewell the tranquil mind! farewell content . . .
. . . Othello's occupation's gone!
                              (Act III, Scene iii)

The point is, not that ill fame will disqualify him from the

        Pride, pomp and circumstance of glorious war,

but that his humanity is inseparable from his social role and both are attainted.

But here we are on the same ground with the classic portrayal of jealousy in the Old Testament, that of King Saul. Again, our purpose is not premature conclusions from narratives that in many respects are incommensurable. We are interested rather in the prior question. What can we learn about the modern sensibility, the climate of our peculiar subjectivity and its interests and disinterests, with the artistic corollaries that follow? It appears at least that Proust locates the coordinates of jealousy or other dynamics of behavior differently. Perhaps I may anticipate and say that we find in him a masterly evocation and analysis of the penultimate orders of good and evil.

Certainly in the Hebrew story we do not have to do with sexual jealousy as in the cases of Marcel and Othello. Saul's jealousy is directed towards David as a rival and merges with envy. The roots of the passion in Saul go back again into his "occupation," his identity as the one first called to be the king over Israel and then rejected. When he heard the tributes to the exploits of David

> Saul was very angry, and this saying displeased him; he said, "They have ascribed to David ten thousands, and to me they have ascribed thousands; and what more can he have but the kingdom?" And Saul eyed David from that day on.
> And on the morrow an evil spirit from God rushed upon Saul, and he raved within his house, while David was playing the lyre, as he did day by day. Saul had his spear in his hand; and Saul cast the spear, for he thought, "I will pin David to the wall." But David evaded him twice.
>
> (I Sam. 18:8–11)

The recital of Saul's fall, melancholia, jealousy, attempts on David's life, compunctions, resort in ultimate reprobation to the witch at Endor, and nobility in suicide run through sixteen chapters. Though it is characteristic of Hebrew narrative to scant psychological and subjective states except as they are evoked in action, yet it is remarkable how much is here conveyed of the passion itself in its irrationality and ravages. This appears especially in the way in which Saul's invidiousness against David is turned against his own son, Jonathan:

> "You son of a perverse, rebellious woman, do I not know that you have chosen the son of Jesse to your own shame, and to the shame of your mother's nakedness? For as long as the son of Jesse lives upon the earth, neither you nor your Kingdom shall be established." . . . But Saul cast his spear at him to smite him.
>
> (20:30–31, 33)

Thus although the Hebrew version differs from that of Proust in that jealousy is determined by a religio-political context, yet the malady itself comes before us more recognizably as it does in the case of Othello. Proust's labyrinthine explorations of its pathology hardly repay us for that absent dimension of the self where "occupation" is threatened and where chaos comes again in the inmost fortress of the man's social and historical being. It is true that the society in which Proust's hero has a role lacks any such structure as that of Othello or Saul. This means that Proust's theatre of observation focusses on the heart and the affections in the particular structures of the family and *la vie mondaine.* But if our passions and their fatalities in any society are only fully understood in a wider fabric of social and human ends, as in the cases we have cited, then we would expect that the probing of the modern novelist in such an area as that of jealousy would uncover this dimension of the self, even against the handicaps of his setting. The moral intelligence quickened by the experience would have broken through the order of sentiment and sensibility into that more austere domain of personal reality.

One can discover this dimension in Proust by his occasional recognition of the sway of cruelty not only in the demeanor of his other characters, but in the admission of Marcel himself. Apropos of the sadism and blasphemy of Mlle Vinteuil and her "friend" directed against the former's father, he can speak of "*la forme terrible et permanente de la cruauté.*" From the point of view of a theological criticism one of the most significant features of Proust's moral analysis is that like Gide he can move the question of morality and conscience behind the conventional preoccupation with sexual disorders, lesbianism or blasphemy to the basic issues of inhumanity, coldness of heart and cruelty. Yet one misses the wider context and sanctions that bear upon this ultimate area. Thus there is an insufficient realism in all that bears upon the full personal mystery of love and injury, of fidelity and betrayal, of weal and woe, in short of good and evil.

Going further afield we may say that in modern fiction generally we have a narrative understandably focussed on the dramas of self, on the theatre of the psyche and its affects. However, we do not do justice to modern fiction in its focus on the psychodrama if we see this only as limitation. Without the liberation of the self since the Renaissance and the richness of personal consciousness that developed in the Romantic movement we would not have the contemporary problem in its real promise. The power of the novel in the nineteenth and the twentieth centuries testifies to an irreversible emergence or assertion of the person and his struggle for definition. If we have suggested that Proust's setting in the idealist tradition limits his sense of reality, and even dates him by comparison with our contemporary stance, yet this Romantic overhang in him was one aspect of his best impulse. It operates in more disguised ways in our more disabused contemporary work. A literary study of *À la recherche du temps perdu* will no doubt recognize in the work a history of the decay of the European bourgeoisie and of what Edmund Wilson called "the Heartbreak House of capitalist culture." It will recognize more generally a modern rehearsal of "*sic transit gloria mundi.*" It will also see a peculiarly modern form of the conquest over time, not only in art but in the lived vicissitudes of the self. But it should also recognize that searing compunctions over irreparable cruelty to his mother lie back of the whole analysis and provide its hidden energy. And this moral center of the work in the life of the artist on the one hand endows it with more authentic realism in literary terms and on the other relates it to the deeper quests of our period. It is also at this point that the probing of the heart not only in its sentiment but in its historicity invites confrontation with the biblical narration.

Harry Levin has put together the contributory evidence which shows how traumatic and germinal for Proust was his remembered heartlessness to his mother and to his grandmother together with his general horror at old age abandoned and "*les mères profanées.*"

His guilty fear of having profaned, having outraged, nay having assassinated his mother had come out during his lifetime in the *Confession d'une jeune fille* and shortly before her death in the

95

Sentiments filiaux d'un parracide. In the curse of *Sodome et Gomorrhe,* inverts are condemned as "motherless sons." . . . yet mere self-accusation is not enough; there must be some decisive act of restitution. . . .

Could [Proust] overcome his innate narcissism, which [his mother] had done so much to foster? Just possibly, but only by following her example of self-sacrifice, and thereby doing penance for the suffering that he had inflicted upon her. The years of desecration had to be atoned for by a long and testing consecration. . . .

It has been said that all of Kafka's work constitutes an epistle to his father. So we might say, of Proust's novel, that it may be read as a letter to his mother.[20]

A searching literary criticism of Proust will, therefore, not stop with a study of the significance of his "epiphanies" as solutions of the problems of time and meaning. It will note that these "privileged moments" have a moral context, and that his whole panorama of the human scene is a laboratory for the study of the operations of conscience and obligation. The predicament of modern man, then, is not finally only the "drought of the soul" or vacuity, but heartlessness and a malady of the will. It is not met by aesthetic epiphany alone, but revelations in which as with Marcel the imagination and the heart are equally involved. Levin rightly protests against certain moralistic critics like Maritain who have overlooked Proust's "sympathetic reaffirmation of the parental virtues." Speaking of the intimations that came to Marcel of "a lost fatherland" in the last opus of Vinteuil, Levin writes:

Through his parable of that undiscovered country, Proust interlinks the recognitions of art with those of ethics, the disinterested imperatives of Vinteuil and Bergotte with the unselfish motives of Marcel's [Jewish] mother and grandmother. . . . The pilgrimage has unexpectedly led from the *Almanach de Gotha* to the Old Testament.[21]

20. *The Gates of Horn,* pp. 438–440.
21. P. 442.

In sum, then, Proust stands as one example of our modern disabused and sophisticated humanism. He went beyond idealism and aestheticism. If our modern situation denied him more total apperceptions, yet the history of modern subjectivity—whose positive contributions may be suggested by romanticism and symbolism and by such legacies as those of Stendahl and Flaubert—provided him with an inexhaustible material and task. If he dealt with this by a creative transformation of the genre of the confessional novel or the literary memoir, it is also important to recognize that he was driven by quasi-scientific curiosities, evidenced also by his own omnipresent use of images drawn from the natural sciences. He is in the tradition of Montaigne and de Rochefoucault as well as of aesthetic idealism. For him ultimately art was a higher reality. He wrote in a setting where fiction was associated with a consciously literary expectation. Of his manner it has been observed that it was probably the "most written style since Flaubert."[22] Recognizing all these givens of the situation we can understand why Proust does not tell more of "how things happen to happen" whether in a wider metaphysical context or in the deeper fealties of the soul.

Going farther afield we may say that in modern fiction widely we have a narrative of sentiment, sensibility—either Proust's variety, or the tough kind of Hemingway, or Gide's "sincere" and compassionate kind, or Thomas Mann's comic humanism —all marked, indeed, by a complex sophistication, and all, even when socially realistic, determined by the special horizon of our modern subjectivity. Even any metaphysical or eschatological dimension of such works is in the subjective key, in the affective register. Yet as with Proust, so with others, modern recital seeks a more fateful level than that of "stories, stories." They move towards the existential in the sense of dynamic moral reality; in the case of Sartre, indeed, an existentialism which disengages the reality of ultimate freedom from all others. It is significant,

22. Melvin Friedman, *op. cit.,* p. 98.

however, that in work of the greatest import and scale such writers are still drawn to the narrative mode and thus to dealing with the world of time, and of persons in time and history, even where they radically attenuate the biblical grasp of a teleological history. Though they forego the total orientation of the biblical epos and its wider Alpha and Omega, they nevertheless reflect its prototype of human life as a fateful pilgrimage, even if only in echoes and fragments.

IV. The Symbolics
of the New Testament

A theological criticism oriented to comparative rhetorics must take account not only of genres and styles but also of the particularities of the symbolic imagination. Writers of different settings differ in their mythopoiesis as in other aspects of speech and communication. Here too, fundamental apperception discloses itself. Reality as it is experienced in any time is defined by the scope and repertory of its language and not least by those dramatizations of existence which are a part of it.

Since in Part I of this book I am examining the biblical antecedents of our western rhetorics I must therefore give attention to its imagery. Here too it is possible to go behind dogma in our study of Scripture. But it is not just a question of identifying ancient metaphors and mythological motifs which continue to be cited and manipulated as part of our usable past. More significant is a consideration of the vicissitudes of such imaginative media especially in the modern period. These often survive only in attenuated form, as elements of folklore or literary cliché. Or they may be radically subverted as when certain Romantics identified Heaven with abstract tyranny, fallen Nature with spontaneous innocence, and Hell and the Devil with the creative daemonic principle.[1]

1. Cf. Northrop Frye, "The Drunken Boat: The Revolutionary

But more fundamental is the question of the special character of the biblical mythopoiesis and the structures of its vision. Peoples and epochs see their respective worlds each in a different lighting, and this is related to their arts and all aspects of their creativity. In the title of the present chapter I speak not of the symbolism but the symbolics of the New Testament. This term points to something more than the images themselves. It suggests at least the social-psychological dimension of the symbol and the whole domain of cultural dynamics.

My topic therefore introduces us not to the imagery but to the deeper determinants which have shaped it and lent it power. Here we find ourselves in that unclarified domain associated with myths and archetypes. No study of literature can ignore this dimension of meaning in language. Yet such terms as myth and archetype are used differently in different disciplines and contexts. It is enough here to recognize that there are deeper structures in consciousness as well as the unconscious—the legacies of our cultural past, varying in different cultures—dynamic patterns, which as Denis de Rougemont has said, "preform the inner movements of our sensibility."[2] The affective and cognitive realities so crystallized "dictate—unknown to the authors—the profound rhetorics of their composition."[3]

De Rougemont has in mind such deeply embedded cultural "models" in our western inheritance as those of Tristan, Don Juan and Faust. His studies of love in the western world have shown how such "archetypes" shape literary forms and the "action of language itself."[4] Not only so but his canvass of the vicissitudes of such dynamic images and their literary expression

Element in Romanticism," *Romanticism Reconsidered,* edited by same, New York, 1963, pp. 1–25.

2. *Love Declared: Essays on the Myths of Love,* New York, 1963, p. 17.

3. P. 44.

4. P. 19.

bring to light the deeper theatre of moral transformations in a society.

But we may extend his method as applied to these more recent images to include older and even more fateful patterns and archetypes associated with the Scriptures. Here too there are potent legacies in the western soul which have determined its sense of reality and shaped the rhetorics of its creativity. Any study of the crisis of culture and of language today must take account of the vicissitudes of these residual and still powerful structures and syndromes as elements in our contemporary crucible of images.

Surely one legitimate aim of literary criticism is to contribute to an understanding of our contemporary disorders at the level of the imagination. The student of the arts as we know them today cannot but be concerned with the related domain of cultural dynamics and with the sources and vehicles of cultural renewal. The theological critic especially will be impelled to explore the biblical archetypes and the ways in which they have shaped language and life. As in the case of the biblical narrative so its symbolics should offer a base from which we can better assess the special features and limitations of our modern sensibility.

In my second chapter above I have already called attention to that aspect of the Old Testament story-telling which required a total mythological world-plot and which related it to temporal existence and empirical reality. The present topic gives me an opportunity to explore further this holistic scope of the biblical epiphanies and their plastic media. My chief attention here will be given to the New Testament. What is said about the power and continuities of the biblical mythos, its social role, and its transformations in times of crisis like our own, will further document the resources of a theological criticism. In subsequent chapters, moreover, issues bearing on the survival power of this kind of vision and its dynamic structures will recur.

I.

I shall order this discussion of the symbolic imagination of the New Testament about the two terms, myth and dream.[5] Both point us to the depth of sensibility and creativity with which we are concerned.

At least two phases of the discussion of "myth" in the New Testament have already been worked through. The older Christ-myth thesis of Drewes and others has long been obsolete. The more recent major discussion centering in Bultmann of the "demythologizing" of the New Testament can only be really fresh today if the term "myth" is understood in a less technical sense than he did. More justice should be done to its mythopoetic character and its implicit claim to provide valid world-representation and dramatization of existence. The Christian Scripture is full of myth in this sense. We can therefore pass over the fact that the Greek term for myth, "*mythos*," occurs only five times in the latest writings of the canon, always in the pejorative sense of heretical fables or old wives' tales.[6]

The vocabulary of "dream" and dream-phenomena is more abundant and diversified in our writings than is the case with "myth." In most cases the usages are predictable in these kinds of sub-literary texts in this period. To associate guidance with dreams was traditional both in the Hebraic and pagan worlds,

5. For a wider phenomenological treatment of these terms and the whole question of cultural dynamics see the symposium, *Myth and Dream*, New York, 1970, edited by Joseph Campbell for the Society for the Arts, Religion and Contemporary Culture, New York. The present chapter was written for that symposium though it is here presented with revisions.

6. For example in the First Epistle of Timothy Christian teachers are charged not to "occupy themselves with myths and endless genealogies which promote speculations rather than divine training" (1:4), and again, "Have nothing to do with godless and silly myths" (4:7).

and narrative style employed it as a cliché. Even in more significant instances, as when Paul's campaign is directed across the Bosphorus into Europe by his dream of a man of Macedonia who bids him, "Come over to Macedonia and help us" (Acts 16:9), the interest is in the instruction rather than the psychic state through which it was mediated. Nor do we have in such cases an enigmatic oracle requiring interpretation. In fact dream interpretation (as distinguished from explanation of visions) is totally lacking in the New Testament. Though God himself is hidden, he "does not speak ambiguously. He wills to be understood."[7] "No New Testament witness thought of basing the central message, the Gospel, or any essential part of it, on dreams."[8] This parsimony of dream phenomena corresponds to a main trend in late Second Temple Judaism and contrasts with the luxuriant picture in contemporary Hellenism and even with the revival of such motifs in the rabbinic tradition.

What I have said so far bears on the dream in the strict sense of a disclosure in sleep. On the other hand, the New Testament vocabulary for "vision," whether in a waking state or "by night," is very much more abundant and significant. The canon is full of visions and auditions and this points to what is of main interest to us, the deeper dynamics of our human awareness. Actually, the most significant use in the New Testament of the Greek term for dream "*onar*," is one where it is in parallel with one of the terms for vision, "*horasis*," as quoted in the Book of Acts from the prophet Joel:

> and your young men shall see visions,
> and your old men shall dream dreams. (Acts 2:17)

This passage is part of Peter's discourse at the first Pentecost and is typical in that it has to do with vision of the last things.

7. Article "Onar," G. Kittel, *Theologische Wörterbuch zum Neuen Testament*, vol. V., p. 236.
8. *Ibid.*, p. 235.

We make a fundamental observation here when we say that "myth and dream" in Christian Scripture are shaped by the eschatological consciousness. All the creative symbol is governed by the sense of world-transformation in course and ultimate goals within reach, and these are social and cosmic goals as well as individual. The entire Book of Revelation illustrates this. This work comprises a series of visions and auditions in the wider frame of a single unveiling or *apokalypsis,* accorded to the author and which he "saw" on the island of Patmos when he "was in the spirit on the Lord's day." Though the category of vision here is in the main a literary convention and though the mythological material that fills the book is in good part compositional borrowing, yet the entire work is a *mythopoetic* reading of the contemporary experience of the community. It is an example of what we would call surrealism animated by that sense of total crisis and world-metamorphosis which characterized the beginnings of Christianity throughout.

Our topic has already led us into a recognition of the large place in the New Testament of what the psychology of religion would call supra-normal, ecstatic and mystical experience. A list would include not only dreams, visions, auditions along with related trances, epiphanies, theophanies, but also glossolalia or "speaking with tongues" (which could be understood as the language of angels), raptures to heaven and reports of various quasi-magical transactions. Sometimes we find ourselves in a world of spells and archaic mentality. When Jesus gives a new name to Peter or to the sons of Zebedee we recognize the archaic idea evidenced, for example, among the ancient Arabians, that the sheik had the power to change both the name and the nature of a tribesman. The primitive power of the spoken word appears again in the charismatic salutation of "Peace" spoken by Jesus' disciples as they journeyed as heralds through the villages, a word which if it is not accepted returns to the speaker and leaves the hearers exposed to evil powers. Or this potency of speech can take the form of a ritual doom-pronouncement as in the legend of the death of Ananias and his wife.

An interesting example of what we would call levitation occurs in the account of Jesus walking on the sea. The variety of the three accounts in the Gospels make it possible to trace the legend from its most developed form back to a more primitive stage. The oldest form may well be recognizable in the Gospel of John. Jesus here *appears* to the disciples distressed at night in their rowing to reassure them. It is not said that they actually received him into the boat. The sequel of his manifestation is rather that "immediately the boat was at the land to which they were going." What we have here, as Rudolf Otto says, is "not a mere miracle as such but the quite definite category of an *apparitio,* and especially that of the charismatic figure who in hours of need and of mortal danger appears from afar in phantom form and gives help."[9] The episode is then transformed, first in Mark where Jesus as really present enters the boat, and further in Matthew where Peter also makes the attempt to walk on the water. Thus in both these later versions the memory of an apparition is carried over into the category of a levitation, one which also has abundant illustration in the history of religion. Otto's confidence in the historicity of the original apparition to the disciples need not be accepted, but his documentation suggests the cultural background in which these kinds of reports and their elaboration could take place. Quasi-telepathic conceptions, as of action at a distance, are clearly exemplified in Paul's relation to the Church at Corinth. Though he writes from across the Aegean with respect to a case of discipline, he assures the Church that he will be present when with the Holy Spirit it carries out a formal act of excommunication against the offender, an action thought of realistically as carrying with it his probable death.

9. Rudolf Otto, *The Kingdom of God and the Son of Man,* Grand Rapids, n.d., p. 370.

As I have indicated, all these kinds of motifs and their narrative genres are predictable in popular writings of this period. But the early Christian movement arose from such depths that it was indeed accompanied by many kinds of charismatic and psychic phenomena, so much so that discrimination among them became a prior concern. Such supra-normal experience was commonly assigned to the Spirit, that is, the Spirit of God, but some of its operations were more significant than others, and there were also false spirits. In the Corinthian Church, for example, Paul was confronted with a veritable riot of ecstatic manifestations associated with Gnostic or related ideas and with antinomian ethics. He discusses all this under the head of "visions and revelations." He himself, he observes, is as much an initiate as anyone with respect to "spiritual gifts." In fact, either in or out of the body he had been caught up to the third heaven and heard forbidden matters. But, he insists, it is nothing to boast of and leads to phantasies of false transcendence, unless subordinated to down-to-earth responsibility as in the case of Christ himself.

With respect to Jesus, I would agree with the view that he can be called a charismatic.[10] The category of "mystic" varies so in different contexts that it should be used of Jesus only in the most guarded way. Certainly if it implies emphasis on a psychological state for its own sake or the use of special techniques and disciplines for the attainment of such a state it does not apply to him. Yet in the case of Jesus as in that of St. Francis we have an interesting case of the seer with visionary sensibility and at the same time the clear-headed realist. He sees the connection of prodigious matters in the twinkling of an eye and can crystallize such vision in a parable or metaphor of the utmost simplicity. In this connection it should be borne in mind that the accounts in the Gospels of certain of his visions such

10. See the author's *Eschatology and Ethics in the Teaching of Jesus,* rev. ed. New York, 1950, Chapter XII, especially pp. 202–214.

as those ascribed to him on the occasions of his baptism and his temptation as well as that of the three disciples on the Mount of Transfiguration have been extensively reworked by the tradition. Yet these instances as well as the epiphanies reported in the Gospels recounting his Resurrection appearances testify both to the dynamic power of the movement that began with him and to the momentous mythopoetic language it called forth.

To conclude this section, the Christian Scripture gives us a wide documentation on dreams, visions and associated media of revelation and wisdom. The styles and literary forms reflect these deeper dynamics. Our writings confirm the importance of the pre-rational dimension in human experience. But the modes and conditions of such phenomena are not dealt with in any sophisticated way. Their origin and operation are referred to the Spirit of God, and their import is construed in terms of the message and mythos of the movement which of course had its tap root in the history of Israel.

II.

We turn now to the category of myth and mythopoetic representation. One feature of Christian Scripture that is significant for our wider critical undertaking is the continuity of its mythos from ancient times. We have a prime example here of the stubbornness of social symbol through cultural change, its time-binding character, and the way in which it provides coherence to human society. This may be recognized despite the mutations it undergoes, as for example in the transition from Judaism to Christianity. It is as if a kind of life-line of meaning and orientation ran through the millenniums, identified with the oldest Hebrew archetypes. This is all the more remarkable when we note the survival of these images and ritual motifs down into the present day. The political imagery of divine kingship and covenant which underlies Jewish and Christian worship today goes back even beyond the Hebraic foundations to the ancient Near East. No doubt there was a radical reconception of the old Hittite and Mesopotamian antecedents by Israel, as there was of Jewish and Graeco-Roman antecedents in the rise of Christianity. But there is an underground continuity, as is evident in the Scripture itself.

To know the way of life of a people or a society one must enter into its myth and dream, its folklore and its art. Political doctrine alone, or social ideology, is not enough. The same holds true for a religious community and its faith. The dogma or the confession tells only half the story, that part of it which separates and stresses discontinuity. One can illustrate from the Old Testament. Scholars have identified in the Pentateuch an ancient confessional formula which they call the "credo of Israel." Here Israel's origin, its "adoption," is connected with the events of the Exodus from Egypt. This credo served to establish the identity of this people and its loyalties as against other cultures. But the deeper connections of Israel with all mankind come to expression in a rich mythos of origins also in the Pentateuch and in the Psalms and the prophets.[11] The iconoclasm of Israel always remains indebted to its antecedents in the ancient Orient.[12]

11. To give one example I cite Is. 51:9–11. Here the deliverance of Israel at the Red Sea is colored with ancient pre-Israelitic creation-myth, that of the slaying of the dragon and the establishment of world-order. These overtones in the rehearsal of Israel's election are invoked to convey the full meaning of the eschatological fulfilment now promised to the exiles returning from the captivity.

> Was it not thou that didst cut Rahab in pieces,
>   that didst pierce the dragon?
> Was it not thou that didst dry up the sea,
>   the waters of the great deep. . . ?

12. "One aspect of the dynamic which animates the universe of mythic representations [is the iconoclastic]. This iconoclastic tendency

The same consideration holds for the apparently discontinuous character of the corresponding New Testament credo or kerygma and its all but exclusive focus on Christ. Essential as it is for Christian self-understanding it is only an abbreviated pointer to the faith. By overemphasis on it theologians isolate the Gospel in its origins from both Judaism and paganism. The deeper richness of the Christian consciousness in that period and its continuities with the past are recognized only when we enter into the mythic legacies with which the kerygma clothed itself. Again, the iconoclasm of Christianity always remains indebted to its antecedents and rivals. It is only so that it could ever make any claim to universality.

But there is one further point here. The long lineage of early Christian myth back through the centuries and millenniums says something about its contact with humanness and secularity. The first Christian imagination, myth and dream, had archaic roots in the life of mankind and direct relation to the most ancient epiphanies. If this was true historically, on the horizontal plane of time, it was also true phenomenologically, vertically, in the individual. Indeed, Paul Ricoeur has shown how the New Testament symbolics of evil and purgation include psychic strata

---

appears whenever history occasions a confrontation of rival symbolisms. This conflict leads to refusals and pitiless exclusions; it also brings about reciprocal enrichments. In the Old Testament the conflict of symbol with symbol attaches itself to the interpretation of the history of Israel as a history of salvation. It transforms that history in a 'crucible of symbolization,' a crucible which appropriates from the religious universe of the civilizations which surround Israel representations which it demythicizes, and others which remythicize the history of Israel. This recovery of archaic symbols, whether obsolete or still surviving, takes place most often thanks to retrospective interpretation of the ancient symbolic language in the light of a new 'experience of the sacred.' "Pierre Barthel, *Interprétation du language mythique et théologie biblique,* Leiden, 1963, pp. 298–299 (summarizing a section of Paul Ricoeur's "La Symbolique du mal," in *Philosophie de la Volonté,* Part II, Paris, 1960).

which go down into primordial human categories. He notes that the long way back of reflection on the successive layers of the great cultural symbols can alone match psychoanalysis and co-operate with its regressive exploration.[13]

Mythical motifs in the New Testament having a long pre-history can be further illustrated. Let us take, for example, the Christmas story. The birth of the Divine Child, the discovery of his hidden birthplace by the humble, his persecution by the usurper, his inauguration of the Golden Age: for these elements in the nativity stories of Christ the Gospels draw on world-wide myth and folklore. Note especially the analogies to the birth of Horus and to Vergil's Fourth Eclogue. The version of the nativity that we find in the twelfth chapter of the Book of Revelation sets it in a cosmological drama that goes back to old solar myth and the primeval war with the dragon. In this case all such myth and dream is now transparently related to actual events in the Roman provinces, and reordered to interpret the birth of Christ, his being "caught up to God and his throne," and the persecution of his church. Thus always the poet uses old archetypes and symbol to inform present experience.

All such dynamic imagery in the New Testament has this vital relation to situations and events. It is not merely decorative, literary or free-floating. Moreover, what is borrowed becomes both old and new. It is new because it is used in a new system of symbols and because it is related to this particular history. Even such a general archetype as death and rebirth takes on a stubbornly different meaning, as in fact it does in every culture. The various vegetation cults of the ancient Mediterranean and Near Eastern world were all very different, as Henri Frankfort has shown. Where the church adopted pagan or Hellenistic motifs like that of the Divine Child, or those associated with the sacred meal, or such images as those of Dionysos

13. "The Hermeneutics of Symbols and Philosophical Reflection," *International Philosophical Quarterly,* 2 (1962), p. 195.

turning water into wine, these elements are all transformed by the power of the new myth. Yet there is a continuity.

I cannot leave this theme of the continuity of Christian myth without noting the problem created today by the radical discontinuity in our own cultural crisis. The modern arts widely reflect a sensibility which not only disowns symbolic legacies but prizes immediate atomistic perception without interpretation, happenings, the unrelated epiphany, emancipation from sequence of any kind. There is hardly any parallel in the past to this extreme revolt, even in the age of the sophists or in the solipsism of the Romantic movement on the continent. Gnosticism's world-loathing still had its myth, its house of being. No doubt we should understand the present atomization and "dry mock" of all ordering symbol as a ruthless testing of reality, pushed to the limit, to be followed by a reconstruction of authentic structures. After all the human body has its stable form, and the human psyche is no less stubborn in its basic gestalt. There is in it something which resists any such radical change of consciousness as would constitute mania or chaotic phantasmagoria. Therefore it appears to me that those very ancient structures of consciousness that have provided orientation and stability for man in existence and have served as a kind of lifeline of order and survival will again reassert themselves.

III.

I have tried to show in the preceding section that our early Christian texts provide us with an example of the long continuity of myth through cultural changes. But they also document what happens to myth in a time of crisis, and this should be of special interest to all of us in our modern situation. In the first century both Judaism and paganism were passing through a radical challenge and the emerging church was caught up in

111

the creativity on both sides and in the war of myths of the period. The early believers represented an eschatological sect of Judaism and continued its ancient war on pagan myths, idols and rites. Yet it also developed powerful imagery drawn from Jewish apocalyptic, from Jewish Hellenistic syncretism, and from the dualistic and gnostic impulse in paganism. We see continuity and discontinuity throughout, mythoclasm and mythoplasm.

In a time of crisis like this a new mythical impulse or mythopoesis is engaged on two fronts. It has to speak to the situation of the loss of roots, the faded myth, anomie. But this brings it into conflict with social authority and establishment. We see both aspects in the Christian Scripture.

1. *Mythopoeic impulse in a situation of faded myth and anomie.* We have an example of this in the explosion of the Christian eschatological myth and its community-building power in the disarray of the Hellenistic world. The new faith arose out of a momentous epiphany in the first-century world and its creativity was manifest in a wealth of dramatic imagery which answered to the prevailing hungers. The astonishing prestige of the gnostic fabulations in this period is a parallel phenomenon, and its relation to the Hellenistic anomie has been impressively set forth by Hans Jonas. At this time the ideology of the Greek polis had long been in trouble and, as today, the masses craved for some new crystallization of meaning and community. The Christian movement related itself to the unconscious dynamics of the time and so created a new language, or rather metamorphosed the existing rhetorics, styles and symbolics. We have here an example of what has been called a language-event, that is, an epochal revolution in the gamut and power of language, including imagery, a liberation of human speech and a new grasp on reality. Such a mutation cannot be explained, but it is helpful to use the tools of social psychology. It is evident, at least, that the psychic structures or archetypes of a long past had broken down together with their symbols. The new Chris-

tian myth and dream met the situation both by rejection and appropriation. Old dream was quickened at a greater depth thanks to a new experience of the holy.

I have cited the dynamic motif of the Birth of the Divine Child known throughout the Mediterranean world in diverse forms. I could also illustrate by the old cultural image of the hero-deliverer or divine man (*theios anēr*), typically represented by Hercules and his legend, many of whose traits were later absorbed into the portrayal of Christ. Or I could point to the whole phenomenology of rebirth and renewal in the pagan world. All such legacies were now quickened from the depths by the Christian mythopoesis, unified about a center, and publicized in rhetorics both celebrative and narrative which engaged with the contemporary idiom and sensibility. As the great classicist Wilamovitz observed with reference to the long decay of the language of the Greeks and speaking of Paul: "At last someone speaks in Greek out of a fresh inward experience in life," though to him "all literature is a bauble."[14] It is worth noting by way of comparison that Tannaitic Judaism in that phase in which it prosecuted a mission to the Gentiles entered into no such radical and dangerous encounter with the psychic structures of paganism. Where some forms of speculative and heretical Judaism did so their venture into syncretism failed either to safeguard the Hebraic roots or to renew the classical inheritance. The Christian church did both and laid the basis for a new world-order in the Empire.

One question that always haunts any discussion of myth is that of "broken myth," and the disparity between genuine primordial epiphany with its irrecoverable naivete, and "myth" in such a relatively advanced culture as that of the first century. Civilized man, we are told, is forever debarred by his "*oubli du sacré*" from this kind of autonomous mentality. It is true that

14. *Die griechische und lateinische Literatur und Sprache,* Berlin, 1905, p. 157.

when we speak of the mythological elements in the New Testament we have to do with much that has passed from the state of genuine archaic myth into that of culturized symbol—whether democratized myth or historicized myth or even folklore or literary allusion. Nevertheless, the true epiphanic and ecstatic potential survives in mankind and is creative, world-creative, in given situations. The power of such an impulse in the midst of first-century Judaism and Hellenism related it to primordial epiphany and was such as to organize many forms of secondary myth into a unified vision corresponding to its similarly fashioned ritual.

What holds true for the Christian impact on Hellenism also applies to the beginning in Galilee. In this case the situation of faded myth and anomie refers not to Judaism as a whole at the time of the ministry of Jesus, but to the disoriented groups suggested by the term "sinners" in the Gospels. For these the meaning of the inherited patterns of Jewish life and their sanctions had been eroded by social changes. They lived on the margin of the official cultus and of the movement of restoration represented by the synagogue and the Pharisees. The vigor of the eschatological groups in this period, including the sect which left us the Dead Sea scrolls, testifies both to disaffection with the existing authorities and the impulse to renewal. The power of Jesus' initiative among the unchurched groups was inseparable from the dramatizations he employed. His language drew on old archetypes and more recent imagery in such a way as to ignite the dream and incentives of his relatively few followers. It was only secondarily that Jesus found himself at odds with the official orthodoxy and those circles for whom traditional images were still vital. The death of Jesus, as a famous poem of Allen Tate ("The Cross") suggests, threw a blinding light on what was at stake, and inevitably led to a situation that resembles a war of myths, though it was a conflict within Israel still. But this leads to the other aspect of which I have spoken.

2. *Mythopoeic impulse and social authority.* Myth-making in the rise of Christianity not only meets the problem of the breakdown of older myth but inevitably enters into conflict with existing authority. I note this first as regards what we can call the "establishment" in the Roman Empire and its cities. This war of myths is dramatically orchestrated in the Book of Revelation with a full repertory of ancient cosmological motifs. We have here something like a cosmic opera whose dramatis personae include all the powers and agencies in heaven and earth and whose plot is conceived in the tradition of the holy war. Though we shrink from the gory detail and the unfairness to the humanistic values of Rome at its best, yet we should recognize what is at stake in these surreal tableaux. The eighteenth chapter contains a list of the products exchanged by the merchants in this great emporium, Rome, the new Babylon: cargoes of "gold, silver, jewels and pearls," all "articles of ivory, all articles of costly wood, bronze, iron and marble," also incense, spices, wine, oil, fine flour and wheat, cattle and sheep, horses and chariots, and finally, "bodies" (that is, slaves) and "human souls." The items in this list are taken mainly from the famous taunt-song against Tyre in the prophet Ezekiel. The Greek translation of Ezek. 27:13 reads, "Hellas and the regions about traded with you for the souls of men." But the Book of Revelation has set all these same wares in an ascending series with this as the climax. Sir William Walton, the composer, has used this climax with tremendous effect in his oratorio, *Belshazzar's Feast.*

This example shows that where primitive Christianity became involved in a war of myths issues like human slavery were at stake. This goes right back to Jesus who said, "Of how much more value is a man than a sheep" (Mt. 12:12). Surely any myth and dream of any age or inspiration must finally be answerable to this kind of test.

I turn now from the conflict of early Christian myth with

115

paganism to its conflict with Judaism, beginning with Jesus himself. This is usually presented as a conflict over the Jewish law and is, of course, a highly sensitive and controversial topic. But we can, at least, seek to go behind the usual terms of the discussion. Whether as regards Jesus or Paul the issue as to the law can be illuminated if studied as one example of a crisis in social symbols and archetypes. Normative Judaism in Jesus' day was dealing with this problem in one way and certainly safeguarded much of the cultural dynamics of the tradition. In this same crisis Jesus and his followers selected differently out of Israel's past, both conscious and unconscious, impelled by a new and momentous epiphany or experience of the sacred. Both movements felt themselves to be faithful to the law and the covenants. But each related itself differently to the deeper structures of the past, and this meant different ways of dealing with the present.

I can present this divergence in two ways. At the level of the imagery one can show that Jesus of Nazareth reordered the symbolic and mythic legacies of Israel and established new priorities, especially by a leap back to the oldest covenant imagery, especially the covenant of creation. In the second place, at a level that underlies the first and that requires the use of social-psychological tools, one can show that Jesus dealt more fundamentally than his contemporaries with the deeper strata of human existence. For this second level I refer to the phenomenological study by Paul Ricoeur of what one can best call the psycho-dynamics of the ancient world including the period with which we are concerned.[15] This second analysis, however, I must assign to a concluding note.

The focal image of Jesus' message was that of the Kingdom of God viewed as imminent and constituting both grace and

15. *Philosophie de la Volunté,* Part II, *Finitude et Culpabilité,* Paris; 1960, II," La Symbolique du mal," with its two sections, (1) The primary symbols: stain, sin, guilt; (2) the myths of origins and end.

total demand. It is not enough to say that Jesus goes back to the prophets. The ultimate reference of his message and vision is that of the creation itself. This is suggested by the cosmic-eschatological character of the Kingdom which he announced, in this respect different from the eschatology of the Pharisees associated with the age to come and the national hope. It partakes of the total Alpha-Omega scope of apocalyptic without its curiosities and phantasmagoria. Jesus identified the opposition to the Kingdom with Satan and the demons and this central symbolism confirms the creation-archetype. It is as though for Jesus much of the intervening cultural strata in Judaism with their long sedimentation of social and psychic habit had collapsed like so many floors. We may take as illustrative his appeal back of Moses to the "beginning of creation" in the words assigned to him in the dispute with the Jewish teachers about divorce (Mk. 10:6). Jesus' attitude to moral evil was one that recognized its ambiguity and its close relation to possession, one of Ricoeur's archaic symbols for the experience of alienation.

This depth in the sanctions of Jesus explains the implicit universalism in his position, as in his attitude to the Samaritans; his attitude to nature and the creatures (for example, the flowers of the field and the birds of the air); his appeals to reason, common sense and the processes of nature; and the quasi-secular tone of his parables and much of his teaching.[16] I am not saying that Jesus reverted to the creation-motif alone but that his imagery met the current dilemma by reordering all its symbolics in depth. One aspect of this is the convergence in him of the various roles and styles of the three main types of Israel's spokesmen, prophet, sage and scribe.

I have been speaking in this section about the conflict of a new mythical impulse with social authority and illustrating it in the case of Jesus. Jesus went behind the particular symbol-

16. Cf. the author's "Equivalents of Natural Law in the Teaching of Jesus," *Journal of Religion* 26, 2 (April 1946), pp. 125–135.

structure of his time and this meant a critique of the law as then understood and its patterns both in the unconscious life and in public institutions. We have an example here of the restructuring of myth in close relation to social and cultural change. As the breach with the synagogue developed we find that Jesus' use of the creation archetype is carried through. Paul's decisive framework is that of creation and new creation, just as his basic category for interpreting Christ is that of the new Adam. In the Gospels the corresponding category is that of the Son of Man. This image with its apocalyptic and universal roots and implications is related to that of the First Man and dominates the Gospel of Mark.[17] The Jewish category of Messiah is entirely subordinated to it just as it played little role in Jesus' own imagery. It is important, however, to make clear that the revolution in images initiated by Jesus should not be viewed as a war of myths between Judaism and Christianity. The divergence then as to this day is within the same household of faith. Not only Jesus but also Paul understood themselves to be faithful to the law and the covenants. But it is of interest to note that that same radical appeal to older archetypes which occasioned the conflict with the parent faith made possible an effective encounter with the universe of symbols of the Gentile world.

IV.

I have sought to discuss myth and dream in Christian Scripture in dynamic terms rather than theological. We have found illustration here of the power of the mythopoetic impulse and some

17. It is related to this that in Mark's account of the temptation of Jesus the scene suggests Eden before the Fall; Jesus is in the company of angels and "wild beasts," the latter harmless in the Paradisal state. In this same setting the first Adam fell, the second did not.

of its phenomena. We have concentrated upon the issues of continuity and discontinuity: the unbroken life-line of older archetypes offering orientation to culture; yet the vicissitudes of such symbol in the course of cultural change. There is, however, one feature of our material which requires a closing comment.

The myth and dream of Jewish and Christian origin is unique in its nexus with man's social experience and his historical life. This is a commonplace in all study of comparative religion. The most radical discontinuity we have had to recognize was that in which Hebraism historicized the older mythos of the ancient Near East. The new myth and ritual of Israel was oriented to time, to the birth of the people in time, and to its promise and obligation in time. The mythology of natural cycles was largely overcome. The Christian mythos, indeed, looked to the end of history but in such a way that the historical experience of man was still validated.

All this has meant that, as against some other kinds of world vision, the Jewish and Christian myth has been inextricably involved in the pragmatic vicissitudes of the West, in its social and political as well as cultural life, disasters as well as achievements. This means also that its original epiphanies and symbols have been often distorted, overlaid and given false theoretic formulation. If our basic concern is with the problem of cultural dynamics today, the sources and vehicles of cultural renewal, it is important that this particular mythology should be dissociated from such distortions and understood in its origins and total context. To this end the kind of social-psychological approach represented in this chapter can make a contribution.

In the foregoing discussion of the symbolics of the New Testament I have had occasion at various points to suggest implications for contemporary literary assessment. If, as de Rougemont observes, inherited archetypes "preform the inner movements of our own sensibility" and even dictate "the profound rhetorics of

119

our composition," we can well ask how far this is true today in the case of these once dynamic apperceptions. Their continuity through earlier vicissitudes has been noted as well as their power for cultural order and literary creativity. What is fundamentally distinctive about their basic theophanies and their *mythos* is their concrete universalism. A teleology of the world process is envisioned in inseparable relation to the moral dimension of personal existence in time with all its social realities. As we have insisted this kind of epiphany was one that required historization and embodiment, though not without its own forms of psychic and spiritual transcendence. Wherever in the classic period this vision of the world became involved in a war of myths, what was at stake was some such issue as that of human slavery. Here other visions and their rhetorics can be tested including those of the present day.

In the three chapters that follow dealing more directly with the crisis of language in our time the viability of all the classic archetypes of the past including the biblical will continue to demand our attention. Even where the conditions of our epoch tend to mute the voices of the past, and even though the dramas of the self eclipse the wider theatre of the classics and the Scripture, yet we shall find accents and metaphor to suggest that the very constitution of the human being demands a more total vision.

Note

I have referred to Ricoeur's phenomenological study of the issues with which I have been engaged in this chapter. It is carried out in the context of his wider investigation of the evolution of man's moral consciousness, especially in the section entitled "The Symbolics of Evil."[18] By the first century of

18. See the full title, footnote 15, p. 116 above. We give

our era Israel like pagan antiquity had long passed through the
two earliest stages of man's sense of rift or alienation from the
order of the sacred, each stage with its own strategies of expiation. The first stage was that in which his unrest was alone
identified by such non-moral symbols as stain or impurity or in-
fection calling for cleansing. Survivals of this stage are reflected
in texts of confession from the oldest cultural records we possess.
The second stage, also very old, corresponds to a new level of
culture in which we have a communal consciousness of sin as
deviation from the order of things or group-offense against God
or the gods, all suggested by symbols of bondage or possession
and calling for deliverance or atonement. Language of the earlier
stage is carried along into the new. The value of those ancient
symbols was that they recognize that evil is a part of the history
of being and of social being. Evil is already there, is not the
opposite of good; it has an external aspect or is an enslaving
power that cannot be dealt with by the will alone.

But by the time with which we are concerned Israel like
Greece had long passed to a third stage, that of the interiorized
guilt of the individual, evoking images now first of all not of
stain or sin but of burden. In the Old Testament as a whole
the deeper sensibilities of evil as a mystery had been carried
over into this third stage. But before the common era this depth
became attenuated with a new focus on the individual and his
obligation to the law now taking on an increasingly juridical
character. Thus we can understand the structuring of the
Judaism of our period about this third stage, and the categories
of law, transgression, obedience, repentance, gratitude, reward.
The Pharisees carried through their admirable ethico-juristic
and casuistic program enriched by the haggada, and the ethics

---

references to the French edition. See also Pierre Barthel, *Interprétation
du langage mythique et théologie biblique*, Leiden, 1963, Chapter V,
"L'Interprétation symbolique des représentations d'origine et de
structure mythiques par Paul Ricoeur," pp. 286–345.

of the people was the loftiest in the world of that time with its emphasis on freedom and responsibility. Yet in terms of cultural anthropology it was the ethic of an epoch and it was now in crisis, as we can see by the diverging sectarian movements and circles identified with apocalyptic visionaries or wisdom speculation. Like the mythology of the Enlightenment in our modern period, the symbolics of this stream of Judaism had forfeited connection to some degree with the earlier strata of man's experience of evil, including the pre-ethical and pre-rational. Thus Ricoeur can ask whether the "will to complete and exact obedience, even sustained by the joyous acceptance of a grateful heart, carries over fully the God-relation expressed earlier in the conjugal symbolism of the prophets."[19] And he asks whether the spiritual regime of the Law espoused by the Jewish teachers "could recognize its own abysses."[20]

It is to be remembered that such an analysis is proposed not at a theological level but a phenomenological. A comparative study of the symbolics of evil is carried out to throw light on the deeper structures of meaning, and the role of cultural myth. It is suggested that the imagery of Jesus represented in part a recovery of older archetypes, especially of those evoking the "non-ethical face of evil," thus de-moralizing the patterns of his day. That Paul should focus so much of his debate with Jewish opponents upon the theme of justification shows that he too found himself necessarily dealing with the Judaism of this particular epoch. His preferred Jewish categories and symbols drew on older levels of Israel's consciousness. In conclusion, lest Ricoeur's study appear partisan, it should be noted that his method can disclose analogous vicissitudes or what he calls *gauchissements* in other religious traditions including those of Christianity.

19. *La Symbolique du mal*, p. 129.
20. P. 134.

PART TWO

Vicissitudes of the Word in Our Time

We do not see our signs.

Ps. 74:9

New modes of expression must be found to dominate the mental complexity in which we struggle, these clashes of civilization in our spirits, their oppositions, their fusions—to solve these problems and beyond them once again to find footing, truth and a reasonable society.

Michel Butor

V. The Confusion of Tongues

Suchen ist irren.

Goethe

The wrestle with language is a universal feature of our world. In it all the incoherences and impasses of our age disclose themselves. The broken continuities in our culture represent no less than a seismic disturbance, affecting not only our intellectual life but our political substance and all that it means to be human, as testified particularly in the arts and in religion. We must understand culture here in its deepest sense of life-orientation and psychic and social sanity. But the disjunction in cultural tradition is so radical that our sense of reality becomes tenuous; our access is obscured to that nutriment of impulse that "incites men to go on living."

McLuhan's way of describing our situation is to say that man or human consciousness today is like a caravan just coming around the corner of a mountain-shoulder and suddenly becoming aware of a totally new reality that confounds all his measuring rods, categories and apperceptions. The present phase is the shock-phase, characterized by a sense of vertigo and weightlessness, but also of ontological dynamism. It is a phase fertile in new perceptions but these are inevitably atomistic.

125

Paul Tillich characterized this extreme situation by saying that our contemporary arts "show in their style both the encounter with non-being, and the strength which can stand this encounter and shape it creatively."[1] One test of a valid renewal of language today, whether in the arts or in religion, will be whether it bears the marks of such direct encounter with primordial realities today exposed.

The French poet Pierre Emmanuel has observed, "Why yes. Since the earth quakes, the most heroic thing that the artist can do is to dance!"[2] Certainly the most authentic language of such a time whether in style or image will testify to these elemental dynamics. And the most adequate mastery of the occasion will evidence both baptism in the primeval waters and an ordering of violence all the more miraculous—what has been ascribed to some modern poetry as a "furious calm." Here in any case we see the occasion in contemporary utterance for the apocalyptic mode, for surreal vision and paradoxical styles, not only in poetry but in the novel and the drama.

Yet if the arts today often exhibit such dynamism one thing that may give us pause is the difficulty with which the imagination retains its hold on any stable reality. McLuhan uses the term "weightlessness." Father William Lynch finds a principal theme in the gap between word and thing. Perhaps this is due, as Lukacs says, to the reification of the world which has accompanied our modern economic and technological changes. Lynch cites the tension in the cinema of Antonioni between private fantasy and public reality, and invokes Buber's formula: "Imagine the real!" We are out of touch and will resort even to violence to assure ourselves of some relation to things. The cliché of the hippie, "Get with it," is highly significant.

1. Cited by Cleanth Brooks with special reference to Ernest Hemingway in *The Hidden God,* New Haven, 1963, p. 7.
2. Cited by P. R. Régamey, *Art sacré au XXᵉ siecle,* Paris, 1952, p. 25.

Another aspect of this weightlessness and gratuity of experience is defined by the term, "The Protean man," assigned to the modern anti-hero. With the gap between the inner and the outer worlds the artist and his spokesmen lose their identity and pass from role to role and mask to mask. Robert Lifton, writing on this theme,[3] characterizes this "omni-attentive" man as one whose spine is made of plastic napkin rings. The widespread kaleidoscopic effects in current cinema, musical composition and fiction answer to his attenuated sense of reality or the discontinuity of his vision. Lukacs, again, in his discussion of the ideology of modernism, sees such scattering of the personal center in terms of an "eternal incognito." Citing Gottfried Benn's extreme dichotomy of thought and being he observes how easy it was for this type to be absorbed by Nazism.[4] But we should not judge too hastily even the extreme symptoms of our contemporary disarray. The necessary exploration of language in our time will inevitably take many forms.

I. MODULATIONS OF THE WORD

Man first came to consciousness in language which with all its changes remains the register of meaningfulness and reality. One biblical analogue for this is found in Genesis 1:2–3: "the earth was without form and void . . . and God said . . ." Or, we can say that man came to consciousness in myth and ritual, in those primordial experiences or epiphanies in which space, time and society began to be defined and organized. In Genesis 15:7–21 we have an Hebraic instance of an archaic epiphany in which to Abraham in a "horror of great darkness" the world-plot of his seed was disclosed.

3. "The Protean Man," *The Partisan Review,* vol. 20 (Winter 1968).

4. *Realism in Our Time,* New York, 1964, pp. 26–28.

Today also language and society and world are interrelated. Language is the register of coherence and orchestrates our sense of reality. For our reality-sense has to do not only with self identity—whether psychic or metaphysical—but also at the same time necessarily with our social and cosmic involvement. If we speak of language in this way it is evident that we have in mind not only vocabulary and names, but also images, fables, myths.

But the transmission of language in all these aspects is not a smooth, uninterrupted process. The language world can be disordered as a given society is disordered. This can come about in relation to cultural changes in human groups. It can also come about through disturbances caused by the impact of other language groups. Our biblical analogue for such disturbances can be found in Genesis 11:1–9 which begins: "Now the whole earth had one language and one speech," and ends, "There [at Babel] the Lord confused the language of all the earth." The history of cultures shows an alternation of coherence and incoherence, of meaningfulness and anomie. All the media of speech may become stale or empty, particularly the focal images and myths. Again we find biblical analogues for this situation: "And the word of the Lord was rare in those days; there was no frequent vision" (I Sam. 3:1); or, "We do not see our signs" (Ps. 74:9).

This is the situation we face today. Archibald MacLeish has stated it in its extreme form:

A world ends when its metaphor has died.

Evidently the whole language phenomenon of our modern world and the reality sense it reflects is transitional and disordered. Our wrestle with language and meaning is carried out in a situation of incoherence occasioned not only by the many layers of language behind us, but also by the confluence of many alien legacies. The complexity of contemporary poetry and literature evidence this.

Yet in such language situations of incoherence, when the basic securities provided by tradition are attenuated, there is a profound impulse at work towards the renewal of authentic speech, towards the emergence of a language conferring meaningfulness upon the chaotic actuality. It is as though man wants to keep on living, and since he has to live from the depths the primordial mystery renews itself from the depths. And here the arts have their perennial importance, a role analogous to that of the cultic epiphany of earlier societies. And, indeed, the modern arts in this world-making role inevitably relate themselves to the focal images, fables and myths of the past.

Among these focal world-images of the past are those of the great religions, and for our situation those of the Bible. Just here appears one of the striking features of the language problem today. Culturally speaking, the biblical archetypes are only one feature of the usable past, yet any new imaginative language and symbol adequate to our situation today cannot ignore them. But Christianity for its part cannot reappropriate its basic mythos without full engagement with the other images which carry meaning in the life of today. The renewal of language in our time, therefore, involves an interplay here. The impulse in our times to articulate adequately our new world experience will always be driven by a demand for totality of meaning. The analogy of Pentecost as narrated in the Book of Acts is illuminating. We seek a universal language and universal communication. But man is also incurably eschatological in the sense of positing ultimates. The fables of the tribe demand a background of cosmic myth. The renewal of language today, therefore, in its wider sense means the projection of a world myth, an eschatological myth, and this will no doubt involve a continuation of the war of myths that has characterized our whole cultural tradition.

There are two areas of intense concern with language today which interest us particularly, those of modern letters and re-

129

ligion. In the area of letters we observe the writer wrestling with the medium of contemporary speech, and in the process often actually commenting on the task. Thus to cite only the best known example, T. S. Eliot in "East Coker":

> here I am . . .
> Trying to learn to use words, and every attempt
> is a wholly new start . . .[5]

But we see also the literary critic concerned not merely with changing rhetorics in the usual sense but perforce occupied with the wider cultural determinants of our language situation. And since language is so fundamental a human gesture, such critics are inevitably involved in depths they may well wish to avoid.

In the case of religion likewise, it is a question of the modulation of its traditional language, the actualization of the faith in speech and vehicles at home in our own sensibility, and in engagement with the life-forces which determine our actual situation. Malcolm Boyd, speaking of the communication of the faith today, writes:

Evangelism requires finding and establishing points of contact with the unchurched. It must result in a breakthrough—through alien cultures and a vacuum of outmoded Christian words and symbols in post-Christianity. . . . The Church is finding one area of breakthrough in art forms.[6]

Thus we see about us in various quarters today the unpredictable emergence of new religious rhetorics from the depths. The life-tradition of faith, the underground movement of the Hebraic revelation, in both its main branches, renews itself and re-articulates itself in our new cultural configurations as it has done

5. *Four Quartets,* New York, 1943, p. 16.
6. *Focus,* New York, 1960, p. 37.

in the past. These transformations can be seen emerging not only in religious idiom but also in liturgy and in sociological patterns, and outside the institutions as well as within. And this involves clashes and schisms between new and old as well as all manner of mediation and interpretation.

But in distinction from such fundamental change from within there is also the accompanying theological activity. And today the focus of all theological work lies here in the problem of language. Religious leaders talk today of little else but of the problem of communication, of a new evangelism, of making the Gospel relevant, translating the message, getting out of the ghetto, renewing the ecclesiastical arts, liturgical renewal, as well as the value of new versions of Scripture.

The institutions, by and large, cling to their inherited formulas, categories, idiom. Poetry and art have learned some time since to come down off their pedestal. Religion has been slow to come down from the high hourglass pulpit and the stained-glass windows. The language of Zion needs to be reactualized. After all Jesus did not speak in Hebrew, but in the popular Aramaic. Paul did not speak in classical Greek but in the koine, that is, popular Greek. St. Francis did not speak, and Dante did not write, in Latin, but in the new Tuscan vernacular.

Our main point here, however, at the outset is to urge that all wrestlings with language and meaning in today's extraordinary situation are mutually related and have much to teach each other. What is going on in modern literature both in art and in criticism offers an inexhaustible documentation on the vicissitudes of language today, and one that is of decisive importance for the theologian. What the renewal of the word means for our culture is exhibited in various and compelling ways in the modern poet, novelist and dramatist as well as the critics. For the Christian witness or theologian to ignore this is fatal. Not least do they learn here to recognize the changing audience, the changing world reality to which they must address themselves and, indeed, of which they are part. But the concerns of the modern theologian with language and the whole meaning of the word in the biblical tradition also has a contribution to make today to the general task. Indeed, some Christian poets and artists have crossed the frontier and merged the two tasks.

II. SENSIBILITY AND GENRE

If we speak of the renewal of the word or of language today we may well reflect upon the scope and ramifications if the task. We may associate with it the expression, "the rebirth of images," or even the biblical promise of new tongues or a new song. On the religious side we may recall the remark that the question of a revival of religion is "almost a question of rhetoric."[7] On the secular side we may recall Ezra Pound's injunction, "Make it new!", or Eliot's "We cannot follow an antique drum"; or Archibald MacLeish's mandate to poets, in view of the death of our world-metaphor, "Poets, invent the age! Invent the metaphor!", or Stevens' plea, "Make the bread of faithful speech."

To speak of the renewal of language supposes some sort of failure of older media or some break in communication. Words and images have gone stale; some dislocation or geological shift has occurred between inherited symbols and speech-forms and the way things now are; there is unreality and consequent emptiness in our familiar media of communication. The inadequacy may not be universally felt or felt in different ways. We have not only discontinuities with the past or with various pasts, but confusion of tongues today—all calling in any case for a renewal of language that will quicken the traditions and order the chaotic present. And all with a result that language may speak for and to our actual *Lebenswelt*.

Surely we know that this result cannot be brought about by

7. T. N. Wilder, in Foreword to *The Angel That Troubled the Waters*, New York, 1928, p. XVI.

calculation. Only in our integrity as talking creatures or as artists can we serve the process as midwives, by our disposition and our alertness.

We also know that the renewal of language can be more than a matter of vocabulary or even images. Speech is a primordial gesture of man and its many aspects are related. The literary artist and the critic are concerned not only with the dictionary and the figure of speech. They are concerned with the total phenomenon of language, and therefore with its various modes, conventions and genres; their social context and transformation; the presence or absence of particular rhetorics in a given situation; the rise and fall of particular literary conventions. They know that there is a time for the epic and a time for the satire; a time for iambic pentameter and a time for alliterative verse; a time for the allegory and a time for the philosophical poem; a time for free association and a time for the litany; a time for the tragedy and a time for the apocalypse. New epochs call for particular kinds of voices, rhythms, stances of the author; particular strategies with respect to the past; and highly diverse forms of publication, whether by public recitation, by handbills, by private circulation, by the printed book, by recordings, or by radio script.

Certainly one of the most revealing indices of a new sensibility is to be found in the vicissitudes of literary forms. I leave aside here the wider question of styles and raise the prior question as to the great classical genres themselves. Professor Tom Driver has drawn attention in a most illuminating way to the dilemma of the drama in our day and its cultural implications. The paper in question is entitled, "The Loss of the Histrionic and the Modern Quandary of Theology."[8] Traditionally the drama presupposes social imagination and a sense of inherited

8. A paper presented in Atlanta, November 18, 1967, at a Conference on Literature and Theology sponsored by the Graduate Institute of the Liberal Arts of Emory University, published in *Soundings*, vol. LI, no. 2 (Summer 1968).

relationships between man and man and man and his world. In this context a dramatic action is meaningful and the audience can relate itself to plot, story and character. But today the basic presuppositions of such an art have been eroded. Indeed those unconscious attitudes which gave ritual its power are attenuated, and the drama has always carried with it its roots in ritual. As Driver points out, our modern disinherited man has been thrown back on his own subjectivity, and the question of reality for him is narrowed to the thirst for authenticity. The dramatic imagination is one of the more visible casualties of this situation.

Here then we can recognize one aspect of our language dilemma. This shift in sensibility makes all but impossible demands upon the traditional art of the theatre. The novel and the film lend themselves more easily to the urge for immediacy, for the phantasmagoria of the unrelated self and the kaleidoscope of broken awareness. The playwright is impelled to move towards the open theatre, the happening, the play or gesture without words, and the documentary. Subjectivism, psychologism, existentialism, solipsism invent their own vehicles and language, as man in this extremity finds it necessary to invent himself. Even Arthur Miller in *The Price* gives to the harassed Walter in an otherwise old-fashioned play the line, "We must invent ourselves." But again we remark, all such explorations, whether of genres or other features of language are inevitable. In any case they call for assessment at another point. We shall return to this when we examine the new rhetorics of our day.

Of course one of the most critical features of language in a time of change is that of image or symbol. Even in a few years our repertory of plastic expression renews itself. Any attention to the prints, engravings, illustration, say of the eighteenth century, would remind us of a host of emblems and pictorial conventions which carried a world of meaning to that age and which today are largely meaningless. At a more significant level still, the images with which our fathers evoked religious, patriotic or domestic sentiments are often today quaint if not embarrassing, like a collection of old valentines in the attic.

But even more important than such semantic fashions we have to reckon with the great world-images of an epoch, the way in which men have dramatized existence for themselves and the course of time. Here we touch religion as well as general culture. Here the fading of language raises our greatest problem. But at this level as well as the others changes in imagery do not go on at the same pace throughout a society. Here we have one chief cause for the confusion of tongues especially today when varying forms and stages of tradition are brought so close together by our facilities of communication.

III. THE COSTS OF EMANCIPATION

When we face the present language dilemma we cannot but ask the question as to its causes. But this means that we are pushed back upon the question as to the origin and significance of our modern cultural disorder. Everyone likes to play word games with such terms as Enlightenment, Romanticism, Victorianism, Modernism, and to assign various values to one or the other. We do not propose here to assess all the familiar analyses of modern alienation, secularization, dehumanization, desacralization, the breakup of the Christian synthesis, the dissociation of sensibility, the death of tragedy, and indeed, the death of God. But I would like to point up a certain convergence of literary-critical and theological analyses of our western antecedents, especially when it is seen as a revolution in language and in imagery.

This convergence appears in a refusal to look upon our disorder and the state of modern arts, as attributable to some kind of Fall. Culture-historians offer moralistic judgments on western man's rebellion and hybris. As we stand

Musing upon the king my brother's wreck
And on the king my father's death before him,[9]

we are supposed to repent of a Promethean revolt against older European traditions of order. Our confusion of tongues is traced to the attempt to build a modern tower of Babel and to make ourselves as God.

It is true that we are indebted to poets and artists themselves for our most adequate portrayals of the special anguish and aridity of modern life. They also define the epoch. We all recall certain phrases and titles: Valéry's "civilizations have learned that they are mortal"; Eliot's *The Waste Land,* Yeats' loss of ceremony and innocence; Auden's "Age of Anxiety"; Sitwell's "Song of the Cold" and "Song of Cain"; Kafka's labyrinth; Robert Penn Warren's portrayal of man as "Brother to Dragons"; Faulkner's watch without hands; Robert Lowell's slave-ship, a new "heart of darkness" (*The Old Glory*). Such portrayals may often imply a lapse from a more perfect order. But no simple moralistic conclusions should be drawn from these imaginative works, other than that the human condition presents different constellations in different times. Thus Yeats' classic reading of the age, "The Second Coming," sets the modern epiphany of evil in a wider myth of recurrence.

If one says with Eliot in prose that "the world is trying the experiment of attempting to form a civilized but non-Christian mentality," with the implication that modern disorder and the "dark ages before us" are the consequence of a wilful assertion of autonomy, one can answer in a number of ways. One can ask whether the older western world was as truly Christian as all that. Or one can say: what else could the West do in the seventeenth century and later but explore new frames for the changing *Lebenswelt?* Or one can even say, as we should, that the modern experiment in autonomy was obscurely prompted

9. T. S. Eliot, *Poems 1909–1925,* New York, n.d., p. 95.

by the same God whose traditional image had come to misrepresent him. Eliot can speak differently in poetry. We know that *The Waste Land* should not be read as an expression of post-World War I disillusionment. But neither should it be read as an indictment of post-medieval humanism. It is one thing if our literature offers us a nostalgic confrontation of modern ill and ancient health, and it is another to locate the cause or to seek out scapegoats. What is most characteristic of modern literature is the deeper vision which superposes contemporary man upon older annals of the race, and so seeks to see man in a planetary and universal way. So we find it in any case in Eliot, Pound and Joyce.

Yet let us look at two less familiar texts about the modern situation. In his Preface to the *Dynasts* Hardy is speaking of the superb confidence that animated the periods that gave us the Greek and the Elizabethan drama.

But [today] the meditative world is older, more invidious, more nervous, more quizzical than it once was, and being unhappily perplexed by

> *Riddles of Death Thebes never knew*

it may be less ready and less able than Hellas and Old England were to look through the insistent, and often grotesque, substance at the things signified.

George Steiner, who cites this theme in his *Death of Tragedy*,[10] connects it with the modern lack of such superb confidence to create, especially in the genre of poetic drama. Hardy no doubt diagnoses one aspect of the situation today, but the handicaps of a particular genre should not be the barometer of the world's health or even of the state of literature in general. If we confront "Riddles of Death Thebes never knew" it may be a sign of

10. New York, 1961, p. 120.

maturity, and our stammering in a different mode may have its own eloquence.

Again, Edwin Muir describes the modern situation in his poem "Prometheus." Prometheus after ages of his ordeal reflects on changes in Olympus and in religion on earth.

> Now time's storm is rising, sweeping
> the sons of men into an emptier room,
> vast as a continent, bare as a desert,
> where the dust takes man's lifetime to revolve
> about the walls, harried by peevish gusts
> and little spiteful eddies; nothing standing
> but the cast-iron cities and rubbish mountains.[11]

This portrayal is true to much experience. But Muir's work as a whole and, indeed, the poem in its conclusion testifies to the unobtrusive operation of those metamorphoses of the dust which older epochs have celebrated more confidently.

The disorders of modern society do not mean that the world has become worse than it was in the Enlightenment or in the Middle Ages. Men have had new problems to wrestle with and these transitional struggles have inevitably disrupted older achievements of order and thereby obscured some highly visible aspects of man's greatness. One aspect of this limitation has appeared in the arts of literature. We may illustrate by the genre of tragedy. In his volume *The Vision of Tragedy,* Richard Sewell rightly points to the recovery of this vision in major literary expression in Faulkner, especially in *Absolom! Absolom!* On this point a recent testimony of Allen Tate is corroborative.

We must not fall into the historical trap where, immobilized, we apply a doctrine of historical determinism to poets, and pretend that after a certain date a certain kind of poetry could not be written. I fell into the trap thirty-five years ago when I said that

11. *Collected Poems, 1921 to 1958,* London, 1960, p. 215.

138

after Emerson had done his work, the tragic vision was henceforth impossible in America. I am glad to have been proved wrong.[12]

And Tate then cites a passage from Robert Lowell's poem, "The Severed Head."

Sewell's discussion of the rarity of the tragic vision in the modern period points to social and ideological factors. For a long period circumstances have not been propitious for that kind of cultural homogeneity which can give birth to great representative works in such genres as tragedy and epic, or which can, for that matter, favor major and massive religious repossession. But this is only one instance of the law of alternation.

It is too easy for moralists and traditionalists to make capital of modern disarray. The story of the modern world is the story of rapid change and emancipation. And this has inevitably occasioned iconoclasm and conflict, the repudiation of authority, and the costs of anomie and alienation. The changes in society have had their inevitable accompaniment of changes in language, whether image or rhetoric.

We still live in the great epoch of revolt and emancipation which dates especially from the late seventeenth century, though this phase belongs in the wider arc defined by the Renaissance. The liberation and autonomy claimed have been associated throughout with temptations to self-sufficiency and pride. The whole constellation has taken on new forms in every generation. The struggle of the individual to affirm himself against one or another kind of constraint, tradition, custom, law or conformity is a feature of the whole story of modern culture.

Literature has been eloquent of this story of revolt and its cost. The literature of the Romantic movement offers us the convulsive struggle of revolutionary man, and his consequent disillusionment, solitude and loss of footing. The example of

12. Quoted from "The Unliteral Imagination; Or, I, Too, Dislike It," *The Southern Review,* vol. I, New Series, no. 3 (July, 1965), p. 542.

139

the young Wordsworth is familiar. More recent literature presents us with a new phase, the efforts of those who would break with bourgeois patterns, with modern conformities and stifling cultural conventions. The situation in this country in the first decades of this century is well suggested by Norman Pearson in his paper on "Anderson and the New Puritanism."[13] In the Winesburg stories and the novels "the blind gropings and beatings against the walls of personal inhibitions and social conventions, seem to have a violence of desperation. . . . Always there is the same timid trembling of the hands towards the apple (a thing of beauty and a seed of knowledge), which Anderson describes in the foreword to *Horses and Men*."[14] Here as throughout the whole period of modern emancipation we see both the lonely heroism and the moral anguish attendant on the revolt against authority. In our more recent literature the typical heroes are the exile, the resistance fighter, the alienated, the Isolato, the haunted rebel, the clown, the Christ-figure, the expatriate, the Wandering Jew. In all of them we recognize alienation and the vision of a "world without governors" since the older sanctions have faded.

When this period is under review literary criticism has a wide field of observation as to changes in rhetoric, in noting how western man's voice has changed. Some literary forms and styles are obsolete. Some have come to the fore—the conversational voice, the stream of consciousness, the epiphany, the psychological drama, the surrealist fantasy, the international-hero-narrative. So the theologian, for his part, observes the hard death of pulpit oratory, of the resonant prophetic diatribe, the Emersonian meditation, the sententious aphorism, the subjective hymn, the plangent confession, the illustration from the preacher's file, the nostalgic cadence. Religion finds it difficult today to change its voice to accord with a disaffected public. Apart from the question of symbol, it is only beginning to speak

13. *Four Studies,* Verona, 1962.
14. Pp. 14–15.

in authentic contemporary accents and vehicles, born out of new stresses. Yet here and there in the church or at its margin we observe the emergence of such speech—whether tone, idiom or medium—for example in new liturgical texts and musical settings, or in the sobered rhetorics learned under totalitarian persecution or in other frontier situations, as well as in the wider use of Negro spirituals and the new folksongs born out of racial conflict or the menace of nuclear destruction. Such new speech-forms, as in the case of Stravinsky's music or Rouault's paintings, will take up both classic religious elements and contemporary secular idiom.

To return to the main dilemma of our revolutionary age. Men in the West have been impelled by a passion to understand and a convulsive struggle to breathe freely. The whole story has been marked by veritable paroxysms of revolt. This impulse has inevitably swept its prophets and scapegoats beyond the law, and been associated with Promethean defiance. The quests and revulsions have inevitably brought disorder in their train. Over the whole history to this day one can write Goethe's formula: *"Suchen ist irren."* To seek is to err, to go astray; morally as well. But we have to seek. And with the erring, and through it, we also find. Thus I would place a positive sign over against modern cultural change and the modern arts.

Robert Frost takes sides with all such modern exploration and urges a good conscience on those wrestling with these ambiguities.

> Go on to know
> More than you can sing.
> Have no hallowing fears
> Anything's forbidden
> Just because it's hidden.
> Trespass and encroach
> On successive spheres
> Without self-reproach.[15]

15. "Kitty Hawk," *In the Clearing,* New York, 1962, p. 51.

141

The whole story is epitomized in Hölderlin's poem, "Lebens-lauf." The poet speaks for his age intoxicated with new hopes of emancipation, that sought life beyond the law; an age that then passed through the terrors of the consequent loss of norms and sanctions, through the metaphysical anguish of having no ground beneath its feet—therefore, as Auden puts it, "scared of the unknown unconditional dark"—and yet an age that refused to take the false courses of cynicism or escape or reaction. In Hölderlin we have a paradigm of the rebel who has aspired limitlessly, has encountered the inflexible limits of the Promethean spirit, and who nevertheless has refused to be embittered. The gods teach the poet acceptance of the givens of life without defeatism. The poet addresses himself.

> You, too, aspired after greater things
> but love and its earthly bonds and the law of the creature
> proclaimed their ancient rights,
> and suffering bows us down with irresistible force.
>
> The rainbow returns to the earth from which it arose
> but it is not in vain or without meaning.
>
> Whether we soar or fall, a divine justice presides,
> whether in the womb of the unborn
> or in deepest Orcus.
>
> This I have learned.
> For you, O heavenly powers that maintain all that is,
> you, as I well know, have never led me by smooth paths
> as did my mortal Masters.
>
> Let man prove all things—say the heavenly ones—
> so that he may be mightily nurtured,
> and learn to render thanks for all;
> and, whatever his own course,
> be taught, notwithstanding, to hail the dawn of freedom.[16]

16. *Hölderlins Werke,* edited by Anton Brieger, Salzburg, 1954, p. 276. My translation.

I have here focussed the vicissitudes of our cultural history upon the artist and the rebel. But this story of modern alienation and anomie applies to society at large. The ordeal of the artist has been representative. We do not mean that all iconoclasm has been wise. Much of it has been motivated by man's ancient avidities. But at its best the ordeal and valor of the modern spirit, right down to the present day, are well suggested by the title of one of Marianne Moore's poems, "He 'Digesteth Harde Yron.' " This poem is an incomparable allegory of the imagination as hero, "the one remaining rebel." Here we see the sparrow-camel, the ostrich; its plumes, eggs despoiled by man's greed and cunning,

> Six hundred ostrich-brains served
> at one banquet,

Yet all such trophies of splendor insolently paraded

> dramatize a meaning always missed
> by the externalist.
> The power of the visible
> is the invisible; as even where
> no tree of freedom grows,
> so-called brute courage knows.[17]

IV. TECHNOLOGY AND THE SPIRIT:
ROBERT MUSIL

If we thus pretend to look hopefully upon our cultural predicament and the language crisis of today there is one sector of it which can serve as a test. There is perhaps no aspect of our supposed alienation that receives more attention than the sway of impersonal and rationalist categories related to modern science and technology. We may look on this analytic habit as a main

17. *Collected Poems*, London, 1951, pp. 102–104.

source of modern achievement. We may see it as a factor in the dethronement of old cultural tyrannies. But we may also be disturbed by the extent to which such abstractions threaten the deeper dynamics of a healthy society and the whole domain of imaginative creation. In any case it is clear that we have here one of the most critical factors in our confusion of tongues.

We shall find documentation of this problem among our most recent writers, but let us return first to an older writer who was preoccupied with it in a way that may still be found exemplary. I refer to the Austrian writer who was also a mathematician and scientist, Robert Musil. In his novel, *The Man Without Qualities*,[18] the author well states part of the dilemma brought to light by the technical mind. "Anyone," it is remarked, "who is in the habit of dealing with his affairs by means of a slide-rule finds that a good half of all human assertions simply cannot be taken seriously."[19] But he can also satirize all such clinical discourse: "on they talk in a special, stiff, out-of-touch extraneous manner of speaking that does not go any deeper down inside than the epiglottis."[20] And speaking more generally:

Here we have the new method of thought, pure intellect, the very well-spring of the times, the fons et origo of an unfathomable transformation . . . a religion whose dogma is permeated by the hard, courageous, mobile, knife-cold, knife-sharp mode of thought that is mathematics. . . . We have gained in terms of reality and lost in terms of dream.[21]

But Musil has the wisdom to keep the problem open. It is true, we read, that mathematics has entered like a demon into all aspects of our life.

18. Vols. I–III, London, 1953–60.
19. Vol. I, p. 37.
20. *Ibid.*, p. 38.
21. P. 40.

It is exactly as if that old-time inefficient mankind had gone to sleep on an ant-hill, and when the new one woke up all the ants had crept into his blood.

He then characterizes our technological man:

The inner drought, the monstrous mixture of acuity in matters of detail and indifference as regards the whole, man's immense loneliness in a desert of detail, his restlessnesses, his greed for money, his coldness and his violence.

But Musil stops at making logical and accurate thinking the cause of all this, or seeing mathematics as "the arch-mother of that spirit from which in the end poison gases and fighter aircraft have been born."[22]

The negative side of what Musil calls "this unfathomable transformation" of our being is powerfully expressed in Rilke's phrase,

das verzehrende Wesen der Rechnung,

which can hardly be translated but means something like the process of schematization and calculation which wastes and devastates the truly human, that obsession with cyphers and series and abstractions which invades the sentient universe of the human mystery like an alien power. Like ice in the unconscious it represents a built-in numbness and an ineluctable limit to freedom and awareness, a take-over of our existence by a kind of cerebral non-being.

The implications of this mentality could lead us far. In the moral field we recognize the perilous borderland of an autonomous science, especially in experimentation on human subjects, which went to such excesses under the Nazis. But this mentality can color the whole range of the sciences of man and

22. *Ibid.*

culture generally, and pretend in its hybris to design the future of man, to usurp upon the prerogatives of the creator and profane the ultimate sanctities of the heart. Here it has confederates in the impersonal structures of our society and even in the neutral habits of scholarship identified by Hugh Kenner as "the true scholastic stink."

It is not surprising therefore that we find contemporary writing marked by and engaged with this aspect of our experience and its costs. The real front here is not in the external world of machines and constructions but in the private world of conceiving and encountering the world, not in the order of public violence but psychological violence, that order for which the arts offer unique strategies for resolution. At the most general level, indeed, we find observations like the following:

The adolescent is probably right in saying that it is difficult to know God in a technical world that worships computers that predict our future, machines that control our present, and bull-dozers that destroy our past.[23]

The computer, the machine, the bulldozer should have their rights recognized along with modern science and technology as a whole. Facile satire answers no questions. But it is at the deeper level of the maladies of the will and the imagination that the issues may be illumined and here the arts are essential.

It is therefore understandable and, indeed, welcome that our contemporary literature finds itself engaged in this arena and, indeed, implicated in all the temptations of nihilism. The imagination must stoop to conquer. Language cannot order experience without entering into it. The word must couple with the real, especially the new and the unnamed. Only so can the irrational be brought under control and the monstrous be tamed. Auden says this effectively in his homage "To T. S. Eliot on His Sixtieth Birthday":

23. James A. Knight, *Psychiatric Spectator*, New York, December, 1–3, 1966.

146

> ... it was you
> Who, not speechless from shock but finding the right
> Language for thirst and fear, did much to
> Prevent a panic.[24]

But if it is true that the poet and artist must name things as they are, yet the true imaginative act is of all things most difficult. It represents a kind of total wrestle with the intractible, a kind of exorcism, and the struggle incident to it requires supernatural resources and disciplines. It has been said of the painter Rouault that he

has painted social themes, judges and the judged, kings, prostitutes and clowns, each painting a sort of powerful stained-glass icon in translucent oil. Rouault's mythical figures seem to have a primitive function, acting as a sort of "Christian" fetish, capturing as if by magic, in powerful staring eyes, the spirits that are to be controlled or worshipped.[25]

If, however, the modern artist must enter into the fateful struggle for meaning and go down among Beckett's "twilight people" and be responsive to what Tillich called the encounter with non-being, it is above all the duty of the critic to discriminate. This is ambiguous territory and there are many artists who lack the passports and the disciplines required, and whose motives may be rather fascination with vertigo and the forbidden, and a hidden complacency with destruction. There is a long tradition in the arts which assigns them ultimate autonomy and makes creativity its own law. The valid iconoclastic role of the arts in some situations becomes a pretext for total denigration, inspired by diffused resentments or morbid world-loathing. The disinherited man of today can again fall a prey to antinomian phantasies such as have been known in the past and which give a good conscience to any profanation. Robert Musil envisages

24. *Nones,* New York, 1951, p. 71.
25. Guide to an exposition of African art.

one such extreme doctrine as possible in the climate he describes: "Rob, murder, fornicate—our teaching is so strong that it will transform the cess-pools of your sins into clear sparkling mountain rills."[26] Recognizing all these possibilities and confusions in today's crucible of images we can also gauge the difficulty of the task of criticism.

But we have been specially concerned in this section with those unresolved stresses in our modern reality occasioned by the analytic mind. It will be remembered that Auden dealt delightfully with these issues in his *Christmas Oratorio* in those sections dealing with the wise and their vacuous and sterile thought, climbing on glassy slopes where there was no foothold or "stuttering on an obsessive note."

More recently these abstract and cerebral aspects of our modern alienation have become a marked feature of our literature. Whole novels and plays are written which present a puppet-world dominated by these kinds of bloodless categories, sometimes with the collaboration of the tape-recorder or the computer or the stereo-speaker. No one can understand Samuel Beckett who does not recognize the large place that this incubus occupies in his work. And in Beckett the stakes are very serious and the art is a match for them as not always elsewhere. He goes deeper than satire or irony to a tragic encounter with post-Cartesian man struggling with his solipsism and tormented by the vanity of ratiocination and a logic that has no hold on things. In the discourse of his characters we find frequent obsessions with number schemes, statistical games, rehearsals of mathematical series, hallucinatory struggles with computations that always end in a surd.

This is more than a "dry mock" of rationality. Nor should we say that in such contexts Beckett is sheer nihilist. From within our confusion of tongues, from within our paralysis of authentic speech, he explores the gulf between the tyranny of the im-

26. *Op. cit.,* I, p. 41.

personal in our life and the human voice. That he pushes the dilemma to the utmost limit, the point of *stenachoria,* to use a Greek term—the anguishing impasse—and in mordant style, all this is only the artist's right to present a matter in its most illuminating exposure. In all the arts today we find that one of the recurring strategies is to go behind all existing patterns and to begin over with the first elements of language, at the very zero point of experience.[27]

As we have observed at the beginning of this section, the transformations wrought by mathematics and their sequel represent only one segment of our post-Renaissance experience. There is nothing here to refute the hopeful view we have taken of our modern situation. If the whole mentality of analysis and serialization threatens us we can digest it and humanize it if we confront it honestly as Beckett seeks to do. The neutral laws and impersonalities of mathematics and logic upon which so much of our civilization is erected are only an extension of the objective determinations of our human world with which men before us have come to terms. If it is only in our era that these regularities have been fully uncovered, though as an aspect of thought itself, surely men can deal with them as men have before with the givens of our condition. In this segment of the struggle with alienation the task of criticism is to distinguish between the true artist and the false, or more often between the qualified and the unqualified. There are many writers and shapers of opinion who lack grounding for dealing with these vicissitudes of the word.

27. "Our technical age, our 'modernity' with all its practical tasks, is one peculiarly characterized by *l'oubli des hiérophanies,* the loss of memory of the signs of the sacred, the loss of man himself so far as he belongs to the sacred. . . . It is the epoch in which our language becomes ever more precise, univocal, in a word more technical, more fitted for those integral formulations which are called, precisely symbolic logic, it is in this same epoch of discourse that we wish to recharge our language, that we wish to start again from the fulness of language." Paul Ricoeur, *Philosophie de la volonté,* vol. II, 1960, Part II, "La Symbolique du mal," pp. 324–325.

Their work only mirrors the confusion or voices the destructive element.

How are we, then, to understand the significance and origin of our confusion of tongues? It is not a question of modern pride and its nemesis. It is a question of a continuing revolution against unreal categories and old seasons of the soul, and the consequent crisis of identity and perpetual struggle for new authentic speech. This holds in the arts as well as in religion. Our literary critics study the whole history not only in terms of ideas but of styles and images. In styles, from the Romantics on, we see the break with discursive logic, the turn to a higher logic of immediate presentation, paradox and epiphany. In our century it is the break with the personal voice in its subjectivity and with a rhetoric of sentiment. We hear today rather the accent of a more radical self, often speaking through the mask of the clown, through some Tiresias or Sibyl or crazy Jane or golden bird, admittedly more austere but often all the more eloquent. With respect to the image: since Blake a revolution against the frozen world-symbol of a millennial past, and in our day a further relocation of the archetypes in the world of everyday. But this whole revolution in rhetorics has accompanied the modern experience and represents our response to reality more nakedly disclosed.

The most significant theology today similarly puts a plus sign on this whole cultural history. However much is lost in the dethroning of older authorities, much is gained. Not only in the medieval period but right down through the Reformation into the seventeenth century Greek metaphysical categories ordered the world and structured not only the conception of God and of Christ but of man and the soul, and all in terms of duality. Even humanism, Christian or secular, maintained a two-storey world distinguishing the eternal and the temporal, the supernatural and the natural, the order of the spirit and the order of the visible and tangible. And this duality perpetuated itself down into the Enlightenment and into Romanticism and transcendentalism in secularised forms. In their various ways the world was such that men lived under a sublime canopy of metaphysical reality—the divine, the eternal, the transcendent Good, Beautiful and True; and everything—dogma, sacrament, nature, politics, morality, art—found its substance in this governing apperception.

But theology does not see the collapse of this canopy as a disaster or a consequence of western arrogance. The fate of religion is not linked with this old habit of the soul. Indeed, the Gospel which preceded the Greek metaphysics is congenial with our new empirical humanism today. Grace is properly sought in the secular and not in an overhead dimension of the sacred. The Hebraic thinking out of which the Gospel came is holistic and mundane. Of course the Gospel recognizes the duality of God and man, but this dynamic duality is all the more viable in our world disabused of the older hierarchies.

Therefore we find today an extraordinary convergence between the new theology and the new poetic or aesthetic. In both any dimension of transcendence must be found in the actual and not overhead. Both demand that we relocate the imagination in ordinary life and the spirit in the flesh. Truth and meaning and revelation are first to be sought in their disguise in the secular. If they cannot be found there how can we be beguiled or appeased by assurances of higher geographies or by nostalgias of some more veridical dream? Moreover as the artist can find today the epiphany with Wallace Stevens in an ordinary evening in New Haven, so the believer locates grace with Charles Péguy welling up where least expected, and the re-emergence of the word not only in Zion but in some unthinkable incognito in Nazareth or among the Gentiles of all times and places.

151

VI. Last Year's Language

For last year's words belong to last year's language
And next year's words await another voice.
T. S. Eliot, "Little Gidding"

You never know, captain:
What's under works up.
David Jones, Anathémata

It has already become apparent that a main feature of the confusion of tongues today is the discounting of traditional language. This problem of inherited rhetoric and images is reflected not only in letters but in the religious traditions. As one aspect of the crisis of meaning it represents a formidable difficulty for the creative writer and one to which he will often give explicit expression in his work. The strategies adopted by such authors in dealing with the past and its legacies are, therefore, of special interest.

We can distinguish between the ways in which our writers deal with older idiom and the ways in which they seek to "make it new." In this chapter we shall confine ourselves to the retrospective aspect; the problem of inherited speech, the dilemma

152

presented by the faded metaphor, the demonitized currency, the broken spell. Whether in literature or in religion we find ourselves insensibly drifting out of hearing of the voices of the past, but that also means our moorings in the past. And we seek to come to terms with the hiatus.

I shall note first the more vehement repudiations of last year's language, seen on the one hand as enslaving and menacing, or on the other as corrupted and calling for purification. I shall then turn to more general questions as to dated idiom and image and ask whether we can distinguish between more recent and older legacies. This will lead us inevitably to the basic question of our inherited myth and classic archetypes.

I. DEFECTIVE THERMOMETERS

When the language of the past becomes alien it may be felt as merely empty. But its once benign authority may also be felt as tyrannical. That the outworn metaphor can become a menace is noted in the poem of MacLeish which I have already cited, "Hypocrite auteur."

> A world ends when its metaphor has died . . .
> Empty as the conch shell by the waters cast
> The metaphor still sounds but cannot tell,
> And we like parasite crabs, put on the shell
> And drag it at the sea's edge up and down.[1]

Probably the most radical rejection of traditional language today, what seems a convulsive repudiation of all its modes and signification, appears in Samuel Beckett. Speaking of the Murphys, Malones and other aliases in this author's anti-novels, André Marissel observes: "These virulent derelicts, who all take up the pen (to unwrite), look like Refusal incarnate, and pros-

1. *Collected Poems, 1917–1952*, p. 174.

trate themselves only before the statues of dementia and derision."[2] And he then cites one of Beckett's anti-heroes, the speaker in *L'Innommable*, who is protesting against the language into which he is born and so is forced upon him:

What they want me to do is to witness for them until I burst . . . They think that they have boxed me into the point where I cannot open my mouth without acclaiming them, and myself as one of them. A fine plot! To have plastered me with a language they suppose I cannot use without lining myself up with their tribe. But I'll fix their palaver. Besides which I've never understood a word of it, no more than all the fine fables it sweeps along with it like so many drowned curs. They do not realize how refractory I can be, and they have underestimated my capacity for forgetting. O my precious stupidity—in the end I'll owe it to you that I can be myself. It won't be long before there is nothing left of their brainwashing.[3]

What we have in such passages in Beckett is, at one level, a revolt against the bourgeois soul carried to its limit. Trilling has diagnosed this impulse in his paper on "The Fate of Pleasure: Wordsworth to Dostoevsky."[4] There is a modern asceticism made up of both disenchantment and honesty which repudiates the pleasure-principle and even the noblest gratifications associated with aesthetic enjoyment. It finds authenticity in their very opposite. It may partake of masochism but not necessarily. But we should recognize that, at another level, these novels of Beckett represent a concern not only with recent language, but with all language.

In any case this assault on inherited speech represented by the passage cited should not be read outside its fictional context as Marissel does. Beckett's anti-novels, he writes, "presuppose a

2. *Beckett*, Paris, 1963, p. 44.
3. *L'Innommable*, Paris, 1953, p. 76. My translation.
4. *Romanticism Reconsidered*, New York and London, 1963, pp. 73–106.

ferocious verdict upon, an assassination of the whole body of literary fiction and its naïve Prometheanism which supposes that truth is accessible or that one can at least lift the veil upon reality. The aim of Beckett is to write the book which cannot be written."[5] But I would urge that his program of demolition can still be seen as an ultimate effort to remove all masks as one aspect of a necessary lucidity at the point where he stands. In the right hands the iconoclasm of the anti-novel and the drama of the absurd constitute an exploration of meaning. Since after all the artist in question continues to write rather than fall silent, the wrestle with language is not abandoned. But such an example highlights the language crisis of today in many quarters.

Another aspect of the revulsion against older idiom is found in the call for its purification. To purify the dialect of the tribe had both aesthetic and moral implications for Ezra Pound. The health of the state was inseparably a question of the health and integrity of speech.

The word rotted by commerce affects us all where we live. It has built up a set of counterfeit "idealists" who jeopardize everyman's life, mind and food.[6]

Artists, he said in connection with the use of language, "are the antennae of the race . . . the registering instruments." His image for the corrupter of language is that of "a man selling defective thermometers in a hospital." To purify the dialect of the tribe is to aerate the blood of a civilization.

Martin Jarrett-Kerr speaks of the artist and the poet as the "Lie-Detectors," and cites Pierre Emmanuel:

The function of the poet—and generally speaking, of the creator of values—is to disclose the fatal sickness of his epoch long before it

5. *Op. cit.,* p. 17.
6. *Polite Essays,* Norfolk, Conn., 1940, p. 53.

155

declares itself openly, to unmask, beneath equivocal symptoms, the underlying corruption of energy, and to prevent the latter from flourishing blindly and to divert it from the seductive appeal of anarchy, and from that morbid exuberance which one sees in decaying organisms.[7]

The Church also is concerned today with the betrayal of the word. From the Old Testament it is aware not only of the fatality of the confusion of tongues but also (in Ecclesiastes[8]) of the burden of so much speech in its vanity and hollowness. It recalls Jesus' censure of empty phrases and of idle oaths, as well as Paul's disavowal of lofty and plausible words and his bridling of ecstatic tongues. Today the churchman recognizes that resonant rhetoric and insipid Christian art can be more subversive than blasphemy. It is not only that older images become stale but that morbid vitalities and infected nostalgias operate under the accepted tenor of familiar idiom. Men are deceived by their old loves. In the vacuum of a new situation old sentiments fester and old loyalties become demonic.

Thus traditional language can sometimes be merely innocuous and quaint. But it can sometimes be toxic. Even when it is innocuous it evokes a world that is gone, and suggests a false security. It ill prepares those who favor it for the unprecedented dimensions of modern experience. In the shocks that result the traditionalist cannot orient himself. This leads to panic, and hysteria. Thus we can recognize the immense contribution of the new poet or artist who maps the new reality. He comes up with the right word for the unknown. By his new imaginative

7. *The Secular Promise,* London, 1964, p. 148. The citation from Emmanuel is from his *The Universal Singular,* 1951, pp. 107–108.

8. Cf. W. Zimmerli's translation of 1:8

> All words wear themselves out;
> a man cannot utter it;
> the eye is not satisfied with seeing,
> nor the ear filled with hearing.

act we find our bearings in the hitherto uncharted. In his work
new powers emerge by which we can move in a wider theatre of
being. But all this means a renewal of language and imagery
and therefore often also rebuke of the old.

II. BECKETT'S *THE UNNAMABLE* AND THE PAST

In the current revolt against traditional language and artistic
idiom distinctions need to be made. It is one thing to rebel
against the styles of yesterday, against, say, the Victorian or
bourgeois or idealistic visions of the world and their arts. In
such a case we may say that we reject a recent tradition in favor
of an older and greater one. Here we have differing versions of
the struggle of the son against the father, or the pupil against
the teacher, or the new generation against the old. In such cases
there may well be a recognition on both sides of older models.

But against these various recourses to an older tradition we
find also today a more radical discounting of all tradition. The
new generation rebelling today against the old often betrays a
more fundamental alienation from all cultural legacies. Here we
have a deeper index of the modern disarray. Here it would
seem to be not only the Victorians and the Romantics who are
dethroned, but all the classics and scriptures of the past. And
since some of the most sensitive and involved groups in our
society feel this shaking of the foundations, it is not surprising
that they find their dilemma most immediately presented in
writers like Beckett and Pinter. The appeal of such artists does
not necessarily lie in their intrinsic greatness but in the fact that
their work canvasses and speaks to our crisis. I say "canvasses"
because such writers at their best are not merely negative. At
the same time that they disallow traditional securities, they explore the denuded and disinherited place in which they find

157

themselves, as though man were to begin again at the ultimate roots of his being. Finding himself suffocated, as it were, by the ancient accumulations of man's historical experience, including the structures of his myths and story-telling, he seeks convulsively for freedom and authenticity, but still as an explorer of language even at that very archaic level.

I can illustrate this again by the novel of Beckett to which I have already referred, *The Unnamable*. We have here in the speaker another of those largely immobilized and crippled figures of this author, reduced to a very narrow scope of awareness and communication, plunged in obscurity and isolation. His only reality of any consequence is language. He is little more than a voice. But he is harassed with a sense that the discourse that pours forth from him and by which he seeks to orient himself is not his own but has been foisted upon him and will continue to be. He is a prisoner of someone else's language and victimized by alien fictions which all but take over his very identity and being. In the passage I have quoted, Beckett's anti-hero identifies this as a kind of brainwashing, the purpose of which is that he shall not be able to open his mouth without speaking for the enemy. He does not wish to be a dupe of the language into which he was born. But neither does he wish to be a dupe of the idea that he has been duped! And so to the third degree and the fourth. The blindfolds can never be penetrated. The layers of illusion are endless.

Here, evidently, it is not only recent traditional language that is suspect but older layers of culture and authority. Yet Beckett's protagonist explores this situation at its roots. The novel is a parable of Everyman, the exposed naked creature, sifting the ambiguities about him for truth. But I would not say that all culture is finally repudiated. The novel indeed presents it so. But here the work serves the purpose of a paradigm. It is so with other works of Beckett. The fiction represents an artistic stratagem, the paradigm of an extreme case, an ultimate test. Beckett is not a nihilist. His paradigm rather asks us to wrestle for authenticity with any particular false language-world in which we may be involved. He implies, as elsewhere, that an authentic voice, an authentic gesture, may be rediscovered today—in the mode of waiting, of responsible attendance, which is a strange form of prayer.

The case of Beckett is worth pursuing a little farther. We have a specially good opportunity here to study the depth of our language crisis. Especially in his novels he documents the insecurity of our modern consciousness with respect to any and all tradition, indeed, with respect to any capacity for assured knowing. He has the value for us of a rigorous laboratory test under which unsound hypotheses are placed in question and we become aware of the radical ambiguity of our existence. In these novels we have a kind of fictionalized rehearsal of man's initial effort to orient himself in the world, or as Hugh Kenner puts it, an epistemology in fictional form.

The comedy he has made his province brings something new to the resources of literature. It is prior to action and more fundamental than language; the process of the brain struggling with ideas . . . precisely . . . the process that has landed western civilization in its present fix.[9]

The isolated protagonists of Beckett have, indeed, their model in Descartes, testing consciousness and its appearances and laboring therefore with the peculiar western burden of subjectivity. This modern aspect of the problem of reality is pursued in these works, as we have already noted, as Beckett shows his "twilight men" suffering under the impersonality of rational schemes. But the oppressive and ambiguous language which tyranizes over these characters has older motifs. In *L'Innommable* the speaker exclaims:

9. *Samuel Beckett: A Critical Study,* New York, 1961, p. 16.

159

All lies! God and men, daylight and nature, the impulses of the heart, and how to understand—it is I that have invented all these.

He cannot trust such ideas especially since in him the voice of a malevolent alter-ego, Mahood, is indistinguishable from his own, and "continued to testify on his part as though interwoven with my own, preventing me from saying who I was, what I was."[10] In this uncertainty our monologist must repress any intriguing hopes that might be suggested to him by the case of another victim, Prometheus. Even more significantly we find him evoking the figure and accents of Job. Speaking of his own mythical persecutor he exclaims:

Let him tell me once and for all precisely what he wants of me and for me . . . Let him show me—that's all I ask—that I may at least have the satisfaction of knowing where I fall short. If he would have me say something, for my own good of course, let him say exactly what: I shall trumpet it immediately.[11]

Thus Beckett's representative man relives the older archetypes. But the mould and frame through which the whole exploration passes is that of our modern Cartesian subjectivity. He cannot believe the stories that the western world has told itself or the older stories that lies behind these. This is Beckett's dilemma, or rather that of his cast. It is very much a question of the head and the heart. As Hamm says in *Endgame:* "there's something dripping in my head. (Pause) A heart, a heart in my head." And in *L'Innommable,* the speaker notes from time to time that he is weeping; he doesn't know why; perhaps because of

10. *Op. cit.,* p. 45. I use the original French edition throughout.
11. *Ibid.,* p. 52 Cf. Job, "Make me understand how I have erred" (6:24); "I will say to God, Do not condemn me; let me know why thou dost contend with me" (10:2); "Oh, that I knew where I might find him, I would lay my case before him" (23:3–4); "Oh, that I had the indictment written by my adversary!" (31:35).

his guilt in being born (p. 47); perhaps because he is condemned to live (p. 78).

We have here another version of Kafka's "K" before the invisible judges,[12] and in keeping with this, so far as the novelistic style is concerned, a defoliation of the luxuriance of the conventional novel. The rhetoric represents an extreme sobering of language. We have here a voice that abjures the too confident tone even of the modern novelist and identifies himself with a ghostly ancient mouth named "Worm," surely again drawn from Job (17:14; 25:6). We have the stammerings—"*les balbutiements*"—which have their parallels in other aspects of the modern arts, say in the dumb gestures and extempore attitudes practised today in some worldless drama or pantomime. "If—rather than yield to the way-out of the fable—if I were rather just to say *babababa,* while waiting to know the right use of that venerable organ [that is, the tongue]"[13]

Beckett's mordant irony with regard to language and meaning is too serious and too sophisticated for us to dismiss it as nihilistic. As we know from his later plays and radio scripts the craving for a human voice is a recurrent theme. He employs the strategies of his art with a fine balance in such a way as not to tip his hand in any didactic manner. He plays his own incredible chess games with his own figures yet so that we recognize ourselves to our astonishment in the slightest moves, and so that profound emotion is communicated yet purified by his art of abstraction. Though the world that is given to us by the past has the character of a labyrinth, yet there is never any question about

---

12. "I have spoken for my Lord, I have listened for the words of my lord, never spoken . . . you are acquitted, you are pardoned, never come. My Lord . . . yes, as a matter of fact, there are perhaps several, a whole league of tyrants, divided among themselves in what concerns me, deliberating now for an eternity, listening to me from time to time, then going off in secret to eat or play cards." P. 47.

13. P. 43.

our having a responsibility or an appointment. In his own way Beckett enforces the questions that must be answered before it is safe for us to take up the past into our new present and future.

III. LOWELL'S *PROMETHEUS*

There is one kind of literary art which is specially revealing of a change of sensibility and that is the work of the translator. When a contemporary writer translates or adapts an older model his revision betrays the cleavage between old and new perspectives and documents a shift in language and in presuppositions. This topic could lead us far if we were to consider such matters as the history of the translation of Scripture and the significance of the many efforts to render the Bible in modern speech in recent years. But for our present purposes I suggest that we look at Robert Lowell's version of the *Prometheus Bound* of Aeschylus.

Lowell's full title reads, "*Prometheus Bound,* derived from Aeschylus."[14] What he says about his undertaking in his introductory note is already revealing. He tells that he deliberately selected one of the dullest translations he could find.

Almost never was there any possibility or temptation to steal a phrase. Yet I kept the structure, either roughly rendering or improving on each speech. Half my lines are not in the original. But nothing is modernized. There are no tanks or cigarette lighters. No contemporary statesman is parodied. Yet I think my own concerns and worries and those of the times seeped in. Using prose instead of verse, I was free to tone down the poetic eloquence, and shove in any thought that occurred to me and seemed to fit. My hope was for some marriage between the old play and a new one.[15]

14. *The New York Review of Books,* vol. IX, no. 1 (July 13, 1967), pp. 17–24 (copyright, Robert Lowell, 1967).
15. P. 17.

What we have, then, is an adaptation. As in the case of Thomas Mann's rehearsal of the Joseph cycle from the Old Testament or Camus' version of the story of Caligula or modern variations on the play of Hamlet or the history of Jeanne d'Arc, this play is as interesting for what it introduces as for what it leaves out, for its contemporary tone as well as for its disinterest in older perspectives. For our present purpose I select certain matters which bear on our general crisis of meaning.

This work of Lowell's stands somewhat apart from his other writings. We have here neither the poet of local soil and regional history nor the austere public censor, neither the highly personalized episode or the characteristic baroque diction. But we do have that tradition of exacerbated moral tension which Richard P. Blackmur has traced in New England back to Edward Taylor.

Both are characteristic New England wrestlers with the Spirit. Each has the ghastly sophistication of the Christian Puritan Protestant— a hangnail may be taken as excruciation,—and each is aware of the bottomless resources of Enthusiasm and Antinomianism generally . . . The chasm between them is like the chasm each saw in himself; upon no razor's edge can this be crossed, and yet one's feet are upon razors. One of Taylor's poems is called "The Souls Groan to Christ for Succour" and it is of such groans that the majority of Lowell's poems are made . . . the devil in him wrestles with the man, the angel with the god. . . .[16]

Now in Lowell's *Prometheus Bound* this exacerbated moral tension does not suit with the lofty defiance of Aeschylus's hero. The modern sufferer lacks the scornful confidence of the Greek Titan and his unquestioned role as servant of mankind and Foreseer of human liberation. In the ancient myth followed by Aeschylus Prometheus confers the essential arts of civilization upon men and these have undoubted validity. But Lowell's

16. *University: A Princeton Magazine,* Princeton, N.J., no. 9 (Summer, 1961), p. 17.

protagonist is too much dismayed by the way in which men have used his gifts. Thus the modern imagination here wars against the classic myth but also against the more recent myth in which Faust or modern science take the place of Prometheus. Here we can recognize a representative significance in Lowell's play. For in it our contemporary disorientation opposes tyranny, indeed, but without the Titan's confidence either in himself or in a world eventually ordered for the best by justice or Necessity.

It is true that Lowell takes over the prediction of Zeus's ultimate downfall. But this "secret" of Prometheus is termed by the latter "of no importance." A new order will be just another order.

Before Zeus, the lesser order of Cronus; before Cronus, the still lesser order of Uranus. Still less, still less, still less! An infinite whittling away. The nothingness of our beginning is hard at work to bury us.[17]

At other times Prometheus can speak more hopefully. But beyond the overthrow of Zeus, he says, "I fear something much deeper, something I cannot answer . . . I fear the fire."[18]

The ground and stability of good is, indeed, witnessed in Lowell by a kind of baffled counterpoint. It appears in the immutability of Prometheus's will, in his passion for knowledge, and in his appeal to "Earth, my holy Mother." The ancient Titan seems at one time to be speaking of modern man's drive for knowledge, power and emancipation, but with a sense of its ambiguity.

I remember hunting for . . . what shall I call them? Causes, knots, heads of action? I was a savage head-hunter, then, always hot on the trail of powers I hoped to defeat and take and put to work . . . I was on a fool's errand, and yet I was guided by the great gods of

17. P. 19.
18. P. 23.

164

that day, their most powerful flashes, and later by the steady light of my own mind. That mind was in no way walled in or useless. Each thought was like a finger touching, tampering, testing, and trying to give things a little of my bias to alter and advance. I never felt bound to keep anything to its original custom, place or purpose. I turned the creatures on their heads, and lifted the doors from the hinges of determination.[19]

One of the strongest notes of promise appears in what follows here.

Around some bend, under some moving stone, behind some thought, if it were ever the right thought, I will find my key. No, not just another of Nature's million petty clues, but a key, *my key, the key,* the one that must be there, because it can't be there—a face still friendly to chaos.[20]

Thus we see the modern Prometheus in his ambivalence. The work also enlarges on Aeschylus in its portrayal of mankind's frustration and self-slaughter. Lowell states in his note that his "hope was for some marriage between the old play and a new one." He has achieved this to the degree that he has carried over the ideal of uncoerced thought and reason by which the Greeks kept irrationality at bay, and he has related this theme to our day in its peculiar disorders whether political or psychological. But there is certainly a diminution of confidence. The whole work is a revealing example of the great changes in our modern vision of things.

The fact is that Robert Lowell's gifts, so suited to the portrayal of the personal labyrinth of our modern consciousness and so sensitive to the costs of our public violence, do not stand him in good stead in his wider cultural assessment. That hyperbolic moral sensitivity which Blackmur notes, that baroque dramatic

19. P. 22.
20. P. 23.

vision—evident also in the three plays that make up *The Old Glory*—tends to read our modern fate with the vision of a Breughel or a Goya. But such styles and sensibilities are most at home with rather special genres like satire and allegory.

This aspect of Lowell's treatment appears especially in his version of the story of Io. It will be recalled that Aeschylus gives large place to the sufferings of this heroine, victimized like Prometheus, but by the jealousy of Hera, sister and wife of Zeus. Aeschylus describes the flight of Io, transformed into a heifer and pursued by a gad-fly, so reflecting the ancient curiosity about strange lands and peoples. Eventually she gives birth to a son whose descendent will cast Zeus down from his throne. Lowell moves this saga into a surreal portrayal of suffering, including a macabre vision of men's suicidal warfare.

What is at stake for us in the Prometheus myth is the world-old tradition of *homo faber* and the affirmation of the arts and technics of civilization as they have come down to us. The Hebrew scriptures confirm this as they tell of man receiving dominion over the creatures. Our crisis is radical indeed if in our discounting of the language of the past we place in question the celebrations of man's works and inventions from the beginning. It is our obsession with subjectivity which obscures for us the ancient epic of man's dealing with nature, his husbandries and his building of cities. Lowell's uncertainty might find support in Sartre and his version of Orestes in the *Flies*. Like other heroes of Sartre the liberator of Argos seeks true liberty by abandoning the human city caught in the spell of unreality. Sartre wrestles with this problem in later works but his existentialist view of the free man and the free act qualifies any sympathetic view of man's historical pilgrimage. How different this is, for example, from Ezra Pound's *Cantos,* with their honoring of man's many inventions and ceremonies in many cultures and epochs. We shall return to this theme in our next chapter in connection with David Jones' epic poem, *The Anathémata.*

166

IV. THE PAST IN THE PRESENT:
ELIOT'S *FOUR QUARTETS*

It has become clear that the hiatus between traditional language and that of the present is more than a question of corrupted speech or dated idiom. More fundamentally it is one of social imagination and myth. It is a question of who we are and where we are, matters which are subject to radical displacement, and matters which always take on mythological expression. Subtle changes in culture affect such inherited vehicles of self-understanding and world-representation. Their authority and relevance is undermined. When this happens our sense of order and coherence is attainted, our psychic security is disturbed.

Contemporary poetry for its part reflects the problem of the faded image and the moribund myth in many ways. Since language can never be totally new, the artist must perforce come to terms with the significant metaphor of the past. Even though our world is in travail with new dramatic vehicles of meaning, and draws upon a new repertory of actuality, even so the new must in some way relate itself to the imagination of the past. Otherwise we have a mere notation of flux, a fever chart of the moment, or a mechanical tape-recording of the diurnal, a kind of ephemeral statistic. This kind of supposed veracity to experience is not lacking in contemporary writing. Where we are and who we are is cut off from time and reduced to an instant of sensation. Where such sterilization of rhetoric or of graphic media seeks deliberately to dramatize the vacuity of experience it may serve an ironic purpose. As a matter of fact it is this very atomistic character of much modern experience which occasions that form of transcendence which we recognize today as the epiphany. Here we have the sudden explosion of meaning out of the meaningless which in itself shows that human nature insists on some kind of metamorphosis.

167

We recognize, then, an anomaly in the situation of the modern poet, novelist, dramatist. He works in a time when the older world-metaphors have lost their authority and he gives himself to the real, the ordinary, the actual. Yet when such gestation in the present is brought into relation with the once potent metaphor of the past, both are quickened. The older myth needs such encounter with the new occasion. The aesthetic act of our moment moves towards wider structures of meaning. The mere notation of flux cannot satisfy but in Joyce's *Ulysees* it takes on world-meaning and the ancient fable is renewed. The fever-chart referred to in Eliot's "East Coker" is no longer a statistic but the reading of a world-malady. Even *Krapp's Last Tape* is more than a chattering since its theme, as Frank Kermode notes, is "relation to the past." The power of Beckett's work here as often lies in the tension set up between impotence and obsession on the one hand and the saving myth on the other, even if the latter be suggested only by way of derision or the most tenuous allusion. In *Krapp's Last Tape* this dimension is evident in Krapp's "abrasive evocation" of the current refrain,

> Now the day is over,
> Night is drawing nigh-igh,
> Shadows of the evening
> Steal across the sky.

Moreover, in Beckett's anti-heroes we never miss for long the prototype of Dante's Belacqua, "who could not enter purgation until he had relived his slothful life."

Modern writing offers innumerable illustrations of the ways in which the artist today relates himself to the problem of the faded symbol and the ambiguous myth. Sometimes the poet merely laments the Philistinism which scorns the precious insignia of the past. Thus Elizabeth Jennings comments on the crass pragmatism that presided over the reconstruction of a bombed English town. The poem is entitled "The Lost Symbols."

168

Missing the symbol they restore the fact:
How seven years back this city was burned down
And minds were gutted too. Men learn to act
As though there were no meaning in the town,
And chose at last to make as derelict
All dreams they fostered . . .

It is the fine tradition they have lost
That spoke in architectural styles, that rang
Out with the bells when all the bells were tossed . . .

Now they assemble all the facts to learn
New symbols . . .
    The only style,
The only symbol is in each one's will.[21]

Again, the poet may simply document the profaned or neglected image or sense of the sacred. Here we are in the line of Pound's Mauberley or of *The Waste Land.* But the disinherited modern may only be puzzled and made reflective rather than deeply grieved. So Philip Larkin as he enters an empty church and meditates in "Church Going." He observes a

    tense, musty, unignorable silence,
    Brewed God knows how long.

He is much at a loss,

    Wondering what to look for; wondering, too,
    When churches fall completely out of use
    What we shall turn them into . . .[22]

One can find any number of more drastic reflections upon the lost authority of the house of God. Maurice Lindsay writes "A Cathedral" of which I cite the first and last verses:

21. *A Way of Looking: Poems,* London, 1955, p. 33.
22. *The Less Deceived,* Hessle, East Yorkshire, 1955, p. 26.

169

Half-sunk in silence the cathedral stands,
its very stillness an unshaken prayer,
as if that confidence the Faith defends
was still the essence of our smoke-filled air ...

This bubble in time, this long-held visible pause
still keeps at bay what yawns outside its door,
while still-processing priests chant as it was
in the beginning, and shall be nevermore.[23]

It is relatively easy to satirize the weakened symbols of an older order, whether religious or patriotic or cultural. Any more significant dealing with the past is taken up neither with nostalgia nor with indifference nor with iconoclasm. It sounds the true elegiac note as in well-known poems of Allen Tate, or the tragic note as in Faulkner or in Robert Penn Warren's long narrative poem on Thomas Jefferson's dreams, *Brother to Dragons*. At the same time it turns to the renewal of the myth, or attendance on the new language-event which will take up into itself all that seems to have been lost. As transition here we may recall again MacLeish's "Hypocrite auteur":

A world ends when its metaphor has died.

An age becomes an age, all else beside,
When sensuous poets in their pride invent
Emblems for the soul's consent
That speak the meanings men will never know
But man-imagined images can show ...

Poets, deserted by the world before,
Turn round into the actual air:
Invent the age! Invent the metaphor![24]

23. *Snow Warning and Other Poems*, Arundal, 1962, p. 11.
24. *Collected Poems, 1917–1952*, pp. 173–175.

But it is not so easy to "invent the metaphor," and MacLeish here telescopes the deeper task that Eliot speaks of in "East Coker" as

> the fight to recover what has been lost
> And found and lost again and again . . .
> For us, there is only the trying. The rest is not our business.[25]

In his *Four Quartets* T. S. Eliot meditates upon the meaning of time in many registers. This leads inevitably to reflection on the problem of suitable words and language, and three of the quartets include passages which deal directly with rhetorical strategies. I have taken the title of this chapter from the lines in the last of them, "Little Gidding":

> For last year's words belong to last year's language
> And next year's words await another voice.[26]

In the first quartet he speaks of how "words decay with imprecision, will not stay in place," and in the second, "East Coker," he characterizes one way of putting his theme as "a periphrastic study in a worn-out poetical fashion." He has been trying to learn to use words in the period between the two world wars,

> and every attempt
> Is a wholly new start, and a different kind of failure
> Because one has only learnt to get the better of words
> For the thing one no longer has to say, or the way in which
> One is no longer disposed to say it. And so each venture
> Is a new beginning, a raid on the inarticulate
> With shabby equipment always deteriorating . . .[27]

25. T. S. Eliot, *Four Quartets*, p. 17.
26. P. 35.
27. P. 16.

171

Though Eliot disavows "last year's language" he recognizes that the valid speech of today must take up into itself the experience of the past and the language of the past. There is a total pattern of the dead and the living of which we are a part, and we may not elude this by some private ecstacy of our moment and its truncated utterance.

> Not the intense moment
> Isolated, with no before and after,
> But a lifetime burning in every moment
> And not the lifetime of one man only
> But of old stones that cannot be deciphered.[28]

What this means for the language of today is most fully stated in the last quartet, "Little Gidding." The new language takes up the old in it

> And every phrase
> And sentence that is right (where every word is at home,
> Taking its place to support the others,
> The word neither diffident nor ostentatious,
> An easy commerce of the old and the new,
> The common word exact without vulgarity,
> The formal word precise but not pedantic,
> The complete consort dancing together)
> Every phrase and every sentence is an end and a beginning,
> Every poem an epitaph.[29]

What we must highlight here as to our strategies with the language of the past is that miraculous outcome:

> An easy commerce of the old and new . . .
> The complete consort dancing together.

28. P. 17.
29. P. 38.

The solution in Eliot corresponds to what we have found in other writers. It would be another question to ask what in man's past Eliot actually cherishes and how he construes the concrete annals and vicissitudes of man's life in time. We have noted earlier his use of *The Waste Land* saga as an ordering myth for our confusions. But at the center of the *Four Quartets* is the theme that true reality and wisdom are located outside time and make themselves known to us only at the point of the intersection of the timeless with time. All mere succession is unredeemed, and apart from the timeless moment the course of the world is "driven by daemonic, chthonic powers,"

> while the world moves
> In appetency, on its metalled ways
> Of time past and time future.[30]

"Time is no healer," and meaning is not to be ascribed to either succession or development. Time is conquered only momentarily in rare glimpses, but ultimately only by that baptism of fire which is the one discharge from sin and error:

> The only hope, or else despair
> Lies in the choice of pyre or pyre—
> To be redeemed from fire by fire.[31]

What shall we say then finally about Eliot's understanding of the language of the past? In his case surely we see the devaluation of last year's language, that of the immediate past. Again, surely, we see the leap back to older symbols of order, in this case clearly the Incarnation. Yet, as we shall see in the case of David Jones, the Christian imagery is conflated with that of other traditions of prayer and wisdom; for example the figures

30. P. 7.
31. P. 37.

of Krishna and Artemis are evoked in "The Dry Salvages."[32] The chief difference lies finally in the degree to which Eliot discounts the significance of the human story in itself. He so polarizes reality proper over against the unredeemed course of all men's works and days that significance attaches only at the boundaries, our end and our beginning, outside of time. Within history, "the way forward is the way back," and there is no pattern here.

But Eliot is not really as negative as this. The *Four Quartets* are written from the special perspective, we may say, of Good Friday and this accounts in good part for the other-worldliness which colors the whole. Moreover, in the third section of the last quartet, "Little Gidding," the poet overcomes the sharp polarity in a moving passage. As we are liberated from attachments to our human world yet our detachment is not indifference. Through memory and love these human bonds become "renewed, transfigured in another pattern." Thus that true reality which is otherwise beyond our servitude nevertheless can bless our mortal days with its charities and its promise that "all shall be well."

Whether a modern writer employs such Christian archetypes or not, we shall not today find any artist speaking to our condition unless he has wrestled with such fatalities as those recognized in different ways by Eliot, by Robert Lowell in his *Prometheus Bound,* by Beckett and many others. What I would like to insist on, however, is that the greatness of man in his works and in his cultures should be brought into the total vision. All the issues associated with man's mastery of nature, his building of cities, his arts and his symbolics, including that

32. Note the opening of section IV:

> Lady, whose shrine stands on the promontory,
> Pray for all those who are in ships . . .

> Figlia del tuo figlio,
> Queen of Heaven.

(P. 26)

superb garment of fable and language which he has wrought at such cost over the millenniums—all this should be honored. No vision of redemption which eludes or disparages man so understood can long persuade. As William Blake wrote, "Eternity is in love with the productions of time." It is for this reason that the language of the past and its fabulations whether of Prometheus or Ulysses, whether Abraham, the father of peoples, or Adam—to whom was assigned the naming of the creatures, the tilling of the ground and subduing of the earth—it is for this reason that the language of the past must always be a part of the language of today and tomorrow.

VII. New Rhetorics

Teilhard de Chardin proposes to "carry Christ to the heart of
the realities reputed to be the most dangerous, the most
naturalistic, the most pagan." For the father [Teilhard]
wanted to be "the evangelist of Christ in the universe."

Mircea Eliade

I have a vivid memory of an occasion in which Paul Tillich
posed to me a crucial question about modern art. Granted the
presence of the religious dimension, the manifestation of the
holy, in contemporary art forms—identified by him as is well
known with such features as distortion and other departures
from realism—beyond that, he asked, where can one today
identify more positive evidences of celebration, the crystallizing
of new motifs and symbols indicative of the future?

I have quoted at an earlier point Tillich's observation that
our contemporary arts "show in their style both the encounter
with non-being and the strength which can stand the encounter
and shape it creatively." But he also scanned the arts and all
the creative activities of our age for signs of more specific out-
comes. He knew that a gestation was in process.

To understand the present means to see it in its inner tension
toward the future. In this field also, there is such a thing as spiritual

perspective and the possibility of finding amid all the infinite aspirations and tensions which every present contains not only those which conserve the past but also those which are creatively new and pregnant with the future.

Tillich like all of us recognized that our kairos is one of baffling complexity, and yet a transition. He knew that the arts have an essential role in illuminating the situation and in bringing it home to us. But he was eager to recognize the point at which the arts move beyond our present disarray to suggest the shape of things to come.

No doubt we should be on guard against too hasty an answer to this question. It may still be more important for us to clarify the past and the present than to make blue-prints for the future. Certainly much of the most serious literature of today continues to dissect our maladies, our alienation and our illusions. This is still a time for the oracle of judgment rather than for the vision of the New Jerusalem, a time for the surgical probe rather than the confident prognosis.

We can therefore appreciate theatre like that of van Itallie's *America Hurrah,* which, using the image of the motel room and its horrible dolls, dramatizes for us the insidious modern lust for destruction. We can appreciate Ionesco's parables of subhuman obsession in which words and languages are totally vacant of significance. We can appreciate Pinter's spectroscopy under which as in a biologist's slide the passions and attitudes of a family are exhibited in a sterilized objectivity. We can appreciate Albee's unflinching exhibits of the intolerable banality, the *Dreck* and *Ekel,* of much modern existence, and the recourse to symbolic violence and to rituals of human sacrifice to overcome them. We can appreciate the Gothic narratives of Robert Penn Warren—as in his "Ballad of a Sweet Dream of Peace"— and the hallucinatory overtones of his *Brother to Dragons.* We could cite many other contemporary works which continue

177

to expose our condition, and which in the order of art do not allow us to forget those realities which are all too actual for us in the horrendous public violence of the last decades and the present.

No doubt, I repeat, we should not be too forward in projecting the shapes of hope. As Eliot wrote,

> wait without hope
> For hope would be hope for the wrong thing.[1]

There are indeed those who continue to affirm older conventional designs for the future but who themselves have escaped initiation into our modern shocks. Their uncontaminated dreams are out of touch with reality and most often turn to fanaticism. There are blue-prints old and new which are inspired by nostalgias or virulence.

Louis Simpson has probed the dilemma of our national hopes in his poem, "Walt Whitman at Bear Mountain Bridge."[2] Simpson comes upon the statue here of Whitman and is reminded of the contrast between the American dream and the twentieth-century actuality. So he mildly reproaches the older poet:

> "The Open Road goes to the used-car lot.
>
> "Where is the nation you promised?
> These houses built of wood sustain
> Colossal snows,
> And the light above the street is sick to death.
> "As for the people—see how they neglect you!"

But to this Whitman demurs: he gave no prescriptions or prophecies; it was "Myself" he had advertised.

1. *East Coker*, p. 15.
2. *At the End of the Open Road*, Middletown, Conn., 1963.

This leads our contemporary poet to reflect upon the futility of blue-prints, and to express relief that the future is not bound by any model even that of Whitman; yet he notes that some cherish blue-prints because they can exploit them:

> Then all the realtors,
> Pickpockets, salesmen, and the actors performing
> Official scenarios,
> Turned a deaf ear, for they had contracted
> American dreams.[3]

We recognize therefore the cautions that are in order if we are to look about us for authentic auguries of renewal and the first crystallizations of a new order of life. One thing is sure and that is that no such new-found-land will be reached except by those who have made the voyage of the modern Ulysses. No such release will take effect save for those who like the Belacqua of Dante and Beckett have spent their season of wrath and compunction in these lower circles of our purgatory. That incalculable renewal and liberation of language and new myth-making power which we await will only arise among those who have shared fully the costs of the modern ordeal.

Thus forewarned, however, we may inquire as to any auguries for the future, examine the new idioms and rhetorics that have been emerging, and consider what may be portended today by the imagination of this our ever wider world dreaming on things to come.

As a suggestive analogy it may not be amiss to cite what Erich Auerbach wrote about the gestation of new styles in the earliest Christian movement. "What we witness is the awakening of a new heart and a new spirit . . . It sets man's whole world astir." And further he observes in the new literary impulse "a

3. Pp. 64–65.

spontaneous generation of categories which apply to epochs as well as to states of the inner life."[4]

Is it too much to hope that just as literature and language itself have been inescapably involved in the fragmentation of modern culture, so their very honesty during this ordeal will enable them to provide shape and coherence to it again in the future?

Georg Lukacs, the Marxist critic, rightly pointed to the disintegration of traditional literary forms and of literature itself in those writers from Flaubert on who represented the "ideology of modernism."[5] The loss of a hierarchy of significance was accompanied by an isolation of the individual from his social bonds and from any significant relation to history. Thus Lukacs sees in Kafka, Gide, Proust, Beckett and others a destructive nihilism whose central focus was on psychopathology. Hence too the destruction of literary forms. Over against this he rightly asks that the writer should portray man in his significant web of social and historical relations, and cites the example of Brecht. On this view the new rhetoric we are looking for, and the new myth of the future, would be socialist.

But Lukacs fails to see that the dilemma of the modern self has deeper causes than modern capitalism. Nor can it be met by socialism just as the wholeness of literature cannot be restored by socialist realism. The fact is that the disorder in literary forms that we have witnessed has been a necessary strategy of the artist in this period. And it is for this very reason that we may count on the new writers to assist in the renewal both of the world of meaning and the heritage of letters.

The Marxist attack on modernist writing has an interesting parallel in that of many Christian interpreters. This is not surprising since both Marxists and Christians disapprove of seemingly nihilist views, both insist on the social character of

4. *Mimesis*, Princeton, 1953, pp. 43, 44.
5. *Realism in Our Time*, New York, 1964, Chapters I and II.

man, and both have, traditionally, a chart for the future of man. Like the Marxist the dogmatic Christian critic sees our western time of troubles in moralistic terms. The Marxist blames our situation on capitalist exploitation; the Christian, on pride and self-sufficiency. But as we have seen in our fifth chapter our dilemma has deeper causes than revolt against authority. A less rigid Christian view will recognize that the arts must perforce have associated themselves with the vicissitudes of the epoch. And such a view will anticipate an outcome to our ordeal in which all the dimensions of human nature will be validated.

The modulations of language now in course are predictable in the light of those reactions from traditional speech which I have been canvassing. I have already had occasion to anticipate some of the new directions. We note on all sides the demand for new idiom, new styles, new explorations in all aspects of art and communication. The gamut of such new initiatives is so wide as to baffle generalization: from a merely stylized traditionalism to an extreme pulverization of speech; from the empirical plain style to the hermetic; from solipsist mania to the mosaic of many cultural voices; from the naive folksong or the Blakian treble of the child to the infinitely nuanced psychological monologue. All such new utterance, tones, media seek to push through the ambiguity of our inherited language-world, to repossess meaning, to remarry the word to actuality.

Nor can these aesthetic explorations be separated from the generally human and ethical. It is a question not only of the renewal of the arts but of a total life-style. The modern Ulysses in Ezra Pound's *Cantos,* for example, is a man who is finding his way home to an ordered ceremony after having departed "from a heap of smouldering boundary stones." The ardors of the pure artist in our time, the rigors of Pound and Stevens, the life-long cult of the difficult in Henry James and Valéry—living at what Theodore Roethke called "the edge"—all such disciplines have been driven by an impulse to lucidity, mastery of the inchoate,

181

the purification of both language and awareness. It is in this sense that Pound invoked his Chinese ideogram: "Name things accurately!" And all this wrestling of the artist has flowed out into the general consciousness of the times and crystallized a gestation going on there. Literary criticism has cooperated in the process.

All such exploration of reality on the part of the artist is important for the renewal of religious language. After a long divorce the time has come for the church to attend to the modern artist. In a recent discussion Meyer Shapiro reviewed this relationship.[6] During the last hundred years the most significant movements in the arts have been rejected by the churches. During this period the artist had had to break with the ikons of the past and to follow his own call. In this way he continued to bring forth works that were authentic, and though he departed from the recognized motifs of the religious group he "lived the basic content" of its tradition. But the church was not able to honor the resulting work. Shapiro noted the resistance offered in ecclesiastical circles to the church at Assy, and the fact that the name of Rouault was not even mentioned in a Catholic study of modern religious art. But the situation is changing today and the church is beginning to recognize that what arises in secular culture can be of the first importance to it.

But this is especially clear in the arts of language. In our complex Alexandrine epoch, the fate of religious discourse is linked with the most sensitive registers of meaningfulness. It is in the poet and the image-maker that our new world-in-the-making discloses itself.

In the present chapter I shall select three areas of observation, in all of which light can be thrown on the renewal of language both in modern letters and in the religious tradition. I shall

6. In a discussion of "The Religious Imagination and the Contemporary Artist" at the Museum of Modern Art, New York City, February 5, 1965, at the first annual congress of the Fellows of the Society for the Arts, Religion and Contemporary Culture.

deal first with the passion for the real and the concrete. I shall then illustrate the continuing sense of the power of the word even in the contemporary confusions. And finally I shall ask about the fate of the great mythical legacies of the past.

I. THE ELOQUENCE OF THE SECULAR

Even when we recognize the bewildering variety of modern voices we can identify one recurrent impulse. Modern letters have been marked negatively by a revulsion against false spirituality, against all that suggests angelism or abstraction. Positively this means that speech, idiom, image arise from the ordinary or the immediately given. This urge for the authentic can be illustrated by many examples, some of which have now become clichés, whether the phrase cited by Marianne Moore, "literalists of the imagination"; or Wallace Stevens' "the poem . . . is part of the res itself and not about it"; or MacLeish's "Ars Poetica" ("a poem should not mean/But be"); or Robert Frost's "the fact is the sweetest dream that labor knows."

This concrete given, however, is not just the here and now in its grittiness. It develops its own metaphysics. As Wallace Stevens writes in his "An Ordinary Evening in New Haven,"

> The eye's plain version is a thing apart,
> The vulgate of experience.

But this vulgate then calls forth its commentary, and the eye's plain version takes on endless fulgurations:

> As if the crude collops came together as one,
> A mythological form, a festival sphere.[7]

That the ordinary transmutes into its own metaphysics is a

7. *The Auroras of Autumn,* New York, 1950, pp. 110, 111.

recurrent theme in the work of Theodore Roethke. Thus in his homage to Yeats he has the latter say:

> I am the clumsy man
> The instant ages on ...
>
> What sensual eye can keep an image pure?
> When figures out of obscure shadows rave,
> All sensual love's but dancing on a grave.[8]

But in another sense this concreteness is not just the local here and now. It can include a total human experience horizontally and vertically. Horizontally, in the sense of a global consciousness; so we get the international hero, the poet of many tongues. Thus Greek and Russian and Spanish poets of our period break down our parochialism and help define our world moment. Vertically, in the sense of contemporaneity with older records, all the way back to primitive myth and ritual. The cosmic awareness of a scientist like Teilhard de Chardin or a poet like St.-John Perse helps to rebuke the household sentimentalities of our western soul. In any case the passion for the real in contemporary art envisages the totally human. Its language would be time-binding and space-binding, but now without false transcendence.

Thus one feature of contemporary work is its hospitality to the most varied styles, its transcultural character. The modern monologue in prose or poetry can be a montage of vocabularies from many languages living and dead, eastern and western, and not only of words but of tones, motifs, symbols. Karl Shapiro well suggests the world-citizenship into which we are entering when he writes:

English is a dying language. The new language that is to come is in its birthpangs. The cure is not in the "campus muse." English is in

8. *Words for the Wind,* Garden City, 1958, p. 188.

the making in a pluralist direction: Joyce, Eliot, Crane, Pound did what was right, not "purify" but "complicate" it, giving it the gift of tongues.[9]

Our new concern for the concrete and the actual is not to be understood as naturalism or a shallow kind of realism. It may be true that older versions of spirituality are excluded. But the anticipation is that all such orders of transmundane significance will disclose themselves more authentically in honest commerce with our actual givens. Nor again is it just a question of expedience as though the artist must accommodate himself to a Philistine culture which denies all super-sensual reality. It is a question rather of the whole language-fate of the West. It is a question of our struggle to unify our world. Transcendence must be located in the flesh. The new rhetorics answer to this situation.

But all this applies also to religious language. Here too the metaphysical categories have become unreal, not only those of the ancient creeds but also those of modern idealism. So far as God and his action have been apprehended in these structures he has become unreal and his image misrepresented. But his reality can come to speech authentically again in our here and now. And at this point the believer can learn much from the poet and the artist, if not about God directly yet about the world in which he can again be named.

What illustrations can we give of this commitment to the concrete here and now in the new rhetorics, this focus on the natural? Of course every generation has its idea of what is "real," and we only have to go back to Masefield for what was then a shocking program of poetry in engagement with ordinary life and language, or farther back to Wordsworth. But Masefield went slumming, as it were, under a rainbow of idealism, and the

9. *The New York Herald-Tribune, Book Week,* January 10, 1965, p. 11.

accents of Carl Sandburg's "The People, Yes!" are colloquial but full of the resonances of an older dream. What makes the new realism different is a more radical alienation and disenchantment. But this is not first of all a question of pessimism or disbelief. It is a question of locus, of where we stand, and the appropriate language.

One aspect of the new rhetoric is the use of the plain style and idiom, the colloquial, the unliterary, the common speech-rhythm, the conversational voice. This is not just a matter of being "democratic" but of getting rid of what William Carlos Williams calls the "grammar which stultifies, the prose or poetical rhythms which bind us to our "pet indolences and medievalisms." It is a question of getting the "power of thought back through a new minting of the words."

For the liberation of religious communication we find the matter felicitously stated by Auden:

> the Holy Ghost
> does not abhor a golfer's jargon . . .

> Our magical syllables melt away,
> our tribal formulae are laid bare: since this morning,
> it is with a vocabulary
> made wholesomely profane, open in lexicons
> to our fees to translate, that we endeavour
> each in his idiom to express the true *magnalia*.[10]

All such use of colloquial idiom and current tone and speech-rhythm has the effect of naturalizing whatever is evoked, bringing it all into our horizon. It unifies our total experience and liberates us in our own actuality. This need not mean the loss of older "spiritual" reality. Such dimensions are, rather, renewed precisely by being brought into our own field of action in the authentic speech of today.

10. "Whitsuntide in Kirchstetten," *About the House,* New York, n.d., p. 83.

The parallel in the arts and crafts is the use of contemporary materials, media and processes. Workers in these arts today as in sculpture have a very special new kind of vision of matter and substances, a heightened awareness of the inanimate order. They hear the stones cry out, and they pursue their researches into the elements of the tangible, as composers do into the elements in sound, and painters into the elements of space, line and color, and poets into the elements of articulation. The artist craftsman is concerned with such things as the shock of new media, the textures of surfaces, the raw qualities of stone and metals, the torsion and fine grain in glass fragments, the exploitation of light and motion. When traditional ritual is served by such arts it is naturalized for us and two worlds are brought together.

Contemporary idiom, of course, means more than just popular usage or colloquialism. It also carries constant allusion to the life about us and the properties of our world. Thus John Wain can write a "Villanelle: for Harpo Marx" and mean more than clowning:

> True oracles say more than they suppose.
> The clown may speak what silent Hamlet knows.[11]

And John Wain, again, can write a "Poem Feigned to have been written by an Electronic Brain." Here the computer misbehaves and steps out of the function assigned it, a parable of the poet today who rebels against the tyranny of the impersonal.

> You set me like a cactus to draw life
> From drought, in the white desert of your mind,
> Your speculative wilderness of charts;
> What went you to the wilderness to see?
> A matrix made of glass? An electric thought?
> Come quick! I snow down sheets of truth; I print
> The sleep of Socrates, the pain of Christ!

11. *A Word Carved on a Sill,* London, 1956, p. 34.

A man, white-coated, comes to switch me off.
'Something is wrong with our expensive brain.' ...

Yes, switch me off for fear I should explode:
Yes, switch me off for fear yes switch me off
for fear yes switch me off for fear yes switch
(finis)[12]

But the passion for the real today is more than a matter of current idiom and diction in the narrow sense. Authenticity requires much more than slang and topical allusion. All dimensions of language are affected, tone and voice, style and genre, as well as metaphor and fable.

As regards tone, or the attitude assumed by the writer to the reader, note how disinfected it is today of intrusiveness and false intimacy. It can be austere or ironic or corrosively sardonic, or it can adopt modes of naïveté and comedy, but as in other modern arts it addresses a perhaps disabused but deeper self. This world is exorcised of older complacencies now felt as disingenuous. The matter of the voice or "persona" is closely related, and we are familiar with the way in which writers resort to the masks of the clown, the angel, or the aged crone—all as ways to circumvent that all too voluble spokesman, the ineffable bourgeois "personality" who is still too much with us.

The question of new genres could lead us far. It is enough to say here that modern writers aware of their field of action continue to transform the drama into meta-theatre, the novel into the anti-novel, just as they modify satire, eclogue or lyric. What Pound said in his poem, "To Whistler, American," continues to hold true, that the painter

Had not one style from birth, but tried and pried
And stretched and tampered with the media.[13]

12. *Ibid.,* pp. 14–15.
13. *Personae. The Collected Poems of Ezra Pound,* New York, 1962, p. 235.

II. IMPROVISATION: PERSE, "OPEN VERSE."

We turn now to our second observation about the new rhetorics. Despite the confusion of tongues today the poet and fabulist can still believe in the power of the word. Not, indeed, in the Romantic sense, say of Shelley, but in a primary, an archaic sense. We men of today have been stripped of our Romantic layers, the sensibilities and reflexes of the whole era of idealism. This matter of a change of sensibility goes very deep. It has the character of a universal fate, affecting the intimate character of all perception: aesthetic, moral, political. So the chorus can chant in Eliot's *Murder in the Cathedral:*

> What is woven in the loom of fate,
> What is woven in the councils of princes
> Is woven also in our veins, our brains,
> Is woven like a pattern of living worms
> In the guts of the women of Canterbury.[14]

The point for our purposes here is that as men and women of today we inhabit a special kind of reality. Certain disabused apperceptions penetrate our whole existence, though not necessarily to our loss. Though stripped of those old layers and more naked we have good company in still older epochs and may return to the archetypes. Even if we are no longer eloquent in the styles of our fathers, even if we improvise and stammer out of the roots of speech, yet we still know that the word has power, in the true primary or archaic sense.

Take the example of St.-John Perse. Here still is dithyrambic speech, but not the Romantic afflatus. Here is the immaculate Word of the surf on the shores, the snows on the prairies and the roofs, of man in his prehistoric migrations and artifacts. I translate from a few sections in *Chronique.*[15]

14. New York, 1935, p. 65.
15. Bilingual edition, New York, 1961.

So the times have been moving not towards ashes but a hearth of glowing coals, and all things point us beyond familiar categories and equations. We live of that which is beyond death; we live of death itself. You great Forebears with your tablets of stone—your lips move but you have not spoken the definitive word. But God who sees not glitters in the salt and the obsidian. (Section 2)

Our annals are many and ancient. We come from riddling ways. Masterless, how often we have overthrown our altars and burned our standards. O tell us at least what hand it was that clothed us with this burning tunic of fable, and from what abyss we were carried along for good and for ill by this rising tide of dawn. (Section 3)

The great age at length opens to us as we return from the high seas of fable. We shake off the phantasms of our sleep and enter on a great lucidity as we are caught up in a prodigious blast and tide of things to come. (Section 5)[16]

Perse concluded his Stockholm address at the time at which he received the Nobel Prize with a passage in which he set the clay lamp of the poet over against the atomic hearth as no less potent for our age. It was his theme that science and poetry pursue a common interrogation of the same abyss. The mystery is common to them both. The great adventure of the poetic imagination yields in no way to the dramatic break-throughs of modern science.

Refusing to divorce art from life or love from knowledge, it is action, it is passion, it is power, a perpetual renewal that extends the boundaries. Love is its vital flame, independence its law, and its domain is everywhere, an anticipation.[17]

It is clear that Perse's work, for all its orgiastic character, cannot be accused of angelism or of gnosticism. Modern poetry, he

16. Pp. 5–7; 8–10; 13–14.
17. *Two Addresses,* New York, 1966, p. 12.

observes, "is concerned with man in the plenitude of his being. In such a poetry there is no place for anything Pythian, nor for anything purely aesthetic." The modern fabulist, we repeat, has a sense of the power of the word, as he renews it, and it is a power associated often with archaic and primordial utterance. It goes behind the cultural rhetoric of our recent past or even of a longer tradition. It would find its way to the first springs of speech, and draw on the voices and tablets of many tribes and peoples. It employs myths and fables that represent, as it were, the seeds of many cultures. In these and other ways it would break out of our more restricted sense of reality into a different space-time, and thus speak for man in a more total way.

We recall at this point the question raised by Paul Tillich as to where in the contemporary arts one can recognize the crystallizing of a new order of life and a new shape of culture. The passion for the concrete of which we have spoken is only a pre-condition for any such emergent. Similarly the contemporary confidence in the power of the word can only be a step in this direction. But here there are discriminations to be made.

I come therefore to a very typical and widespread aspect of much creative activity and its new rhetoric, an aspect whose phenomena I would gather up under the category of the improvisation. In a situation where the continuities with the past are eroded, significant experience is understandably identified with revelation in the moment, with improvisation and ex-tempore language and gesture, with the epiphany and the happening.

In anticipation I would make several remarks. (1) The kind of authenticity associated with all such untrammeled voice and action is to be prized, and no doubt must be a necessary element in any more coherent and total language. (2) A caution must be voiced against this whole conception of the modes of creativity and aesthetic in that it is difficult for it to recognize any law except its own dynamics. (3) If by this way some eventual design of human life is to emerge there will needs be some eventual intermarriage of its unrelated epiphanies with the older archetypes of the race.

The literary phenomena in question here are varied. The common feature is a focus on immediacy apart from context, on happening without interpretation. But such immediacy can be at various levels. It can mean a mere naked presentation of totally contingent sense-impressions, as though we were obscurely impelled to assure ourselves not of the whatness but the is-ness or there-ness of things and their multifariousness. Associated with this is the collage in the visual arts, or the method of the anti-novel with its chaotic juxtapositions or chosism. Any such kind of raw immediacy may be defended as a step in the re-education of vision.

At a more significant level is the immediacy of the sudden epiphany or moment of intense revelation exploding out of meaninglessness. In either case it is as though our encounters with a post-Einstein world could only be reported by appropriate improvisations. What is so evident in modern painting has its parallel in modern letters. It is again as though our new reality cannot be mapped; all we can do is to put down markers at points of contact. Wider meanings cannot yet be portrayed but scattered soundings can be registered. Literature must therefore come close to life and experience at the risk of artistic distance. So we get the open theatre of Peter Weiss as in *Marat/Sade*. Or literature must cling to the contours of the dream as in the cinema of Bergman. In these forms also the category is that of happening and improvisation since the experience so presented is taken in isolation.

We should, however, recognize that this impulse and the new rhetorics it employs can serve a genuine renewal of the word. The fragmentary acts of the imagination are not condemned to a claustral sterility. Some of our greatest modern works offer us their own versions of the discontinuous epiphany and the polarity between absurdity and vision. We have only to think of

192

Eliot's burning moment arising out of the "waste sad time/Before and after," or of the way in which Theodore Roethke like Yeats could transcend the merely sensual eye. In Wallace Stevens we have a notable demonstration of the changed conditions under which the imagination today finds its starting point in our reality. But this leaves us still with many questions.

One example of the new rhetoric of improvisation is found in the program for poetry today defined by Charles Olson as "projective" or "open" verse, and represented in varying degrees by the work of Robert Duncan, Robert Creeley and Denise Levertov. This language experiment deserves attention because it appeals to the authority of Pound, Stein and W. C. Williams for its poetic and to Whitehead and contemporary scientists for its view of modern reality, as well as to corresponding movements in contemporary music and painting. It is evident for one thing that these poets propose to adapt their art to the new reality that modern science has opened up.[18] The first axiom of Olson speaks of "composition by field" and "kinetics" and "an energy-discharge," and we hear of "a different space-time for content," and an indebtedness to Whitehead for a sense of the multifariousness of the world and thus a "multiphasic" art.[19]

18. Norman Pearson, writing on "The American Poet in Relation to Science," in *Four Studies*, Verona, 1962, well states the problem of language created by our new understanding of nature. "Science . . . has provided us with a new topography of definitions . . . The laws of Newton, the logic of Aristotle, and the geometry of Euclid no longer obtain except on the lowest level of familiarity. The world as we see it today through the mind's eye of the scientist is no longer a familiar and substantive mechanics but a helter-skelter of electronics out of which we can extract only equations of infinite variables. . . . The poet has had to look upon a new physical reality and learn not to accept what has been thought about it simply because it has been thought. He has to learn a new vocabulary and syntax for giving extension to his conclusions. Pp. 29–31.

19. See his statements on poetics in Donald M. Allen (ed), *The New American Poetry, 1945–1960*, New York, 1960, pp. 386–400. On the importance of Whitehead see Duncan's remark on p. 435.

Projective verse, then, can be understood as an attempt to renew the word in our modern reality. Its character as improvisation is insisted on in sophisticated terms. Olson would take speech back behind all that is "literary" and behind the space-time premises of older grammars and their humanistic riches to "inherent speech (thought, power)" and the etymological roots of words. Indeed he urges that original utterance is connected with the breath itself, with the throat: therefore "breathing rather than listening"; "the line comes from the breath." Thus poetry rejoins nature itself, and the poet causes "the thing he makes to try to take its place alongside the things of nature." The relation to the visual arts today is evident in his purpose: "the replacement of the Classical-representational by the *primitive-abstract*," the term primitive here meaning "primary."

Thus one is equal across history forward and back, and it's all levy, as present is, but sd that way, one states . . . a different space-time. Content in other words, is also shifted—at least from humanism, as we've had it since the Indo-Europeans got their fid in there (circum 1500 BC)[20]

This view is interesting for the way in which it deals with the available past, and in effect relativizes its features, or at least subordinates them all to the idea of the one perennial creative voice. One finds analogous formulations of this programme in Robert Duncan who characterizes poems not as achievement but as "fountains," "doors of language" and "adventures."[21]

This view of the poem can be confirmed again in the work of Robert Creeley. In the Preface to his *Poems, 1950-1965*,[22] his term for what we have called improvisation is to "stumble." The poems are "places . . . stumbled into . . . and too, a sudden

20. "Letter to Elaine Feinstein," *ibid.,* pp. 398–399.
21. "Pages from a Notebook," *ibid.,* p. 400–407.
22. London, 1966.

194

instance of love, and the being loved, wherewith a man also contrives a world (of his own mind)." We also find here the purpose to bring the poem as close as possible to living: "I want the poem as close to this fact as I can bring it; or it, me."

We may applaud all such intentions to conform language as closely as possible to the living reality of the poet who thus "contrives a world (of his own mind)." But then for any public importance whatsoever all depends upon who is speaking, and just how significant a "life" or person it is who speaks!

That this kind of poetry rests its case on the creative act of improvisation itself, upon "the poem supreme," rather than any traditional content is evident in Creeley's "The Dishonest Mail-men."

> They are taking all my letters, and they
> put them into a fire.
>
> I see the flames, etc.
> But do not care, etc.
>
> They burn everything I have, or what little
> I have. I don't care, etc.
>
> The poem supreme, addressed to
> Emptiness—this is the courage
>
> necessary. This is something
> quite different.[23]

Here the modern poet sees himself deprived of messages and communications to or from the existing culture and commits himself to a new creative word.

Of course all this sounds like just another version of very old mantic or even more recent Romantic ideas of the poet. It proposes to be different, however, by its identification with a modern

23. P. 29.

195

sensibility, modern science, modern psychology, and the use of
modern styles. Yet all such arts that appeal to the idea of
creativity, novelty, iconoclasm, finally meet the stubborn problem of the image. Communication involves something recognizable, therefore image or symbol. It need not be representational.
It can be subliminal. Consider the stratagems of recent painting.
At the extreme we have sheer random improvisation in shapes
and colors, which, as in John Cage's deliberate productions of
noise, are intended only to dishabituate us of our old ways of
seeing and hearing. We have impact and shock alone, not design. But apart from this the contemporary painter intends some
kind of meaning if only to himself and this involves significant
motif, if only at the level of the unconscious. Contemporary
poets employ the stratagem of shock by various iconoclasms, by
typographical device and by nonsense rhetorics. But the arts of
language since they employ words cannot avoid images and
therefore cannot create out of nothing and cannot escape the
past. The more ambitious the poem is, or the novel or play, the
truer this is.

The fact is that the poems written according to the programme of projective verse—or other ideas that stress the
moment and process of becoming, as when Heidegger is invoked—are all repetitions of each other. They all deal with the
one experience, that of the beginning of speech, the phase of
becoming, the break-through of vision. Hence the recurrent
images of the flowing fountain, the opening door. There must
be no content! If images, motifs, myths are used they are uprooted from their traditional reference. Their connotations and
the patterns that adhere to them must be dissolved so that they
can enter into the untrammelled improvisation of the present.
Fortunately these poets are not always faithful to their method
and their best poems are the result. Works of art whether in
writing or painting which celebrate only the experience of improvisation convey no reality except that of a moment of liberation.

In the poetry that Robert Duncan writes and in what he says about it[24] one cannot but prize the impulse towards an authentic voice and the urge to uncover "the spore of what we are becoming." But any student of the history of religion soon recognizes in what he says about mystical wisdom and occult revelation—with his indiscriminate evoking of Plato and Augustine, of Dante and Blake, of Gnosis and Freud—a very familiar and questionable form of spirituality. All ancient images of the struggle between light and darkness, whether God and the dragon, Apollo and Dionysus, Yang and Yin, all dramas of the soul whether from East or West, whether Buddha or Christ, Krishna or St. John of the Cross, are taken on the same level. It is in keeping with this that Duncan speaks of poetry as "magic, a drawing of the sorts," and as having the character of a rite. But discrimination is in order here.

We may agree that creativity in any time or place has its correspondences with all other fabulations. But there are differences in their presuppositions and meaning. These differences should not be ignored even in the interest of a contemporary vision. The past has a right to speak for itself, and the past is multiple. This kind of stress on improvisation runs the danger of exalting the creative act of the artist above all other forms of knowing and wisdom. The elation that goes with immediacy and the power of the word operates in a total freedom if not in a void, without recognizable controls. Such "projective" or "open" poetry or art is prompted by the idea of beginning anew in our only lately discovered "real" world. It would extricate itself largely unconsciously from the givens of any human creativity: the conditions and limits of the imagination, the hidden fabric of relatedness that every man carries with him both as a fate and as a resource.

24. For a statement of Duncan on poetics see Allen, *op. cit.*, pp. 400–407. Also "The Truth and Life of Myth in Poetry," *Parable, Myth and Language* (A Meeting of Poets and Theologians), a pamphlet edited by Tony Stoneburner, published by The Church Society for College Work, 2 Brewer St., Cambridge, Mass., 1968.

The issue that we face here transcends the particular programme of "open verse." It is an issue that has been with us a
long time in all the artistic movements associated with surrealism. Many of our contemporary writers and painters appeal
especially to those artists in France who broke with impres-
sionism and who sought a higher reality in some deeper process
of creativity, automatic composition or visionary apocalypse. We
can recognize that in men like Apollinaire, Cocteau or Dylan
Thomas a breakthrough could thus occur in our habits of vision
and that an order of transcendence was disclosed in a culture
that had widely lost this dimension of experience. The artistic
styles associated with this movement have been correspondingly
novel. But again the crux of the matter is that of meaning, and
therefore of relationship to the language of the past. All such
work has an aspect of improvisation and iconoclasm about it. In
some of it this goes to the point of the loss of all significant context. So we get the hermetic or the phantasy. In the best work,
however, these new rhetorics open up an order of insight which
can be related to traditional experience.

At this point it will be relevant to adduce an illustration of
this whole impulse to improvisation from the art of painting.

I condense here remarks of Robert Motherwell in a conversa-
tion with art students at the Fogg Museum at Harvard. In much
of his work Motherwell embarks upon free improvisation, without any sketches, project in mind, least of all model of any kind.
One could call it a higher kind of doodling, and he even used
the term playfully. A dozen such ventures into the unpredictable,
raids into the inarticulate, may be unsuccessful and are discarded.
But at times in the abstract gestures so initiated, most often in
black and white, something compelling breaks through, a reality
which speaks to the painter and to which he responds.[25] A

25. "Sensing quality in a work of art is like finding an answer to
one's seeking self. Such consciousness of growth is the great revelation
in life." Lawrence W. Chisolm cites this remark of Max Weber in his

human experience thus registers itself in the work of art, a work which is meaningful, satisfying, which as it were conveys health —and, note, in the actual contemporary situation.

Observe that such a transaction as Motherwell describes depends on the spontaneity of the painter, his refusal of borrowings, his total openness. It is this that enables a "speaking" kind of artistic transcription. Moreover, Motherwell used the term "ethical" of this kind of work of the artist. Not "moral," he said—that means tribal—but "ethical." No doubt he meant that what arises in such open but disciplined encounter with reality carries meaning and order. That such ethical content can have a very real historical reference is suggested by the title, "Elegy for the Spanish Republic," which is given to the considerable series of paintings which are among his best known work.

Evidently, it is not everyone who can "doodle" or improvise with such significant outcome. There must be something in the artist behind the quasi-automatic activity, some inexorable honesty, some life-long discipline both of the artist and the man, some craving for order, some appetite for stature. I found it significant that Motherwell acknowledged not only earlier affiliation with the movement of Dada and automatism but also with the surrealists. But I was most struck by his suggestion that the modern artist may well shun the reflexes of familiar representational painting in the hope of achieving such austere or momentous shapes as are suggested, say, by Stonehenge or similar prodigious visions. Evidently the spontaneity of which Motherwell spoke had hidden roots. In conceiving of his art as totally unprogrammed he is detaching himself from played-out habits of see-

---

study of Fenellosa, and continues: "Weber is convinced that this grasp of the creative imagination proceeds from within outward, that the growth of plastic intelligence unites interior experience with wider vitalities in ways which renew individual life, and further, that this renewal is an ongoing process, a continual search for new relationships whose 'synthesis' enables man to link finite and infinite." *Fenellosa: The Far East and American Culture,* New Haven, 1963, p. 231.

ing, so as to bring a total experience into play and to let this total experience find its contemporary idiom. Not all artists will work in the same way, nor, indeed, does Motherwell himself always so work, but there should always be this immediacy, this emancipation from rehearsed responses, and this recognition that the concrete present must have its part in the crystallizing of the word and the ikon. We have the highest authority for this procedure!" "When they deliver you up do not be anxious how you are to speak or what you are to say; for what you are to say will be given you in that hour" (Mt. 10:19).

My main point in citing Motherwell, however, was to illustrate the impulse for authentic experience, for the archaic or fresh word of power. This represents an anti-cultural attitude in the sense that it must by-pass old aesthetic and spiritual habits. But in so doing it may take hold of a deeper tradition. All this has its analogy in religious language. The Christian seeks today to recover the primordial power of the Word, a speech from the depths capable both of assembling a community but also of reconstituting the meaningfulness of our world. But here also the question of the inherited image becomes pressing.

III. BACK TO THE ARCHETYPES:
JONES's *ANATHÉMATA*

In this closing section I urge that the ancient structures of the imagination, the myths and archetypes of the past, must have their place in the renewal of the word today. The life-line of language and meaning that comes down to us through the whole history of culture must continue into the new rhetorics of today and tomorrow. We have seen this theme emerging at a number of points in our surveys. It is not enough that the artist should explore and celebrate our modern reality by his own emancipated vision and utterance. If our passion for the real is truly desperate we shall not be satisfied with even our most authentic contemporary epiphanies and symbols. A genuine love for man and all creatures will require a total language including memory and the voices of the past.

To suggest how this is possible today I shall turn to a book-length poem or modern epic of the Welsh poet and artist, David Jones, entitled *The Anathémata*.[26] This book, which Auden has called "very probably the finest long poem written in English in this century," is a rehearsal of the gesta and rites of western man from the ice-age down. The text and notes are a dense tapestry of pagan and Christian lore, calendars, blazonry. It is a book of signs and hieroglyphs: old runes, the names of gods, heroes, cities, shores. As he looks into the bottomless well of the past and the obscure annals of tribes and peoples the poet studies the many ancient sacrifices and auguries seeking, in company as he says with James Joyce and Picasso, "to uncover a valid sign," to "lift up an efficacious sign."[27] Jones calls his poem *The Anathémata*, meaning, "the offerings," the gestures and prayers spoken and unspoken of man to the powers. He is a Christian. He focusses his book of rites upon the days in Jerusalem "when time turned" and upon the liturgy of the Mass. But he finds analogies to the site of Calvary not only in the mount of Abraham's sacrifice but at the navel of the world identified with Delphi. He finds a prototype of Christ in the archaic Greek statue found on the Acropolis of the man with the ram on his shoulder as he does in the child of Vergil's Fourth Eclogue. He sees resonances of the death of Christ in that of Hector, and of his assumption to heaven in that of Romulus. He sees anticipations and echoes of the mother of Christ in the sixth-century B.C. Athenian statue called "the beautiful Kore," as well as in representations of Artemis, Cybele and all the

26. New York, n.d. (English edition, 1952).
27. Pp. 27, 49.

201

Mediterranean images of the mother goddess and the later divine patronesses of the Celts.

I have thus suggested the character of Jones's poem so as to indicate for one thing the context in which he construes the myth of Prometheus and man's acquiring the arts of civilization. In a section dealing with the oldest artifacts and the cave-painting of 20,000 B.C. he speaks of the discovery of fire. This liberation of man was so great a mutation that he sets it in relation to the event of the Resurrection of Christ. He reminds us that in early Christian liturgy on the Saturday night before Easter the Paschal Candle was lit from a fire of charcoal newly kindled by striking flint. And he associates this with man's first discovery of fire which he calls "the Easter of technics." How long before Easter itself!

> What ages since
> his other marvel-day
>   when time turned?
> and *how* turned!
> When
>   (How?
>   from early knocking stick or stone?)
> the first New Fire wormed
>   at the Easter of Technics.
> What a holy Saturn's day!
> *O vere beata nox!*[28]

Thus David Jones's poem is a celebration of man the maker in a way that contrasts with Lowell's view of Prometheus. The implications would be different for the whole story of technology down to the present. Yet Jones also writes as a modern. He acknowledges himself as indebted especially to James Joyce. His style is close sometimes to that of *Finnegans Wake* and at other

28. Pp. 60–61. The Latin line from the Exsultet at the liturgy in question.

times to that of Pound's *Cantos*. We see in him, therefore, a radical transformation of older rhetoric. He too can recognize that the human pilgrimage today is uncertain. On the first page he presents a picture of the dethroned sanctities of the past, and the lonely role of the cult-man standing guard in *The Waste Land*. He pictures churches of today whose designs are only "cramped repeats of their dead selves," in which the old *numina* are weakened, and "dead symbols litter the base of the cult stone." Speaking of the liturgists, he writes,

These, at the sagging end and chapter's close, standing humbly before the tables spread, in the apsidal houses, who intended life:
      between the sterile ornaments
   under the pasteboard baldachins
   as, in the young-time, in the sap-years
      between the living floriations
   under the leaping arches.
   (Ossific, trussed with ferric rods, the failing numina of column and entablature, the genii of spire and triforium, like great rivals met when all is done, nod recognition across the cramped repeat of their dead selves.)

These rear-guard details in their quaint attire, heedless of incongruity, unconscious that the flanks are turned and all connecting files withdrawn or liquidated—that dead symbols litter to the base of the cult-stone, that the stem by the palled stone is thirsty, that the stream is very low.[29]

One would have to go far to find a better example of the modern writer conscious of the crisis of language and symbols, yet who unashamedly makes his discourse a tapestry of archaic symbols. We have here no doubt a clue to the literary and religious dilemma of our time: we can best overcome the break with the past by linking the very modern with the very ancient. It is in

29. Pp. 49–50.

this light that Jones speaks of James Joyce: "this artist, while pre-eminently 'contemporary' and indeed 'of the future,' was also of all artists the most of site and place. And as for 'the past,' as for 'history,' it was from the ancestral mound that he fetched his best garlands and Clio ran with him a lot of the way—if under the name of Brigit. So that although most authentically the bard of the shapeless cosmopolis and of the megalopolitan diaspora, he could say

> 'Come ant daunce wyt me
> In Irelaunde.' "[30]

It was again something like this marriage of modern tone and movement and style with archaic legacies that T. S. Eliot affected. Our own best dealing with the language of the past may well be similar. When the ice begins to crack under our feet we throw a rope back to the more stable footing where we started, to the great ancient epiphanies of mankind, mysterious but prestigious. Our contemporary anomie and vertigo make us distrust all more recent modern ideologies and their idioms and images; a long past is compromised by our maladies and revulsions. It is there-fore very evident that "last year's language" is compromised but not, if we may use the phrase, "last millennium's language": such as the saga of the Holy Grail or the early liturgies; nor the language of the early millennia before Christ: the language of Troy and pre-Christian Rome. David Jones goes still farther back and establishes our footing on the oldest runes and memo-rials of man's earliest habitations, migrations and navigations, man's earliest rites and ceremonies, back to the archaic burials and cave-paintings which already testified to a universal *pietas* and reverence before life and death. Thus Jones appeals back of even our greatest western classics to what he calls the "deposits" of the human quest. But he uses contemporary utterance and

30. P. 26, from the Preface.

provides a counterpoint of the genuinely modern with the ancient residues. In his poem it therefore comes quite natural for him to cite the saying of Jesus about the "scribe who is like a householder who brings forth out of his treasure what is new and what is old."

He can fetch things new and old: the tokens, the matrices, the institutes, the ancilia, the fertile ashes—the palladic foreshadowings: the things that came down from heaven together with the kept memorials, the things lifted up and the venerable trinkets.[31]

One can add to the modern writers who so deal with the past the name of the poet St.-John Perse. His *Anabase* (1924) celebrated man at the farthest horizons of history and pre-history, in his earliest dealings with time and space, and so with his early artifacture, fabulation and migrations. His poem *Exil* (1961) again dwells upon the lengthy past and the mysterious origins and gropings and milestones of his pilgrimage. Again, as in Joyce, Pound and Eliot, the inevitable subject of modern art is universal man, universal both in the global sense and in the vertical dimension of cultural history. Self-understanding today must be sought in the long retrospective view as well as in the sophisticated introspection pursued by other contemporary writers. Perse's style is, indeed, very different from that of Joyce or David Jones. Yet this eloquent voice is a modern one and divorces itself sharply from what we have called "last year's language."

These examples suggest that Robert Lowell's treatment of Prometheus as founder of the arts of civilization is exceptionally negative. He uses the past for other purposes. In returning to the world of ancient myth and fable he finds a text for the in-

31. P. 50. Note also what amounts to a self-portrait of this poet: "More precariously than he knows he guards the *signa:* the pontifex among his house-treasures, (the twin-*urbes* his house is)."

conclusiveness of man's struggle to subdue nature and build an ordered life. David Jones, on the other hand, is in awe at the marvels of man's successive masteries of his theater of existence and the conditions of his life and links these with the pre-creative Word. We are reminded again of William Blake's aphorism, "Eternity is in love with the productions of time." Yet Jones recognizes the jeopardies of man's pilgrimage. It has always been a close thing, he notes. In a section which fables the first Phoenician voyage to the tin mines of Cornwall and suggests the diffusion of Ionian humanism to Britain, he portrays "the whole argosy of mankind, and, in some sense, of all sentient being, and perhaps, of insentient too"[32] as like a ship finding its port through perilous reefs and storms. As his narrative passes from the archaic epochs to the origins of Europe he writes:

> Down we come
>   quick, but far
> to the splendours
>   of the skill-years
> and the signed and fine grandeurs.
> O yes, technique—but much more:
> the god is still balanced
>   in the man-stones
>   but it's a nice thing
> as near a thing as ever you saw.[33]

For this Christian author the argosy of mankind is related, as he indicates in a note, to "what is pleaded in the Mass," which is "precisely the argosy or voyage of the Redeemer, consisting of his entire sufferings and his death, his conquest of hades, his resurrection and his return in triumph to heaven. It is this that is offered to the Trinity . . . on behalf of us argonauts and of the

32. P. 106, note 2.
33. Pp. 93–94.

206

whole argosy of mankind."[34] Yet the poem in this section gathers up with Christian prayer the petitions of the ancient Mediterranean sailors to Artemis, Cybele and the mother goddesses of the East.

I have noted earlier that the vicissitudes of language today can be studied by the way in which older texts are translated or adapted by contemporary writers. Many such writers understandably use older classics as vehicles for our present preoccupations which they thus see as universal or as recurrent. In the case of David Jones, however, as with others, there is a greater willingness to let the past speak for itself, a greater reverence for the archetypes, in the sense again of Herman Melville's lines,

> Not innovating wilfulness
> But reverence for the Archetype.[35]

It would seem that a renewal of the word today, as one strategy, requires a leap back to those fables and epiphanies in which mankind came to itself and by which it found its way long before our modern confusions. How far that world is from the world of so many novels and plays today whose characters agonize in the various labyrinths of contemporary alienation deprived of any ancient road-signs or rituals! But those ancient mappings of existence can still offer us guidance if they can be incorporated into our own experience by the power of the Spirit and the imagination.

That renewal of language which we await today, that rebaptism of images profound enough to make possible a marriage of things new and old,

> The complete consort dancing together,

34. P. 106, note 2.
35. "Greek Architecture," *The Works of Herman Melville,* vol. XVI, *Poems,* London, 1924, p. 287.

any such language-event, evidently, will emerge from impulses deeper than particular literary combinations and strategies. Even the most prestigious world-determining images crystallized out of the ancient experience of the race only operate to block any such integral celebration if they are not reactivated, resmelted, in the moral experience of the present. The wisdom of the past, conscious and unconscious, can only be rightly grasped and appropriated in the vicissitudes of the present; and the vicissitudes in question are to be understood at a depth analogous to that of those fateful ancient transactions. Yet how are we to become aware of this primordial travail in the present and its meaning if not at the level of the imagination and in the "first-order" language of the arts? Thus we can recognize today as always the two-fold indefeasible role of artist and seer, to bring into view the pregnant realities of the present and so to open the way to repossession of the past.[36]

36. "Imagination is therefore ineluctably bound up with the historical possibilities of human being. With that imagination is not a license to invent *ex nihilo;* it cannot, in an undemented self, intend a world that is not bound to the historical past it renews; indeed, renewal means the disclosure of ontological possibility funded in the ontic, temporal past, that now must be brought forward historically. Ray L. Hart, *Unfinished Man and the Imagination,* New York, 1968, p. 225.

PART THREE

Secular Repossession

The cult-man stands alone in Pellam's land: more precariously than he knows he guards the *signa:* the pontifex among his house-treasures, (the twin-*urbes* his house is) he can fetch things new and old: the tokens, the matrices, the institutes, the ancilia, the fertile ashes—the palladic foreshadowings . . .
David Jones, The Anathémata

since this morning
it is with a vocabulary
made wholesomely profane, open in lexicons
to our foes to translate, that we endeavor
each in his idiom to express the true magnalia.

W. H. Auden, "Whitsuntide in Kirchstetten"

VIII. Mortality and Transcendence

In these concluding chapters I wish to press further the specific question as to the fate of the biblical archetypes in the disarray of the present, a period when, indeed, time has "turned." I continue to pursue this matter at the level of the deeper dynamics of the West mirrored in the life of the imagination. Even at this level it is not a question of identifying specific norms, and we must shun all archaism and immutable authority. There is, however, a homeland of the heart in the bleakness of existence and in the mindless cataracts of appearances which has long been established, and this clearing in nescience and confusion is constantly to be repossessed. Like a rude map of consciousness and conscience it has ever to be corrected and clarified in the light of the present, and its master images continue to nourish us only because they lend themselves to continued transmutation.

The difficulty of such repossession today and the travail involved in the rebirth of images is abundantly testified in our modern classics. The problem arises out of the fact that recent experience has outrun the inherited vehicles and structures of the faith and found itself under necessity of solving its problems apart from the older recognized patterns and guidelines. But as I have urged in an earlier work,[1] the vital tradition still operates

1. *Modern Poetry and the Christian Tradition*, New York, 1952.

in many unrecognized ways. The stream has gone underground but continues to nourish and inform our secularized age. Furthermore, it becomes clear that much of the most significant literature of our century documents the process by which our emancipated age by a costly integrity explores its new reality and shapes a language in which the living not the dead tradition of the past can again be brought to speech. These chapters will therefore continue to scrutinize aspects of this secular exploration of the human mystery, and show how essential this kind of immediate engagement with our contemporary actuality is for any valid repossession of our older epiphanies.

To further this scrutiny of changing categories and idioms I turn in the present chapter to modern versions of transcendence. More generally stated it is a question of how mortality and immortality are dealt with in contemporary letters. We may well recall at the outset that in all ages men have recorded certain responses to death and mortality that vary little. The universal themes of dread and stupor, of grief and compunction, of transience and corruptibility—such poignancies of our finite condition underlie whatever special cultural or even religious influences come into play, or whatever particular hopes are projected. It is for this reason that elegies for fallen heroes and laments for toppled cities and broken hopes, in Job or Homer, are still moving, or the heartbreak in a papyrus letter, or the plangent grief of Catullus as he comes across many seas to his brother's grave,

> ut te postremo donarem munere mortis
> et mutam nequiquam adloquerer cinerem.[2]

Indeed, we must say that it is only in total openness to such common experience of grief and trepidation that other more positive overtones of death can make themselves felt and justify themselves.

2. Carmen 101.

212

Transcendence over our mortal condition comes to frequent expression in contemporary letters. This is all the more significant when the exploration is carried out apart from the formal religious traditions, and I shall confine myself for the most part to such work. Even so my treatment must be highly selective. The following thesis will give a certain unity to the analysis. I am convinced that even aesthetic and Romantic experience can afford valid testimony to transcendent dimensions of our being. The enigma and dynamics of the self so far surpass our understanding that we may well attend to the most diverse kinds of intimations that "we are greater than we know." This holds true today in particular for the experiences of metamorphosis and epiphany prominent in the work of such artists as Joyce, Yeats and Rilke, and for the exceptional kind of visionary apprehensions in our existentialist writers. But more adequate and assured views of eternal life depend upon something that our uprooted moderns lack, namely, a more social understanding of man and of death. It was on the basis of a community understanding of man and the self that Israel came through to its impregnable certitudes of glory and of life in the age to come. It is in terms of the moral tuition of the heart that immortality is fully grasped, through the vicissitudes of our common human endeavor, and not through the psyche, soul or spirit of the individual. Some modern writers indicate awareness of this. But the homelessness and alienation of the modern self often invite other and easier solutions.

As a foil to our characteristic contemporary outlook, I propose here at the beginning of our survey to cite an ancient text at some length. It is the well-known Old English elegy of the eighth century, entitled "The Wanderer."[3] Here we have an

3. Cited from the volume by Charles W. Kennedy, *Old English Elegies,* Translated into Alliterative Verse with a Critical Introduction, Princeton, 1936, pp. 45–51. The MS is from the tenth century, but the poem can be dated between A.D. 700 and 725. I wish to record my thanks to the Rev. John P. McIntyre, S.J., for bringing the poem to

outcast, a lone survivor of the wars, who laments the loss of his companions-in-arms and of his liege lord. We note for one thing that grief is allowed free course. Our own responses too often inhibit this natural impulse through a misprized Stoicism or sophistication, or through a sentimental evasion of the incommensurable reality of death.[4] The poem in question reads in part as follows:

> Who bears it, knows what a bitter companion,
> Shoulder to shoulder, sorrow can be,
> When friends are no more. His fortune is exile,
> Not gifts of fine gold; a heart that is frozen,
> Earth's winsomeness dead. And he dreams of the hallmen,
> The dealing of treasure, the days of his youth,
> When his lord bade welcome to wassail and feast.
> But gone is that gladness, and never again
> Shall come the loved counsel of comrade and king.
> Even in slumber his sorrow assaileth,
> And, dreaming, he claspeth his dear lord again,
> Head on knee, hand on knee, loyally laying,
> Pledging his liege as in days long past.
> Then from his slumber he starts lonely-hearted,
> Beholding gray stretches of tossing sea,
> Sea-birds bathing, with wings outspread,
> While hail-storms darken, and driving snow.
> Bitterer then is the bane of his wretchedness,

---

my attention. In doing so Father McIntyre observed: "We have pretty much the reverse of the modern sense of personal alienation. If, in a real sense, the modern man 'wants to be alone,' the Old English society cursed the unattached man—he threatened the clan or family as a stranger."

4. As a New Testament teacher I was challenged recently to explain the fact that in the New Testament as a whole one finds no considerable passage or passages which a mourner can make his own for the expression and relief of personal sorrow. My answer was that the Christian Bible of course includes and demands Job and the Psalms and other records eloquent of the generic human passions.

The longing for loved ones: his grief is renewed ...
No wonder therefore, in all the world,
If a shadow darkens upon my spirit
When I reflect on the fates of men—
How one by one warriors vanish
From the halls that knew them, and day by day
All this earth ages and droops unto death ...
A wise man will ponder how dread is that doom
When all this world's wealth shall be scattered and waste—
As now, over all, through the regions of earth,
Walls stand rime-covered and swept by the winds.
The battlements crumble, the wine-halls decay;
Joyless and silent the heroes are sleeping
Where the proud host fell by the wall they defended ...
Wretchedness fills the realm of earth,
And Fate's decrees transform the world.
Here wealth is fleeting, friends are fleeting,
Man is fleeting, maid is fleeting;
All the foundation of earth shall fail!
Thus spake the sage in solitude pondering.
Good man is he who guardeth his faith.
He must never too quickly unburden his breast
Of its sorrow, but eagerly strive for redress ...

There are two features of this response to death which may serve as a test of contemporary attitudes. For one thing, there is no tendency to see death as a highly individualized, private matter. In all simplicity the death of the individual is merged with the lot of his companions. And again, it is not thought of apart from the course of the world, from "earth's winsomeness," from what men strive to build, from men's frustrated endeavors. Indeed, the poignancy of this lament for the disastrous fates of his companions refers above all to the unraveling of the fabric of loyalties and the ruin of the work of men's hands and hearts: whether mead-halls and battlements or festal ceremonies fallen silent. Death is here a communal reality. And so it is, indeed, in ⟩

215

the biblical Scriptures and in many ancient and, one may say, healthy records. We have here a test to set against certain contemporary views which revolve about the privacy of the problem. The contrast could not be more sharply drawn than in a passage in Samuel Beckett's *Watt*.[5] Here the unreality of our traditional human bonds, in the view of many moderns, is suggested in the following interchange. Mr. Hackett asks Mr. Nixon what he knows about his old acquaintance, Watt:

> But you must know something, said Mr. Hackett.
> One does not part with five shillings to a shadow.
> Nationality, family, birthplace, confession, occupation, means of existence, distinctive signs, you cannot be in ignorance of all this.
>
> Utter ignorance, said Mr. Nixon.[6]

This modern erosion of our basic structures of identity and "belonging" is seen by Beckett as disastrous. For it cuts the ground out from under the only true fulfillment of our humanity.

I. THE RELOCATION OF THE PROBLEM

The question of death and of life beyond has to be relocated today. Subtle changes have profoundly altered men's outlook and sensibility, and this affects even those who cherish traditional religious images. It is not only that terms like heaven and hell have to be put into quotation marks. Our sense of time has changed; we cannot so easily pass over the temporal in favor of the eternal. The very meaning of the ego or self has changed. Our fathers' view of man as a soul which could be used by Tennyson and Browning, Emerson and Whitman, Francis

5. Paris, 1953.
6. P. 21.

216

Thompson and Vachel Lindsay, is all tied up with views of man and society which for many today belong to old picture books and a very simple world. Even modern translations of the Bible avoid the term "soul" in crucial passages where it is open to misinterpretation.

Moreover, when we envisage the overcoming of death, it is not first of all in chronological terms of an after-life. This dimension must be taken up into one or another version of transcendence or meaning in this life. Modern letters reflect this changed sense of the world and open up appropriate categories and images. Nor is it just a question of obsolete as against authentic language. It is also a question of imaginative depth. The modern voice often provides a more vivid, dynamic evocation of what has been meant by evil, finitude, guilt, suffering, conscience, hell, hope, deliverance.

The issue as to immortality must be relocated today. One reason for this is that our confrontation with nothingness no longer waits upon the moment of death. Meaninglessness, vacancy, non-being has to be dealt with here and now. Modern literature is full of this theme. Modern man is peculiarly naked to his limits, unassisted by those sentiments and idealizations which served as buffers to our fathers. We are conditioned by the shock of our radical alienation from the world as given, the tearing away of the veils of ordinary perception. To cite again a passage already quoted from the English poet, Edwin Muir:

> . . . Now time's storm is rising, sweeping
> The sons of men into an empty room,
> Vast as a continent, bare as a desert.[7]

The question is not one of pessimism or optimism. The situation has its assets as well as its liabilities. One can say that men are

7. "Prometheus," *Collected Poems, 1921–1958,* London, 1960, p. 215.

learning again that in the midst of life we are in death. But it does explain why modern writers take hold of the problem of mortality in terms of the problem of meaning and identity.

There is real precedent for this even in Scripture. In ancient Israel one was engulfed in Sheol not only by actual dying, but by sorrow, abandonment, sickness, disaster, enslavement, sin— indeed, by all forms of weakness. So today the question of death merges with the question of meaning. We are not tied to old categories of present versus future life, or natural versus spiritual, or temporal versus eternal. One corollary of this situation is that secular exploration of nihilism and meaning, or of finitude and transcendence, are highly relevant to theological restatement. Indeed, the secular witness today is all the more necessary because dogmatic answers have become so unrelated to our experience.

The modern feeling about death had in any case become confused because it was made up of so many layers. Dogmatic religious views had been overlaid with various recent strata related to pietism, romanticism, idealism. The way people die and the way they mourn is largely determined by cultural suggestion, and this can range all the way from a morbid necrophilia to a spiritualizing escapism. One is reminded of Hegel's observation that "men die as a matter of habit." So Rilke could conclude that death in our time had become a standardized production. "The wish to have a death of one's own," he said, "is becoming rarer and rarer. Yet a little while and it will be as rare as a life of one's own." Thus we can appreciate the impulse of Sartre when he would convulsively shake off the incubus of false authority, and transcend mortality by a free act of self-determination.

The question of death must, therefore, be dealt with today in new terms. The older layers of cultural habit have been shaken loose. We have been exposed to non-being, emptiness, just at a time when human life has been cheapened by technological war and genocide on a grand scale and when the very survival of the race has become problematical. Recent shocks like this reverberate in the innermost judgment-hall of our being. As the prophet wrote, death is come up into our chambers.

II. DEATH AS CATALYST OF TRANSCENDENCE

For this central section of our discussion, I propose the formula, "death as catalyst of transcendence." The wall of death evokes extraordinary transmutations of our being. This theme can be illustrated in a wide gamut of literary expression. It is of interest to observe how artists of our time explore the unmasked enigma of our condition and testify to this or that version of what we may call secular revelation or secular transcendence. Today when our changed sense of reality can make so little of traditional imagery of the resurrection and the after-life, or even of the enduring life of the soul or spirit, it is highly significant to see these novel probings of the mystery in contemporary images.

It is true that confrontation with death can quench human vitality and impulse. But there seems to be a further point at which some ultimate potentiality in us is shocked or awakened by it in such a way that unaccountable energies and metamorphoses follow.

One can observe how death makes men come alive in even lesser matters. The soldier recognizes and responds to the subtle differences all about him as he draws near to the front, where electric tensions play. As we near the zone of death or danger, men are more alert, more ceremonious in deportment and in dress, more formal, whether in military life, in hospitals, around cyclotrons, or in rituals for the dead. Death puts men on the *qui vive*, arouses them, touches off profound reactions in them.

Death is a catalyst of transcendence. There can be many variations on this theme. "Life emerges at the point of mortification" (Karl Barth). "The inevitability of death accepted at the highest level of passion is an empowering thing" (Kierkegaard). Death is a barrier which calls forth the deeper life of the crea-

219

ture. The image that recurs to me for this transmutation is that of a reef in the open sea. It is against the cruel and adamant ledge that the currents of the ocean disclose their phosphorescence or break into iridescent foam and spray. So it is our finite limits, our inexorable restraints, that reveal us.

This theme has one remarkable statement in a poem of Marianne Moore, entitled "What are Years?" The theme is that of captivity transcended by acceptance and passion. Our limit is overcome by transmutation into another mode. Miss Moore uses the image of a high sea imprisoned in a chasm—a picture of our finitude—along with another image, that of the caged bird that turns its confinement into song.

> ...He
> sees deep and is glad, who
>   accedes to mortality
> and in his imprisonment rises
> upon himself as
> the sea in a chasm, struggling to be
> free and unable to be,
>   in its surrendering
>   finds its continuing.

> So he who strongly feels,
> behaves. The very bird,
>   grown taller as he sings, steels
> his form straight up. Though he is captive,
> his mighty singing
> says, satisfaction is a lowly
> thing, how pure a thing is joy.
>   This is mortality.
>   This is eternity.[8]

8. *Collected Poems of Marianne Moore,* New York, 1955, p. 99. Theodore Roethke has a similar figure in "The Dying Man: in Memoriam W. B. Yeats":

> The edges of the summit still appal
> When we brood on the dead or the beloved;

That the awareness of death lends a special quality to living has had various familiar expressions. In certain cultures a deep-wrought consciousness of the limits of life, of the shadow of the sphinx, acts like a charge, lends a chiaroscuro to existence, confers a richness upon it. This theme appears in the prefatory essay to Glenway Wescott's volume of stories, *Good-Bye Wisconsin.*[9] The author here explains why he and other expatriates went to Europe in the twenties.

It is the Greeks and Romans and the traditions preserved in Europe by the translations of Petrarch and by Montaigne and Goethe which, if one is an American, exasperate the imagination. Traditions of the conduct of life with death in mind.[10]

We have here one diagnosis of the superficiality of much of our American outlook. As John Cheever has said: "How can people who do not mean to understand death understand love, and who will sound the alarm?" And Louis Simpson in his "Poem to the Western World" observes that it is only by our graves that Americans have slowly entered into civilized possession of our land:

> In this America, this wilderness
> Where the axe echoes with a lonely sound,
> The generations labor to possess
> And grave by grave we civilize the ground.[11]

Dylan Thomas gives us an even more specific example of how the fact of death explodes into awareness of eternity. In his

---

Nor can imagination do it all
In this last place of light: he dares to live
Who stops being a bird, yet beats his wings
Against the immense immeasurable emptiness of things.
Words for the Wind, Garden City, 1958, p. 190.
9. New York, 1928.
10. P. 34
11. *A Dream of Governors,* Boston, 1959, p. 15.

221

"Ceremony after a Fire Raid,"[12] referring to the death of a child, he writes:

> ... Forgive
> Us your death that myselves the believers
> May hold it in a great flood
> Till the blood shall spurt,
> And the dust shall sing like a bird
> As the grains blow, as your death grows,
>   through our heart.[13]

In the second section the poet sees the origin of the whole race —Adam and Eve—as present

> In the cinder of the little skull.

And in the last section, the ultimate kingdom of genesis thunders, "Glory, glory, glory."[14]

We may recall also the two well-known poems that begin,

> Do not go gentle into that good night

and

> Death shall have no dominion.

All in all, Dylan Thomas celebrates death-in-life in a neo-Romantic manner. What gives it a certain significance is his breaking away from a banal pantheism and his kinship to the apocalyptic or surrealist grasp of existence.

Rilke is the modern poet who first widely familiarized the idea of life as interpenetrated with death and as therefore shot

12. *The Collected Poems of Dylan Thomas*, New York, n.d.
13. P. 143.
14. P. 146.

through with transcendence. Each one of us as we live is continuously giving form to his own particular death, as though it were a fruit ripening in us during our lifetime. Our present state meanwhile has its momentary flashes of eternity. The outcome is suggested in his poem, "Buddha":

> he who forgets what we know,
> who knows what is withheld from us.

Rilke used the symbols of Death, of the Angel, of Orpheus. The transcendence assigned to these was no mere aestheticism or otherworldliness. In his own words it meant "coming through to the other side of Nature," not an occult escape from Nature.[15] In many of his poems we find an authentic realization of a deathless dimension.

It is at this point that we should pause over the expression, "epiphany." This has become a technical term in critical discussion of modern art and literature, especially in connection with James Joyce. What is in view is the fact that visionary experience in our time is seen as fortuitous and unrelated. By contrast, in the classic passages in Wordsworth's *Prelude* where the poet sees into the heart of things, and feels that "we are greater than we know," the poet nevertheless recognizes a relation between the vision and some ordering Spirit of the Universe. When Browning speaks of the assurances of eternal life evoked by "a sunset-touch, a fancy from a flower-bell, a chorus-ending from Euripides," the same holds true. But the modern has widely lost this sense of enveloping order, so that aesthetic or personal moments of reality have a gratuitous character. The preternatural object seen in glory, or the unveiling of the prodigious, is "just there." God is not in question, nor the life of the soul, nor eternal values. Nevertheless, the epiphany opens up a super-

15. Hermann Mörchen, *Rilkes Sonette an Orpheus*, Stuttgart, 1958, p. 91.

human mystery. Here is where a play of images and correspondences arises, as in the case of Rilke's Angels, or the clowns, dancers and acrobats of Apollinaire, Cocteau and the modern painters, Picasso, Matisse and others. In the travesty of the clown in the garish carnival, or in the momentary perfection of a group of seedy tumblers and acrobats, our whole world with its mechanized obsessions can be metamorphosed for a flash into eternal radiance and pity.

As Erich Heller has stated it,

The humblest object or the tiniest shred of experience may unexpectedly become a conductor of infinity, charged with a force that was once distributed over a whole comprehensive order holding in their right places the great and the little things.[16]

Heller adds that Van Gogh is the portraitist of this situation, and that "it is a mere moment of explosion that separates his objects [such as the old shoes of a laborer] from the distorted fragments of surrealism."

Now such experiences of secular transcendence are important. They have their analogue in meaningful lesser revelations of the average man and woman today for whom religion as traditionally understood is excluded. Such experiences limit the sway of positivism, and keep alive the possibility of a return to the great legacies of faith. Their limitation most often lies in the fact that they are experiences more of the psyche than of the heart. Hence, they provide only a partial enlightenment and nourishment for the human being. In any case, these modern epiphany texts document the conditions to which any more significant understanding of revelation must be addressed, and the categories that would be meaningful.

We must pass over certain writers whose work makes them highly relevant to our theme, poets like Yeats and St.-John

16. *The Disenchanted Mind,* New York, 1959, p. 277.

Perse, novelists like Hemingway and Faulkner. Wallace Stevens calls for brief attention as a poet who sought to define "a fresh spiritual," and to be aware of the "metaphysicals" in a physical world. He knew that for this purpose the poet must find new language. In his "Esthétique du mal,"[17] reflecting on pain and on the answers that have been given to evil and death, he calls out for a savage honesty rather than for traditional comfortings —rather than for what he calls the "nostalgias" or "sleek ensolacings." The shaken realist today awakens to a world without glamor, a world of vacancy in which even Satan is dead. We can no longer impose an outworn magic upon things through "an old and disused ambit of the soul." But the ordinary natural world will open up its mystery in a new direct and humble encounter, through "proverbs of pure poverty."

> . . . Yet we require
> Another chant, an incantation, as in
> Another and later genesis, music
> That buffets the shapes of its possible halcyon
> Against the haggardie.[18]

And he concludes the poem with acclamation of transcendence rediscovered in daily life:

> As if the air, the mid-day air, was swarming
> With metaphysical changes that occur
> Merely in living as and where we live.[19]

The demand for a new language for the supernatural, and new proverbs and new symbols, is a recurrent one. This predicament is put with comic mordancy in Samuel Beckett's *All That Fall.*

17. *Transport to Summer,* New York, 1947.
18. P. 47.
19. P. 53.

225

The two Rooneys are making their way home, and Mrs. Rooney falls into an old-fashioned phrase about their destination.

Mrs. Rooney: No, no, I am agog, tell me all, then we shall press on and never pause, never pause, till we come safe to haven. (*Pause*)

Mr. Rooney: Never pause ... safe to haven ... Do you know, Maddy, sometimes one would think that you were struggling with a dead language.

Mrs. Rooney: Yes, indeed, Dan, I know full well what you mean. I often have that feeling, it is unspeakably excruciating.

Mr. Rooney: I confess I have it sometimes myself, when I happen to overhear what I am saying.

Mrs. Rooney: Well, you know, it will be dead in time, just like our own poor dear Gaelic, there is that to be said.[20]

The point is, that language about "coming safe to haven," or "to heaven," is seen as unusable. So W. H. Auden emerging from a celebration of the Mass in Austria can hail the Christian's emancipation from stuffy language, from what he calls "magic syllables" and "tribal formulae."

> 'Rejoice,' the bells
> cry to me. 'Blake's Old Nobodaddy
> in his astronomic telescopic heaven,
> The Big White Christian upstairs is dead
> and won't come hazing us no more ...

20. Pp. 31–32.

> 'Rejoice: we who were born
> congenitally deaf are able
> to listen now to rank outsiders: the Holy Ghost
> does not abhor a golfer's jargon . . .'[21]

What Beckett and Auden intimate about obsolete usage should not only prepare us for new rhetorics, but should alert us to the possibility that only in this way can older discoveries and celebrations be reauthenticated.

III. EXISTENTIALISM AND THE AVANT-GARDE FRENCH THEATRE

It is in the existentialist writers that we find our most sophisticated working out of the theme of death as catalyst of transcendence. In Heidegger's view of man as being-towards-death we find a formalized statement of much that we have already recognized. In confrontation with death, "transience is completely thrown back upon its own capacities to be." That is, death arouses our deepest impulses. But death here is not just to be understood as a future eventuality to be thought about; it is rather an essential aspect of our transience. To quote: "Death is a way of being which takes over transience as soon as it is. As soon as a man begins to live, he is old enough to die."

Dylan Thomas in his poem, "Twenty-four years," speaks of our being "dressed to die" already at our birth. He carries his autobiography back into his mother's womb where he was

> . . . crouched like a taylor
> Sewing a shroud for a journey
> By the light of the meat-eating sun.
> Dressed to die, the sensual strut begun,

21. "Whitsunday in Kirchstetten," *op. cit.*, pp. 82–83.

With my red veins full of money,
In the final direction of the elementary town
I advance for as long as forever is.[22]

Heidegger holds that our authentic humanity appears only when we resolutely accept and absorb the darkness and shock of our limits. We have already heard this theme in a different bearing in Marianne Moore's "What Are Years?" cited above.

Our interest here, however, is in literary existentialism, and we turn to Sartre for our example. Already as philosopher, Sartre had extended Heidegger's focus on death to one on finitude, and had identified authenticity with man's own free act of self-determination. It is of interest that the theologian Gerhard Ebeling in a discussion of modern atheism praises Sartre for his radical seriousness in recognizing that man is "condemned to freedom," and for his rejection of the standard view that man is a static being with a given nature.

In Sartre's novels we find examples of what we have called "secular transcendence" occasioned by confrontation with death. The sudden revelatory seizures may seem to have the character of "epiphanies," but they have a different context and quality, related to Sartre's categories. Here the absolute split between consciousness and "things" and the radical discontinuity between my consciousness and that of others, both of these accentuate the gratuitous and impersonal character of these revelations. The contrast appears if we set it beside the episode previously noted in André Gide's *The Counterfeiters*. In Chapter 13 of this novel Gide describes the sudden appearance of an angel to the boy Bernard. We have a real intrusion of another world, but the angel comes quite simply as a comforter to the youth in a moment of utter disarray. It is evident that Bernard has a personality to be sustained. But Sartre, Camus and others repudiate the idea of personality. Thus, Camus observes:

22. *Op. cit.*, p. 110.

I don't care about my personality and I am not interested in culti-
vating it. I don't want to treat my life as an experiment, but to be
what my life wishes me. It is I who am the experiment, and it is
life that forms and controls me.[23]

The passage that I cite from Sartre occurs in his novel, *The
Reprieve*.[24] Europe is on the brink of war, and Matthieu is about
to report for service. He sits at a table on the terrace of the
Café des Deux Magots at midnight, and has an hallucinatory
vision of the church across the square, Saint Germain-des-Prés,
bombed along with the City of Paris as a whole, and of eternal
nature replacing the human city. The text continues:

. . . He shivered and thought: "I also am eternal." It had all
happened painlessly. There had once been a kindly, rather diffident
man who was fond of Paris and enjoyed walking in its streets. That
man was dead . . . he had become engulfed in the world's past,
together with the Peace, his life had been put away in the archives
of the Third Republic . . . This man had shaped a future to his
measure . . . a historic and mortal little future: the war had
thundered down upon it and crushed it to powder . . . He relaxed
his grip and let it go . . . and nothing remained but a look. A new
and passionless look, a mere transparency. "I have lost my soul," he
thought with satisfaction . . .
Everything is dead. My look and those stones: eternal, rocklike,
like that white church . . . A look and a delight as vast as ocean—
a great day, indeed. He laid his hands on his knees, he must keep
calm; may I not tomorrow revert to what I was yesterday? But he
was not afraid. The church may collapse, I may tumble into a shell-
hole, or drop back into my life; nothing can rob me of this eternal
moment. There had been, and forever would be, that cold glare
upon those stones under the black sky; the absolute, forever; the
absolute, without cause or sense or purpose, without past or future

23. Interview, cited by Marvin Halverson.
24. New York, 1947. The passage is evoked in another context in
Chapter II, p. 75 above.

save a gratuitous, splendid permanence. "I am free," he said suddenly. And his joy changed, on the spot, to a crushing sense of
anguish.[25]

In Sartre's novels we find an accentuation of a development
in fiction represented by Kafka, Joyce, Gide and others. As the
world itself is not experienced as a meaningful continuity either
of time or of deeply human relationships, so the novelist loses
interest in plot and character in any usual sense. These are unauthentic. The real interest is in explosive "surreal" eruptions
and prodigies. Meaning and eternity are known in moments out
of time, and by the individual alone. But the individual is no
longer a self or person. As we see in this passage the person becomes only a "look," a "transparency," the coming to consciousness of the mystery of being, of what our ordinary human awareness must call the non-personal.

Why do men today have to go so far to find meaning, transcendence, eternal life? Recall by contrast the Old English poem
which we have cited, "The Wanderer." Death and mortality in
that lament have a personal and social character. It is the loyalties of men in life and in ruin which provide the soil out of
which meaning can grow. Through the creaturely bonds of
human brotherhood the heart strikes forth sparks and wrestles
with fate. True grief rooted in love proffers auguries of eternal
life.

We find a modern expression of this theme in one of the
latest writings of Theodore Roethke. We cite the fourth section
of his volume, *Sequence Sometimes Metaphysical*. This section
is called "The Motion," and we are reminded by the title of
Kierkegaard's emphasis in *Fear and Trembling* upon "making
pure movements."

> The soul has many motions, body one.
> An old wind-tattered butterfly flew down

25. Pp. 350–52.

And pulsed its wings upon the dusty ground—

Such stretchings of the spirit make no sound.
By lust alone we keep the mind alive,
And grieve into the certitude of love . . .

Who but the loved know love's a faring forth?
Who's old enough to live?—
Knowing how all things alter in the seed
Until they reach the final certitude.
This reach beyond this death, this act of love
In which all creatures share, and thereby live.

Wings without feathers, creaking in the sun.
The close dust dancing on a sunless stone.
God's night and day: down this space He has smiled.
Oh who would take the vision from the child?—
Hope has its hush: we move through its broad day—
Oh motion, oh our chance is still to be![26]

In Roethke's work it is evident that the epiphany experience of Yeats, or of Robert Graves, indeed, and many others, is carried over decidedly into a revelation of love.

To return to our question: why do men go so far today to find meaning, so far into private and solitary experience? The cause lies clear in our literature. The public, social, cultural life of our time has become impersonal, unauthentic, authoritarian. Even its loyalties are ideological and manufactured, or sentimental; or too abstract, as is too often the case even in our common pursuits of science and learning.

In these circumstances it is all the more significant that death continues to act as catalyst of meaning and of transcendence even in the midst of modern nihilism and atheism, in a Robinson Jeffers, in a Sartre, in a Gottfried Benn. It is banal to say

26. *Sequence Sometimes Metaphysical,* Iowa City, 1963, no pagination.

that all men are incurably religious. It is more interesting to observe that in the final test non-being is excluded a priori by man. Some form of transcendence of mortality or metamorphosis of our being is taken to be in the nature of things.

But the transcendence and eternity witnessed in much of this literature is of a very limited kind. In Sartre it borders on solipsism. In other writers like Yeats and Rilke the solution remains basically aesthetic, even though they have left behind the thin spirituality of many Romantic or pantheist oracles.

It is in this situation that we find a major corrective in an unlikely quarter, in what is called the theatre of the absurd. The treatment of our human extremity in the avant-garde French Theatre is different from that of Sartre and other so-called existentialists. Sartre sees meaning and transcendence as a function of existentialist decision and freedom. Samuel Beckett, Eugene Ionesco and others propose no such intellectual solution. Their novels and plays are not novels of ideas or plays of ideas. As Richard Sherrell writes:

. . . their resolution of the issue (to the extent that there is one) is a theatrical, an artistic one . . . Language and gesture are two of the elements of this theatre through which meaning is disclosed. Didi's compassionate gestures toward Gogo in Beckett's *Waiting for Godot,* are a good example of what I mean.[27]

These writers are basically tortured by the problem of communication, and at a deeper level than Sartre. Here we rejoin our main theme, namely, that the most significant exploration of death must always treat men in their relatedness. The problem is not just one of the finitude of the individual, because no man liveth to himself. Any valid transcendence must have an interpersonal character. This means that the problem of death

27. Personal letter. See his article "The Case Against God in Contemporary French Drama," *Religion in Life* (Autumn, 1962).

is a moral problem. These secular writers in their own way are recognizing the most difficult element in the New Testament teaching about death, namely, its relation to sin: "death came into the world through sin"; "sin reigned in death"; "the sting of death is sin."

Beckett's plays deal with men for whom moral relationships have become unreal or have been betrayed. In these plays the alienation of the modern man is represented, no doubt, at its most extreme: the shrivelling of personal identity. But in the modern situation it is more important for a writer to sound lovelessness to its depths than to dodge the problem by some escape hatch into the absolute. It is more faithful to the facts, and ultimately more hopeful, to open up very modest and painful perspectives of redemption in solidarity with our fellows. Even traditional formulations of eternal life must learn to pass through this kind of honesty. In *Waiting for Godot* one of Vladimir's observations serves as a real challenge to the traditionalist:

We are not saints, but we have kept our appointment. How many people can boast as much?[28]

Beckett is not satisfied to affirm transcendence in terms of aesthetic epiphanies. It is in *Embers,* written for broadcasting, that we get perhaps the most scorching portrayal of man out of relation, of moral torture and of craving for another presence and compassion, for genuine human speech. Henry, as we have noted earlier, speaks of the need that came on him:

. . . for someone, to be with me, anyone, a stranger, to talk to, imagine he hears me, years of that, and then, now, for someone who . . . knew me, in the old days, anyone, to be with me, imagine he hears me, what I am, now.[29]

28. *En attendant Godot,* Paris, 1952, pp. 134–135.
29. P. 23.

233

Beckett opens up an order of meaning, not in terms of psychological or aesthetic seizures as in Sartre and often even in Yeats, but in terms of the resonances of the heart. Out of an excruciating desolation made up of mortality, self-accusation, solitude, there are gestures in the plays, pure motions, towards reincorporation in an absent order of love, the craving for a personal voice, for an awaited visitation.

We must, then, first acknowledge a great debt to all these modern secular wrestlings. Our age has to work through for itself all the great human problems, in our situation and in our language. As Rilke said, "We must live the questions now." The answers of the past must be reconfirmed in our new secular situation.

But in the second place, we must ruthlessly discriminate. Only some of our authors locate the problem where it truly belongs, where the awful reality of death is grasped in its moral depth, where our estrangement from the order of love is recognized as the fundamental datum. In this light even such wonderful disclosures of the human mystery as we find in Rilke and Yeats have only partial validity and can even mislead. As the experience of Israel has shown, any real substantiation of eternal life must ground itself in and wrestle its way through our social realities, man's communal impasse. All other transcendences are too easily come by; they bypass the real death and have little persuasive power, for example, over against our modern holocausts and nihilism. It is for this reason that even the believer today must recognize a special debt to writers like Kafka, Faulkner and Beckett who may remain on this side of triumphant affirmation whether secular or traditional, but who sternly locate the problem, and who prepare the altar where the fire may fall from heaven.

IX. Faith and the Lay Mystery

He is neither priest nor proctor . . .
It is a fresh spiritual that he defines.
Wallace Stevens

I.

Jean Cocteau characterizes the subject matter of the modern arts as *le mystère laïc,* the "lay mystery" or "secular mystery." "Chirico," he says, "is a religious painter without faith," "a painter of the lay mystery." Cocteau holds that the modern artist must deal with the "lay mystery," that is, with secular experience understood religiously. We can translate our phrase again as "secular transcendence." Now we can recognize the importance of the theme for the theologian. We live in an age when any other kind of transcendence or mystery has lost its meaning. The old two-storey world is a thing of the past. Dualistic metaphysics and ontologies can still speak to us through Plato, Dante or Wordsworth, but a poem or a novel written today with this presupposition must be put down as a flashback, as an archaism. To build a new Gothic church in today's life is like disinterring the dead or opening a time-capsule out of a remote past. In an American city of today one can say that the average man walks by such a building without seeing it. It *is* not there for our sensibilities. We have no antennae for it.[1]

If we are to have any transcendence today, even Christian, it must be in and through the secular. If we are to have any mystery it must be the lay mystery. If we are to find grace it is to be found in the world and not overhead. The sublime firmament of overhead reality that provided a spiritual home for the souls of men until the eighteenth century has collapsed. But this need be no loss. I take it that we have been learning this from Bonhoeffer and Gogarten among others. We must take the world more seriously, nature and our nature more seriously, history more seriously.

But all this means that the artists and the poets are more important to us even than before. Not because they preserve for us—as was at first thought—a refuge for dreams and ideals threatened by materialism. But because the artist properly deals with the givens, the primordial givens, of the senses and the affections and the passions. And these still have their transcendence. Even in a one-storey world these still have their theological import. And in the modern situation this becomes all the more significant. Because now the believer and the artist are dealing with the same single reality. And the artist is freer in handling it. By virtue of his craft and by virtue of his embattled autonomy, he gives the voices of nature more directly. The theologian cannot enter so freely into the modern reality, nor can

1. Henry Adams in *Mont-Saint-Michel and Chartres* speaks of Chartres as "a doll-house to please the Queen of Heaven," and as though in warning to nostalgic medievalism writes: "Unless you can go back to your dolls, you are out of place here." Again, nineteenth century attempts to recapture the feeling of Gothic—Viollet-le-Duc in architecture, Sir Walter Scott in letters—are only "a more or less effaced or affected echo of a lost emotion which the world never felt but once and never could feel again." I take the citations from John P. McIntyre, "Henry Adams and the Unity of Chartres," *Twentieth Century Literature,* vol. VII, no. 4 (January, 1962), p. 168.

the conventional religious artist identified with the *art sacré* of the past. They suffer the curvature and the stiffness of an ancient dualistic gesture. Here we have the context of Cocteau's phrase. Protesting to the theologian Maritain, Cocteau says that the artist must deal with the lay mystery and that to deal with it he must be free. This does not mean that such art will be immoral or amoral. He writes: "I believe that art reflects morals, and that one cannot renew oneself without living dangerously and attracting slander." That is, the artist must deal at first hand with life beyond the fences of social or religious propriety.

It is something like this that Wallace Stevens means when he says of the poet or artist today:

> The ephebe is solitary in his walk.
> He skips the journalism of subjects, seeks out
> The perquisites of sanctity, enjoys
>
> A strong mind in a weak neighborhood, and is
> A serious man without the serious ...
>
> He is neither priest nor proctor ...
>
> It is a fresh spiritual that he defines ...
>
> The actual landscape with its actual horns
> Of baker and butcher blowing, as if to hear,
> Hear hard, gets an essential integrity.[2]

In the case of Stevens we can talk about a lay sanctity, a "fresh spiritual," just as in the case of Cocteau we can talk about the secular mystery. We are familiar in Tillich with related views of the religious dimensions in modern painting. And we

2. "An Ordinary Evening in New Haven" XIII, *The Auroras of Autumn,* pp. 134–135.

should not confuse what we are talking about here with romantic or pseudo-religious ideas of nature or art. These interpreters speak as disabused moderns.

Let us say first, then, that the theologian can well put itself to school to the modern artist to free himself from hang-overs of old fashions in transcendence. Not only with a view to better strategies in communication, but also with a view to honesty: honesty of feeling as well as honesty of language. It is a question of where grace is today actually to be found; in old habits and rhetorics or, as Stevens puts it, in

> The actual landscape with its actual horns
> Of baker and butcher blowing.

To avoid misunderstanding we might say that these horns of the butcher and baker relate us more directly to the rams' horns of the Exodus and the Seven Trumpets of the Apocalypse than the ecclesiastical electrical chimes that are proliferating today or the Christmas carols piped through loud-speakers in our shopping centers. The horns of the butcher and baker are not, of course, the Gospel but they are real. Stevens is talking as so often about the primordial givens of our human nature and experience, and this has its "perquisites of sanctity," its genuine coruscations of glory.

Now we go one step farther. If the modern artist often calls modern theology and piety back to an "essential integrity," one can say that art as a whole, the aesthetic order, is always an indispensable corrective and nourishment to faith.

Is it not true that Christianity has a need of recurrent baptism in the secular, in the human, to renew itself? Christianity has to be continually reimmersed in the vitalities of nature so as to be saved over again from a spurious and phantom Christ. And the aesthetic order, art, mediates nature to us.

The Christian faith is recurrently saved from Docetism and

238

irrelevance by immersion in nature, by its wrestling with paganism. Art mediates this order of creation.

The Second Adam presupposes the First Adam. The Christian presupposes the man. Art gives us the First Adam and if we lose sight of him and his true secular mystery and endowments, we cannot rightly identify the Second Adam or the Christian.

Theology and witness today will be impoverished unless they take account of secular man in all his dynamics; of the lay mystery that gives evidence of itself precisely in a desacralized world; of that new kind of transcendence that is made possible today when the category of the supernatural is gone.

To say all this with reference to literature: in the autonomy of the literary arts, precisely in secular literature, we come face to face with the reality of the First Adam, with the secular mystery, and only as we are open to this revelation can we rightly assess theological meaning in itself or in its various articles of belief.

The nourishment and provocation of our religious tradition by doses of paganism, nature, the aesthetic order, can be illustrated through many of its vicissitudes in the past. Faith glows, indeed, when it meets resistance. But I would prefer the figure of fuel. Faith has to have fuel, and this means the stuff of human experience. Faith burns the fuel of nature, the creaturely givens. And art mediates this substance. We may call to witness the fertility patterns of the ancient Near East ordered by Hebrew cult-theology; the Wisdom tradition of Egypt and Edom digested by Israel; the pagan vitalities of Hellenism, transubstantiated by the early church. In certain biblical writings we can observe the process. In Job a disabused look at the irreparable and immitigable occasions a new leap of faith. In John, Hebrews and Ephesians we see Hellenistic Christianity absorbing and surmounting a far-flung pagan encounter with meaninglessness, beyond the horizon of the Jerusalem beginnings. For us today secular strains of the Renaissance, the Enlightenment and the

Romantic movement provide essential challenge, provocation and nourishment. Without these our faith and our theology become cloistered and inhuman. We need ever-renewed exemplars of the First Adam in art and in life. What serves us best is the contemporary instance—more contemporary than Goethe, Nietzsche or Walt Whitman—a Gide, a Yeats, a Rilke or a Faulkner.

II.

We can test our theme by one modern classic: *The Counterfeiters*,[3] by André Gide. We ask the question, in this case, as to literature and theological meaning. Now Gide is a moralist when all is said and done and not an immoralist, and one can find substantial moral if not theological meaning in his work. One can certainly learn a good deal about mistaken theology in any case as one can in the *Portrait of the Artist as a Young Man.* In both Joyce and Gide one learns about the wrong way to commend Christianity to young men. The hero of the *Portrait,* for good and for bad reasons, reaches the point where he says, "*Non serviam.*" In *The Counterfeiters* much attention is given to the baleful consequences of another kind of asceticism, that sometimes found in French Protestantism. We see the "special Puritan savor, the strong exhalation . . . only less asphyxiating, indeed, than in some Jewish and Catholic observances" (p. 131). A particularly horrendous outcome of a sham religious education in the family of the pastor Wedel is seen in the son, Armand, who confesses his savage impulse to desecrate everything. In Edward's diary we can hear Gide himself reflecting:

As the soul habituates itself more and more to religious devotion, it loses all sense, taste, need, love of what is real. . . . For one like my-

3. References are to *Les Faux-Monnayeurs,* Paris, 1925.

self who above all must see clearly, I am horrified at the density of the falsehood in which a *devôt* can indulge himself.[4]

Gide strikes off caustically the Calvinist atmosphere here as having "something of the ineffably Alpine, Paradisiac and silly." With all exaggeration one cannot but recognize in Gide's scenes and portraits the validity of such indictments, as in the case of Faulkner's corresponding evocations of Protestant desiccation in his novels.

But there is a more important theological meaning in this novel as in any first-rank work of art or human document. Theology is provided here with a vision of the children of Adam, the human substance and marrow, man in his enigmatic and prodigious reality. Any theology, any philosophy of religion, has questions put to it by such a work. Human nature is dynamically exhibited here, in all its thrust, explosiveness, fascination, such that many forms of theology will be disqualified. The theologian surely joins the putative author, Edward, or Gide himself, as he exclaims:

I stand before the reality as a painter before his model . . . the reality interests me like plastic material; and I look more for what may be, infinitely more than for what has been. I stoop vertiginously over the possibilities of each being and weep for all that is atrophied under the lid of the mores.[5]

It is true that *The Counterfeiters* is a study in corruption, but it is a corruption that throws into relief the preciousness of human lives, the mysteries of human conscience and aspiration, and the prodigality of human talent. We see, indeed, the basic human drives and relationships off the track—in perversion and inversion—sex, family, friendship, vocation. We see childhood and adolescence solicited into corruption not only by appetite and vanity, but also in consequence of the rebuff of natural

4. *Ibid.*
5. Pp. 147–148.

affection in the child, the overriding of youth's sense of shame, and by brutal shocks to gentleness and loyalty. Gide, like Goethe, sees human life in the context of all natural forms. With the ingenuities, detours and frustrations of human impulse before him he observes:

It seems as though nature had tried by turn every possible way to be alive, to enter into movement, had taken advantage of all the permissions of matter and its laws.[6]

The book contains eloquent examples of tragedy and apostrophe to life. We have the old musician, La Pérouse, who exclaims that all had cheated him, yes, God himself.

He led me to see my pride as a virtue . . . He sends temptations which he knows we cannot resist; and when we do resist he revenges himself all the more. What has he got against us?[7]

This is precisely the searing theme of T. S. Eliot's *Gerontion:*

> History . . . deceives with whispering ambitions,
> Guides us by vanities . . . Think
> Neither fear nor courage saves us. Unnatural vices
> Are fathered by our heroism. Virtues
> Are forced upon us by our impudent crimes.
> These tears are shaken from the wrath-bearing tree.[8]

Even Jeremiah has relevant words here:

> Thou hast deceived me, Lord, and I was deceived.

But the book also has its celebrations of human quality, of endurance, sentiment, affections. These have a radiance. There

6. P. 192.
7. P. 155.
8. *Collected Poems: 1905–1931,* New York: Harcourt, Brace & Co., n. d., p. 44.

is a secular transcendence. Add to this the book itself as work of art, a many-faceted creation. All in all, over against the reality evoked in it the theologian may well be confounded with respect to his premises, that is, his premises with respect to the human creature.

III.

Before proceeding it is necessary to introduce a caveat against misplaced aestheticism in the church. We should not encourage aesthetes in the pulpit or "literary parsons" or liturgical revivals inspired by false views of beauty. We should safeguard the distinctions between the image-maker and the disciple, the creative talent and the religious calling, the spirit and the Holy Spirit. Granted our overdue reaction as Protestants against an ascetic or inhibited type, we should not go to excess on the other side into uncritical eros and a fetish of creative spontaneity without Christian norms. This would be to make the mistake of the Jewish youths of the time of the Seleucid rulers who were captivated by things Greek, who wore Greek garb, went to the circus and the amphitheatre, were ashamed of their circumcision.

Whereupon certain of the people built a place of exercise at Jerusalem according to the customs of the heathen: and made themselves uncircumcized.

(I Macc. 1:14–15; cf. II Macc. 4:9–17)

As Schuerer writes:

A gymnasium was erected below the castle; the young men of Jerusalem exercised themselves in the gymnastic arts of the Greeks. The very priests forsook their service at the altar and took part in the games of the palaestra.[9]

9. *The Jewish People in the Time of Jesus Christ,* Edinburgh, 1890, Vol. I, 1, p. 203.

Schuerer also shows how the Greek styles of architecture penetrated into the inner forecourts of the Jewish Temple as well as the outer court. He notes further that "Grecian music was undoubtedly represented at the feasts of Jerusalem and elsewhere," citing prizes later offered by Herod. And as Josephus tells us:

There were very great rewards for victory proposed [in the games], not only to those that performed their exercises naked, but to those that played the musicians also, and were called Thymelici.

(Ant. XV, 8, 1)

One can see how great the temptation was for the Jewish youths of the time in view on the one hand of the attraction of Hellenic and Hellenistic achievements, and how inhibited in many respects, on the other hand, could appear the existing image of man in the defensive tradition of the Second Temple. So today we awaken to a sense of the stunted image of man widely current in middle-class Protestant ethos. We recognize the immeasurable attractions of certain humanist and secular ideals identified today with the arts and we can easily become confused.

I see this awkwardness—a transitional awkward age among Protestants as they possess themselves of the gospel of the arts today—in two versions. In one case we have the man from a Protestant pietism to whom a kind of subjective release in art is congenial. His aestheticism is a passage from pietism to Romanticism. I have a strong suspicion here of experiments with the religious dance especially, but also with addiction to a kind of oracular-mystical poetry, such as that of Khalil Gibran;[10] or

10. Apropos of Gibran, the following observations make the point, cited from a sermon of Professor William Muehl of the Yale Divinity School in the Harvard Memorial Church, February, 1961.

It is this yearning after generalized and abstract religion which accounts in large part, I am sure, for the popularity of such books as

sentimental representations of Christ or religious subjects in painting which may have superficial aspects of modern style but are essentially governed by pathos or eros.

The other case is that of the man whose background is not pietism but some more dogmatically defined type of Christianity, a tradition involving a built-in asceticism or emotional barrenness. In his case the temptation is not to a Christian romanticism, but to some kind of Christian antinomianism à la Nietzsche, shall we say. Or he may be attracted to some very sophisticated high-church symbolic traditionalism. The antinomian response may take the individual right out of the church as in the case of an André Gide or a Robinson Jeffers: salvation by the epiphany or magic of Beauty prevails over salvation by hearing. Some theological students have a prolonged struggle with this dilemma. The liturgical-aesthetic response, indeed, is an understandable awakening to the symbolic dimension

---

Gibran's *The Prophet*. For here we have the language of things spiritual manipulated poetically in an historical vacuum. Gibran's prophet speaks to mankind without ever having to address himself to particular men and women in specific historical circumstances. He seems always to be preaching to disembodied minds, never to demented bodies. Whatever else may be the condition of this prophet's hearers, we can be pretty sure that they have no ductless glands. Gibran gives us an appealing prophet. One who stands on no recognizable local terrain. One who appears to have winnowed the grain of truth and left the chaff on the threshing room floor.

I have heard it suggested by disciples of this prophet that the Bible ought to be expurgated, not to remove all the violence and fornication . . . but to get rid of that far greater obscenity . . . the particular history of a not too particular people. Anyone who is honest with himself must admit the superficially attractive character of that proposal. If we could with a wave of the hand eliminate the Amorites, Perizzites, Canaanites, Girgashites, Hivites, and Jebusites . . . the Bible would be a lot easier to read. And it would certainly simplify things for Joshua . . .

But we can never completely escape the geography of the historic faith and the unhappy feeling that revelation occurs not *in spite* of the particular in history . . . but in some sense *because* of it.

of religion. It has it in its favor that Christian theological norms may be seriously recognized. But this too can pass into aestheticism; even when it does not, the aesthetic emancipation identified with it becomes too easily identified with obsolete forms.

So much on the dangers of the new interest in the arts in the churches. In my appreciation of the secular arts that follows I am aware of such misunderstandings. But I am more interested in the benefits of this new confrontation when it is wisely worked out by the Christian.

IV.

Let me state the positive significance of our confrontation with the arts and the whole aesthetic order by an analogy drawn from Paul's letter to the Romans as he cites Deuteronomy:

I will make you jealous of those who are not a nation: with a foolish nation I will make you angry.

(Rom. 10:19; Dt. 32:21)

Paul is saying that God's work among the Gentiles will give heart-burnings to the people of God, to Israel, will startle and anger them. Now can we say today that God is using the essentially pagan reality of art—man's often sublime, unbaptized, sensuous and imaginative talents and works—that God is using these today to provoke the church, to needle it, to introduce a ferment into it?

I will make you jealous of those who are not a nation.

Certainly the Bohemia of the artists is not a nation, not a called people; they are individualists, Ishmaelites. But they have uncovenanted mercies and even callings. Do we have here God speaking through people perhaps with strange lips, through the pagan miracle, the secular mystery?

246

Can we say that God is on both sides in the war of the myths, the war of the historical myth of the people of God with the natural myths of Adam, that is, with the secular celebrations of art? For it was precisely in the war of the myths that first Israel and then Christianity has often drawn the resources of language to define itself and communicate itself.

The relevance of art to the theological world today then would be that of its provocation. When the Christian Gospel grows meagre in its imaginative arsenal, that is, in its essential humanity, or with respect to the human dimension of its message, then the imaginations of the world—its vitalities, myths, the stuff of human experience—rebuke and stimulate it.

Let us not be detoured here by the question of the Fall, of man's evil imaginations. For the arts and myths and creativities of unbaptized man have their sound aspects. Professor Mircea Eliade speaking as a student of non-Christian cultures observes that we Christians look too exclusively upon the darker side of their arts and ceremonies. Nevertheless, he observes, by these great societies live.

Our analogy from Romans can be carried farther. Paul goes on now, citing Isaiah:

I have been found by those who did not seek me; I have shown myself to those who did not ask for me.

(Rom. 10:20; Is. 65:1)

Thus the "foolish people"—that is, those given to "vanities," that is, to idols, indeed, to images—those given to man's natural vitalities and creativities, the stuff of the arts—these find God, even though they did not seek him or did not know that they were seeking him. The text is full of relevance for the situation of the secular arts today.

This whole analogy is only valid if we agree as to the nature of art as in itself pagan, natural, representing the endowments of the first Adam. This is said in appreciation of art, not in dis-

247

paragement. We should let art and poetry be autonomous and pre-Christian. We thus avoid parochialism since we do not rule out the aesthetic activity of man in any culture, from the caves of the Dordogne or the artifacts of the paleolithic age to the latest compositions in electronic sonorities. We also avoid false dualisms and spiritualization in our view of art. We do not obscure the basic human sensuous foundation of all art. We maintain the polarity of art and faith, and thus keep open that special reality which art represents. In theological terms we emphasize the doctrine of creation lest we impoverish our doctrine of redemption. We may note the same issue in the case of science. Christianity has most to profit, with respect for example to biblical science or religious sociology, if it acknowledges in them their own autonomous methods and activity.

Art belongs to the order of creation. We have here to do with man the maker, the maker of tools and the maker of images. The dialectic of art and religion, of the aesthetic order and the religious order, of imagination and faith, has all sorts of complexities and inter-relationships. But the artist is first of all *homo sapiens* and *homo faber*.

The great importance of the church's encounter with art emerges only when we envisage the surpassing greatness of man's artistic endowments and achievements and keep in mind the transcending and breathless instances. It is good for Christians to have to make a place in their sometimes shrunken outlook for the formidable energies and realities evident in the arts. It represents a theological provocation which is good for us. In the first age of Christianity the mood and kerygmatic witness of the believers was of a pitch and level to encounter and master and to transmute to its own purpose the dynamic conceptions of pagan antiquity. Its language, its imagery, its symbol were equal to the pagan imaginations of the epoch, let alone the civic and political arts and rituals, all representing the prodigal exuberance of the Roman world. The lowly Christian cells lived by creative powers and community-building "ideology" that in very deed outrivaled the seven wonders of the world, and could battle on more than equal terms with whatever human greatness is represented for us by the names of Vergil, Horace and the classics of the Roman *paideia*.

The arts of our time as indices of man's prolific and consummate powers—quite apart from whatever cultural instruction we may derive from them—should provoke the church to have a life and a message and a lexicon of communication worthy of this mysterious contemporary Adam. When reading some of the best of our modern literature—to take this art—we cannot but feel that we have moved into another dimension in the grasp of our human condition than we find commonly in our theology and even in much of our piety and worship. There is more stature here, more understanding, more reality—a reality wedded with imagination; even though the writing in question is as we say "secular" and non-confessing. It is a question of awareness, of tenor, of voltage, of "breath." Even if our human lot is not seen in Christian terms, it is evoked with a cruciality, a searingness that compels men to take a fuller account of themselves: on the one hand a communication of the fatalities that hem in and block the life-impulse at so many points; on the other hand evidence of man's paradoxical potentialities and incredible works. We learn something here about our creature "man" that is not sufficiently taken account of in our Christian message. These, if you will, pagan arts and outlooks will continue to win and hold the hearts of men whether in constructive or destructive ways so long as we do not have a life and faith which answer to the same dynamics. Fortunately a great deal of this modern literature is on the side of the angels. In all sorts of obscure ways, moreover, it is shaped by Jewish-Christian and humanist legacies resident in western man. But it often towers above our institutional Christian patterns. And our Christian habits of mind and heart seem to inhibit if not cripple our resourcefulness so that we are not able to communicate with the secular mystery of the age.

To illustrate the stature of art in our time let us take the field of poetry. Consider the special handicaps of a poet today either with respect to his world and audience or with respect to the state of the English tongue. Culturally speaking it is an age of incoherence. Linguistically speaking our media of discourse and communication are desacralized. The poets of the past worked in languages that had numinous overtones. I have observed that the chief difficulty in translating the New Testament into contemporary English lies at this point. Our English tongue today at its best—and I am not speaking of journalese or the idiom of Broadway or of Madison Avenue—is practical, or abstract, in any case one-dimensional; it lacks a penumbra of magic or mystery. The translators of the New English Bible, therefore, are hard put to it to translate the Greek work, *thlipsis,* we know as "tribulation"; they translate "trouble." "Mammon" is translated "money." *Peirasmos,* the Greek term for the eschatological birth pangs, has to be translated as "test." Anathema takes the weak sense of "outcaste."

An explicit goal that Ezra Pound set before himself was to cleanse our modern speech. Michel Butor sums it up this way.

Pound finds words perverted and sick, the lie ensconced in their liaisons; it is a question of restoring to them their youth and their grasp on the real, and therefore linking them in potent images. New modes of expression must be found to dominate the mental complexity in which we struggle, these clashes of civilization in our spirits, their oppositions, their fusions,—to solve these problems and beyond them once again to find footing, truth and a reasonable society.[11]

Now with all these handicaps note the achievements of certain modern poets. In face of the special aspects of cultural frag-

11. *Repertoire: Études et conferences, 1948–1959,* Paris, 1960, p. 236.

mentation and incommunicability present today, we have writers who have been able to go beneath and behind our modern anarchy and find images of meaning and order. They can say things for us whether tragic or affirmative by which we can enter into possession of our enduring humanity. I think of the marvellously controlled complexities of our modern experience in the earlier work of Eliot; and of the ordering of both our psychological and political stresses in the work of Auden. I think of the perfection and invention beyond praise of much of the work of Wallace Stevens, a supreme play with language that went on year after year. I think of the crystal-like miracle of a certain vein in Ezra Pound. But more than this, he stands near the springs of life; as Hugh Kenner writes, he provides the "nutrition of impulse." In Pound's own phrase we have the "dance of the intellect among words." One cannot read in his *Cantos* without a cumulative awareness of the aesthetic miracle and wonder at the enigma of man's powers. I have reference to the Protean play, the modulations, the subtleties, the echoes and resonances of a vast register of resources, both of the lexicon itself and of cultural symbol, both of rhetoric and of passion, both of private sensibility and of the fables of the tribe. If we speak of the secular mystery, we have it here, nature in a modern instance in an incandescence to evoke astonishment.

But we could go on to speak of other poets: of the magician-like shaping of our recalcitrant human speech by poets like Yeats and Valéry. And we could speak of St.-John Perse, Marianne Moore and others. We have "lords of language" in our time too, and it evidences what I say about the too easily forgotten depths and dimensions of man and God's hand upon him. Nor would I forget the talents of many poets who are less well known: men and women who report significantly—that is by signs—on what it means to live in the wrestling today between conformity and freedom, the adjusted and the unadjusted, the even and the odd, the sodden and the sensitive, between custom and wonder. The true artist today is the man who has no armor, no second-hand buffers and blinders, and who is therefore exposed and vulnerable, and one therefore through whom the ancient hungers of man can speak, and speak by words and signs both timeless and contemporary.

In our desacralized world, what was once the religious dimension is opened up for many by artistic experience alone. As Robert Spike observed, the symbols have widely lost their power in the church but they still have power elsewhere, for example in the secular Protestant ethos, and in secular artists who quicken these and other potent legacies. A striking example of this secular quickening of Christian imagery is afforded by Beckett's *Waiting for Godot.*

"One of the thieves crucified beside Christ went to Heaven. Do not despair. The other thief went to Hell. Do not presume." It was from these sentences of St. Augustine's that Samuel Beckett, having rejected Christian belief but finding no meaningful aesthetic patterns outside Christian tradition, got the idea of *Waiting for Godot.*[12]

So far as contemporary art is concerned, then, we should be more humble before modern secularity in its creative aspects and see what it can teach us even if we have to divest ourselves for the time being of our own inherited badges of authority. Here is where our thought links on with that of Bonhoeffer in his view of a world come of age and a naked Christ divested of dualistic titles. Our world explores the secular mystery in non-supernatural terms. It is possible for the Gospel to be lived and thought and imaged so as to speak to these presuppositions.

V.

Our topic, however, requires that we give attention also to the work of the Christian artist, to the Christian imagination and

12. Cited from G. S. Fraser, "The Modern Poet and Christianity," *Frontier,* vol. II (Summer, 1959), p. 106.

to Christian imagery. This point can only be made after the first one is clear. We have separated the Christian from the artist deliberately and assigned autonomy to the artist, so that we can then find the fullest relevance of art to the theological world. We have let man as maker and image-maker give us the unbaptized human phenomenon in all its vitality and poignancy, its mystery and miscarriage. We understand better, then, the work of God with Man, of redemption with nature, the meaning of election, calling, responsibility, judgment, guilt, expiation. It is not surprising that our fuller understanding of the Gospel today is opened up for us by a long line of secular artists, by outsiders, by scapegoats and prodigals and victims of the modern experience. It is not surprising that in preaching and apologetics today, we turn perforce to artists outside the camp who know modern man better than we know him ourselves, men who have belonged to the resistance of our time, the anti-Fascist battalions, the anti-totalitarian cells, the anti-bourgeois insecure, the outer or inner emigration of our world. They have had to sustain the struggle for man's moral freedom and imaginative freedom, often with error, in exposed situations, and in a solidarity with their fellows in a way not so characteristic of the Christian. In doing so, as artists, they have restored to us an image of man, paradigms of man in depth, which rebuke our conventionality and expose the inadequacy of our speech.

It is at this point that the *Christian* artist of our time can enter into their labor and reap the benefits. We recognize how a painter like Rouault or poets like Eliot and Auden can speak out of the same depth and with an adequate rhetoric today because they have learned from the secular artist and his achievements in communication. Thus the Christian artist learns how to speak so that modern man can know himself directly addressed when he hears the Gospel today. Of course, there are only a few Christian artists of this stature, but the lesser Christian artists and the faithful preacher and apologist on all the many fronts of the church today increasingly rediscover the

253

stature of man in his secular mystery, in his enigma and in his dynamics, and increasingly repossess an adequate language, a new lexicon of faith, and new manual of communication.

As an example of the way in which the artist conveys the actuality of our world today and provides clues for our own Christian communication, we may select a poem by Thomas Blackburn entitled "Spring-heeled Jack." Under the title is the subscript:

Through the whole of the 19th century there were intermittent reports from various parts of England of violent assaults by a leaping maniac called "Spring-heeled Jack." The reports agree that under a cloak he was dressed in a tight-fitting, silver garment and that he breathed fire.

Thus the poet takes a specimen of the folklore of the country-side redolent of the uncanny and uses it to uncover a very disturbing feature of contemporary experience: where private coercion obtains, there public violence follows; the hidden violence of social conformity brings forth spectacular disorder. Two lines of Auden could serve as a text:

> The average of the average man
> Becomes the dread Leviathan.

The dread Leviathan or totalitarian irrationality and public hysteria have their beginnings in the daily life and gestures of ordinary people. Violence has its origins in apparent order. The theme of the poem is also related to a recurrent topic in William Blake's "Songs of Experience," where he speaks of "mind-forged manacles," and of how

> the youthful harlot's curse
> Blasts the new-born infant's tear,
> And blights with plagues the marriage hearse.[13]

13. "London."

Blackburn's poem uses as an analogy the way in which children are brought up, the invisible coercions of false standards and caste tyrannies imposed upon the spirit—all leading inevitably via subterranean channels to inexplicable violence, irrational disorders, elements of anarchy in the individual and in society. This is a very significant theme for our world, and it can be translated over into the vocabulary of law and grace, of powers and principalities, of wrath and judgment. Note in the poem that when the imagination of children is repressed it has to find play in some other world even if it be one of delusion. When the creativeness, the tenderness, the humanity of men is blocked, pressures are set up and explosions prepared which have their theatre in our public scene: "So nearly to the ghostliness/Is our material kin." The poem here is only saying what Christ affirms that when men are dumb, the stones cry out; indeed, this passage is picked up in the context. In short the poem is about the interwoven web of moral solidarity which includes all that we know as reality, with no cleavage of matter and spirit or body and soul. Thus the imagery of the poem speaks to the modern consciousness which is post-idealist and knows no dualisms.

> Because the white-faced children
> Dare speak no word at all,
> The glasses learn to tremble,
> The picture-frames to fall;
> And nerved by the troubled silence
> Of griefs that lie alone,
> Turn and leap from a childish sleep,
> Tea-kettle, dish and stone.
> For the love and hatred that enter
> The room behind life's back,
> I give you the praise of the murdering ways
> Of a man called "Spring-heeled Jack."

When King Whip and his crooked wife
Are masters of the world,
The children keep their tenderness
Close-reefed and safely furled,
And find another planet for
The rose-tree and the knife,
In Spring-heeled Jack's unpeopled dark,
Beyond the shores of life.
Because tall queens and emperors there
Obey a lightest wish,
Can you believe they lie with dreams
As idle as a fish?
I've seen the mortar fly abroad
And heard the roof-beams crack,
As out of the world of their sleep uncurled
Bounces the Spring-heeled Jack.

Heated by some suggestive word,
Damp wood may burn the skin,
So nearly to the ghostliness
Is our material kin.
If flesh, so plastic, fails its part,
The very stones must cry
Words of the dumb and frightened heart,
Tears frozen on the eye.
So when the newspapers roll back
A long red list of crime
And blame it all on Spring-heeled Jack,
I say that into time
The passion of these innocents
Has slowly trickled down,
And loosens this enamoured man
Like wild-fire on the town.
Because of each unlucky word
No syllable is lost,
And every stifled genesis
Nurses a walking ghost,

Within his brief and sundering hour,
Behind the world's broad back,
I give you the praise of the murdering ways
Of a man called Spring-heeled Jack.[14]

VI.

With all the appreciation which we have expressed here for the
arts and the modern arts, it should, nevertheless, be clearly understood that the obligation to test the spirits is always with the
Christian. The world of the arts and the imagination is even
more fateful for men than that of their ideas and philosophies.
Art often takes the form of idols. There are false imaginations.
If great societies and civilizations really live as they do by
myths, in the sense of compelling world-pictures and their assumptions—and order their institutions and unwritten laws by
them—it is evident how decisive a role is played for good and
for evil by the artist, the image-maker. Christianity is, therefore,
always involved in a war of myths for men's souls. This only
suggests again how important it is that Christian faith in any
epoch should have the dynamic, also in the arena of the arts
and symbolic form, to provide its own compelling images and
potent art-forms over against the prolific and malific magics of
so emancipated an age as ours. The term "myth" is ambiguous.
In one sense one can say that biblical faith throughout was a
war against pagan myths. But it is also true to say that the
emergence of the Gospel meant a renewal of mythical apprehension and communication. Only this kind of plastic conception
could do justice to the depth of men's grasp of existence and
destiny. But such imagery rose out of the drama of the Cross
and was a kind of world-portrayal that inevitably contradicted

14. *In the Fire*, London, 1956, pp. 18–19.

the imaginations of Greece and Rome, while it might borrow from them.

For the war of myths of today and the overthrow of the false ikons of our Romes and our Corinths we can learn from the first believers. The Christian artist may learn where power of conception is born, at the zero point of the flesh which is at the same time the Alpha of a new creation, that is, at the Cross. He may also learn that the Christian speaks to every man and age in his present and in his current idom, for there is no holy language. He may also find an apostleship in the realization that the Gospel prevails not by instruction and argument but by revelation, by bodying forth.

A more general observation finally is called for bearing on the secular repossession of the ancient *signa* and a valid "profane" celebration of the abiding *magnalia*. We have been studying the emergence of a new voice in modern letters in a world largely alienated from the Christian faith. We have also been listening for the new and healing idioms of that faith promised in the Gospel:

These signs will accompany them who believe: in my name they will cast out demons; they will speak in new tongues . . .

(Mk 16:17)

Though these parallel developments are interrelated and sometimes merge, yet the fact remains that a seemingly unbridgeable gulf widely separates whether the church and the world or the biblical and the modern imagination.

But this hiatus—understandable as it is and irremediable as long as the tradition is not renewed from the depth in life and in language—occasions a profound trauma in the psyche of contemporary man. He has so long been shaped by a particular history that this kind of radical discontinuity sets up disturbances

258

and reverberations through all levels of his existence. Of this impasse the major writings of our time disclose the symptoms.

Indeed, the cumulative impression left by our modern classics is that there is today a frustrated groping after some new way of access to our traditional springs of faith, a veritable craving for some viable version of them. The spiritual and intellectual history of the whole epoch has alienated many elements of society from church and synagogue. The religious institutions and the tradition itself are fatefully identified with inherited vehicles, pieties and responses which, for all their preciousness, do not speak to modern ears. A great religious movement, of course, is always a bearer of many layers of older experience and so much the richer. But this stratographic aspect of faith becomes a liability in a conjuncture like the present. Any return to the great theophanies or reorientation in the ancient Way is radically blocked for many.

There are occasions when a youth, or a man like Robert Frost's Hired Man, may *have* to go home, and yet in the circumstances he cannot. I am not thinking here in the first instance of prodigal sons. The spiritually homeless alien of our world is in a parlous state like that of an arrested delivery in child-birth or any blocked organic process. This frustrated situation has all sorts of curious cultural and psychic consequences and they are disclosed to us in much of our recent literature.

Such representative heroes as Stephen in Joyce's *Portrait;* "K" in Kafka's *Trial;* Quentin in Faulkner's *The Sound and the Fury;* Clamence in Camus' *The Fall;* Scobie in Greene's *The Heart of the Matter*—these all carry in their bloodstreams the archetypes of the classical Scriptures.[15] In situations of extremity, or it may be in situations of fulfillment and ecstasy, these aliens

15. In what follows I return to my discussion of these novels in a review of William R. Mueller's *The Prophetic Voice of Modern Fiction,* New York, 1959, a book which selects them for attention. The review-article was published in *The New Republic,* vol. 141, no. 11 (September 14, 1959), and the material is here used by permission.

may be solicited by the older patterns. But if these are not available to them in some viable form a kind of obsessive crisis is set up such as is explored in our novels.

In such works in any case the reader is confronted with formidable exposures of our deeper disarray and at the same time of the defaults and lapses of the religious traditions in their familiar forms. Especially with respect to larger human and ethical issues modern writers bring a disabused initiation and earnestness to bear upon unexamined codes and stagnant or vestigial ceremonies. The reader will recognize oft-cited phrases: *"Non serviam"* — *"Usura contra natura"* — "What shall we do? What shall we ever do?" — "Securitie, that annex of hell." Yet the relation of the speaker in all such works (and indirectly of the author in question) to the tradition is often acutely ambiguous. This anguishing situation betrays itself in various ways including violent repudiation and blasphemy as well as phantasies of reintegration in the eroded covenants. I am not arguing that the modern hero is a latent believer but rather pointing to the radical character of the problem, the impasse which blocks any genuine reappropriation.

The problem no doubt is twofold. At the level of language and categories there is the need to overcome the incoherence of our age including the breach between past and present. But so far as the inheritance of faith is concerned, even when so opened up as a genuine option, there will as always remain the question of response. Actual incorporation in the faith after all means a deep consent to the ultimate charities that lie behind the great transactions of the past and behind their master images as they are carried down through time by the community of faith. But before such consent is possible there must be some common ground of understanding. The hiatus between past and present with its accompanying tensions lies first of all at this level. Modern man cannot live out of the future alone. He cannot live with himself unless the past can be taken up into his own self-understanding and his own categories of apperception. Nevertheless the writings we have in view show that both levels of the impasse are in view.

One illustration of this blocked situation appears in Kafka's "K." In *The Trial* the nub of the matter is presented in the extraordinary parable narrated to him by the priest in the Cathedral, that of the man from the country who through a long life and down to a despairing old age waits intimidated outside the door of the Law only to learn at the point of death that it was not really closed to him. Famished for grace but cowed by the sinister hierarchies that appear to guard the mysteries he nevertheless later becomes aware of the "radiance that streams inextinguishably from the door of the Law." The close of the novel itself suggests that "K" could have cleared himself of the oppressive charges and rejections that weighed upon him and could have saved himself the harrowing years of ever-renewed stratagems and precautions by an original and authentic act of candor and simplicity. We are not to think, however, that the hindrances of "K" were all of his making. If any option of life is offered in *The Trial* it is of the most extreme ambiguity.

In Camus' novel *The Fall,* the monologue-confession of Clamence relieves him of his own torment of guilt by incriminating not only himself but all men. Towards the end his discourse takes on features of madness. At one moment he sees himself in the role of God and at another he voices accents of chastened simplicity and wistfulness for the salvation of all men. Camus crowds the closing scenes with veiled auguries of baptismal regeneration, and thus suggests that this lost soul moves close to deliverance, but these appear finally rather to enforce its impossibility: so near and yet so far.

Camus writes here in the tradition of the French moralists whose aim included especially the exposure of sham. This rhetorical genre favors the stage "type" or particularized "character," a method that operates by generalization and hyperbole.

Clamence is presented as a summation of the "vices of our whole generation," and therefore with implicit elements of allegory. The closing ambiguity recalls the problematic ending of *The Trial*. In both cases the dilemma left to the reader powerfully suggests how the modern anti-hero is estopped from whatever exorcism or vindication may haunt him from the fabulations of the past.

For his part James Joyce's young artist is likewise blocked from espousal of the church as he knows it. We see him convulsively rebelling from what appears to him a formal ceremony but arrested by a vocation to a priesthood of the imagination which represents traditional apostleship only, as it were, modulated into a new register.

What is craved and groped for, we have suggested, is some viable, meaningful version of the historic faiths. On the one hand this does, indeed, call for simplification and the shedding of accumulated detritus that stifles the tradition. In Hawthorne we read of the annual "busk" of old New England in which the year's accumulation of litter, worn out clothes and broken objects were burned up and discarded, and the homes and hamlets purified and alleviated. Romain Rolland in *Jean Christophe* uses the image of the equinoctial storm that sweeps violently through the forest and breaks off the dead limbs, branches and twigs and clears the way for new growth. But those are in error who think that an old faith can be made "modern" merely by removing old foliage. Religions are more like evergreens than like deciduous trees. If the obligation of the agnostic today is like that of Stephen Dedalus to continue forging on his own terms and without benefit of clergy the conscience of a new epoch, that of the church is to renew its own tradition. Of course religion like patriotism must be traditional, but an ever-renewed incandescence should continually transmit and transmute the primal life of the tradition and at the same time burn away irrelevant accumulations and out-dated

262

automatisms. Thus the modern man and the ancient faith may once again draw near to each other like those who tunnel under the Alps from different sides.

Index of Names

265

SOCIETY FOR THE ARTS, RELIGION AND CONTEMPORARY CULTURE, INC.

The Paul Tillich Commemorative Lectureship is awarded annually by the Society for the Arts, Religion and Contemporary Culture in honor of one of its most distinguished founding Fellows.

The 1968 Lectures were made possible through a gift of the Robert Lee Blaffer Trust of Houston, Texas, and New Harmony, Indiana.

The Society was founded in 1961 as a non-profit membership corporation to initiate and foster collaboration between religion and the arts in contemporary life.

The Society furthers this aim through sponsorship of Wine Cellar Conversations, lectures, performances, research, mass media broadcasts and its own publication, ARC *Directions*.

Offices of the Society are located at 35 East 72nd Street, New York, New York 10021.

Officers

Stanley R. Hopper, President
Alfred H. Barr, Jr., Vice President
Denis de Rougemont, Vice President
Luther Noss, Vice President
Amos N. Wilder, Vice President
Truman B. Douglass, Chairman, Board of Directors
Alfred R. Clark, Treasurer
David H. C. Read, Secretary
Finley Eversole, Executive Secretary